Reflective Learning in Practice

To

Rosie, Tom, Gerard, James, Alison
and
Linda

Reflective Learning in Practice

EDITED BY ANNE BROCKBANK, IAN McGILL
AND NIC BEECH

Routledge
Taylor & Francis Group

LONDON AND NEW YORK

First published in paperback 2024

First published 2002 by Gower Publishing

4 Park Square, Milton Park, Abingdon, Oxon OX14 4RN

605 Third Avenue, New York, NY 10158

First issued in hardback 2019

Routledge is an imprint of the Taylor & Francis Group, an informa business

Publisher's Note
The publisher has gone to great lengths to ensure the quality of this reprint but points out that some imperfections in the original copies may be apparent.

British Library Cataloguing in Publication Data

Reflective learning in practice
 1. Employees – Training of 2. Organizational learning
 I. Brockbank, Anne II. McGill, Ian III. Beech, Nic
 658.3' 124

Library of Congress Control Number: 2002100273

ISBN: 978-0-566-08377-8 (hbk)
ISBN: 978-1-03-283755-0 (pbk)
ISBN: 978-1-315-60426-8 (ebk)

DOI: 10.4324/9781315604268

Typeset in 9 point Stone Serif by IML Typographers, Birkenhead, Merseyside

Contents

Notes on Contributors

Nic Beech is Director of Academic Matters at the University of Strathclyde Graduate School of Business. His research is focused on the social construction of people and relationships and the impacts that constructions have on management practice and learning. His is co-author of *The Essence of HRM* (1995) and *HRM: A Concise Analysis* (2002).

Dr Jyoti Bhandari is a General Practitioner in an innovative North London practice serving 13,000 patients. She is an undergraduate clinical tutor and her principal interests are acupuncture and diabetes. She brought to this project a professional and personal concern about the prevalence of coronary heart disease amongst South Asians. She is a graduate of Manchester University.

Stella Binns has worked in the public and voluntary sector for twenty years as researcher, development worker, trainer and manager. She has recently retired from her job managing a corporate training unit in the London Borough of Ealing and is working as a consultant facilitator/trainer specializing in action learning, coaching, mentoring and other personal development activities.

Tom Bourner is a teacher, researcher and writer at the University of Brighton. Currently, he leads the university's Management Development Research Unit and is responsible for leading and developing research into higher education across the university. His main interests are management development, action learning and improving support for learning in universities. He is Professor of Personal and Professional Development at the university.

Anne Brockbank is a learning and development consultant, with clients in public, private and voluntary sectors. She offers learning and development opportunities to individuals and groups through coaching, mentoring, supervision and action learning. Anne is co-author with Ian McGill of *Facilitating Reflective Learning in Higher Education*, published by Open University Press and is currently preparing, with Ian McGill, *The Handbook of Action Learning* for Kogan Page.

George Cairns is a Senior Lecturer in Management in the University of Strathclyde Graduate School of Business, Glasgow, teaching on MBA Programmes in the UK, Europe and Asia. His research focus is on managing complexity and ambiguity across the physical, social, technological and business environments of organizations. George completed his PhD at the University of Glasgow.

Stephen Davis worked in Organizational Development in the NHS before moving to the Bank of Scotland to design their Leadership Development programme. He now heads the HRD team in Thus plc and is working on the development of the people who make the technology happen. Stephen has an MSc in HRD.

Sue Dives is the Managing Director of Dives Consulting and Training Ltd and specializes in people development in call centres and the service industry. Building on a career in banking, Sue has provided consultancy and training support for many organizations across all industry sectors, including Vodafone, the Oxford Group, British Airways, Barclays Bank and Telewest.

Tom Heywood is a consultant and trainer who has managed major learning projects on behalf of a range of blue chip organizations. He has published many articles on learning-related issues. Tom has an MBA from Cranfield and is a member of the Chartered Institute of Personnel and Development.

James Hill has worked in financial services, pharmaceuticals, manufacturing and telecoms industries as a consultant for the past ten years. He has a particular interest in the setting up and delivering of large-scale learning projects. The interaction between change and learning as projects evolve was the subject of his MSc dissertation.

Gerry Kincaid is currently the Information Systems Director of the Datum Group and has been involved in commercial systems development for 18 years. A graduate in Computing Science/Economics, Gerry has an MBA from Strathclyde Graduate Business School (SGBS) and is a qualified Chartered Engineer. Gerry also holds a 5th Dan in Kendo.

Ronnie Lessem is Director of the Transformation Programme at the University of Buckingham, in the UK and Middle East. He is author of some twenty books on self, organizational and societal transformation and consultant to public and private enterprises internationally. His latest book (forthcoming), with Sudhanshu Palsule is entitled *Leadership and Transformation: from Local Identity to Global Integrity*.

Alison Lyon has spent her career in the voluntary sector, apart from one misguided sojourn in a non-departmental government body and a brief foray into the field of commerce. She has enjoyed bringing many improvements to the communications capabilities of several organizations, most recently the leading children's charity, NCH.

Ian McGill is a development practitioner working with senior managers and staff in the public and private sectors. He is a writer who maintains an interest in collaborative working and learning as well as programming professional development groups. Ian also trains and accredits facilitators of action learning.

A qualified accountant, **Peter McInnes** spent ten years providing managerial accounting information in a variety of companies varying in size from partnerships up to blue chip organizations. Returning to full-time study, Peter completed his Masters at Strathclyde University and is continuing his studies in pursuit of a PhD.

David Muskett is Head of Department of Retailing and Marketing at Manchester Metropolitan University. Originally a lecturer in Marketing, his experience with outside clients on distance learning programmes led him to develop an interest in the behavioural and learning aspects of such interactions, using MMU's relationship with Sainsbury's as its basis.

Suzanne O'Hara is a Principal Lecturer in the Faculty of Business in the University of Brighton. She co-leads the Management Development Research Unit and is responsible for managing the self-managed action learning programme for the Health Board.

Nigel Purse founded The Oxford Group in 1987 following a career in HR with the Mars corporation. He continues to work full time within the group supporting colleagues in developing and delivering innovative learning solutions for major clients. He has designed and delivered hundreds of successful training interventions for managers at all levels in business life.

Ian Ritchie is one of the founders of The Oxford Group, the international management consultancy and training company. For the past 15 years he has helped develop leaders for many of the world's most respected organizations. Previously he had a successful career in line management and in HR for a major oil company.

Tom Robertson is a manager with Allied Distillers Ltd. Although working in manufacturing all his life, he has a keen interest in, and has contributed to many, organizational development initiatives. He graduated from Strathclyde Graduate Business School with both MBA and MPhil and is currently a part-time tutor at the school.

Bob Sang is an independent practitioner whose work focuses on learning and development in complex changing systems. By emphasizing the active participation of citizens in the changes and decisions that affect their lives, Bob is working on the design, planning and implementation of interventions that support social inclusion and interorganizational learning.

Dr Sonal Shah is a General Practitioner at the same surgery as Dr Bhandari, with a special interest in dermatology. She graduated from Manchester University and is a community-based clinical tutor for General Medicine and Obstetrics and Gynaecology for the Royal Free, University College and Imperial College Medical Schools.

Anne Sheils is Director of Human Resources at Thus plc. Prior to this appointment, Anne worked with a global technology company with responsibility for both training and development and organization development in the UK and Europe. She has also carried out a number of HR roles in various UK retail organizations.

Joy Wanless works as a management consultant in the voluntary sector. She encourages organizations to use reflective practice to analyse their position. Joy believes her success with organizations is due to the practice of core values of respect, empathy and genuineness. Her recent work with organizations, including Church Action on Poverty, Salford Urban Mission and The East Manchester Voluntary and Community Sector Consortium has enabled them to restructure and meet the current economic and political challenges whilst preserving their core beliefs. Joy also works as a management trainer in post-graduate dentistry. She is a voluntary counsellor with Marriage Care.

Trix Webber is a member of the Management Development Research Unit at the University of Brighton. She lectures in organizational development and change management in

Brighton Business School and is Programme Leader for the MBA degree. She also works on development programmes in public and private sector organizations.

Susan Weil is Professor of Social and Organizational Learning at UCN, Northampton, where she founded the SOLAR centre, internationally renowned for action research in complex systems. Two new books are coming out of this work, including *The Poetics and Politics of Transformative Research* and *Practice: Creating Living Knowledge for a Change*.

List of Boxes, Figures and Tables

1 *Purpose and Themes*

1 *Our Purpose*

Anne Brockbank, Ian McGill and Nic Beech

The idea of a learning organization continues to stimulate the imagination and encourage new approaches to learning and development at work. However, the reality of such an organization remains elusive. Organizations may be moving towards that reality, and may be at different stages of the journey, a journey which can be seen as a continuous and reflective learning process. The kind of learning now sought by organizations addresses the challenges of continual change in a variety of economic, social and political contexts.

The key purpose of this handbook is to unlock the learning process that first leads to and supports improvements in organizational performance and secondly leads to transformational change that so often is elusive or happens serendipitously or not at all. Improvement and transformational change requires a learning process that is explicitly and intentionally created and reflective in approach. We are endeavouring to get into the 'black box' of what the appropriate conditions are to create reflective learning in organizations that consciously support learning for improvement and transformation of products, services, processes and strategies.

We define reflective learning as a process which involves dialogue with others for improvement or transformation whilst recognizing the emotional, social and political context of the learner.

This book is designed in three parts. Part 1 gives the purpose and outline of the book, introduces some of the theories underpinning reflective and organizational learning, and offers some practical ideas for realizing such learning. Here we have sought to give primacy to the data (detailed in Parts 2 and 3), and to draw from them themes and theoretical reflections which relate to practice, as the intention is not to move into a purely theoretical approach, but to seek integration between useful theory and theoretically insightful practice. Part 1 concludes with Chapter 5 which highlights the key themes that are reflected in the contributions in Parts 2 and 3. The themes are presented as questions rather than statements. The reason for this is that the complexity of the topic, the various impacting factors and the possible processes and outcomes of learning, mean that it is inappropriate to offer simplified unitary assessments. Rather, we seek to pose questions which would be useful to those pursuing, contemplating and researching reflective learning. The emergent themes also offer a map of sorts which may be helpful to the reader in deciding how they navigate through the reported learning journeys in Parts 2 and 3.

The aim of the cases in Parts 2 and 3 is to offer examinations of practice which give as honest as possible accounts of the learning processes in the organization concerned. These are real stories of the excitement and struggle which organizational learning implies. Part 2 draws together studies which report on learning processes that had some programmed element at their centre. In some cases there were formal, award-bearing courses, but in most

they were tailor-made programmes designed to serve a particular purpose in the organization. One thing that all have in common is that while the programme may be a starting-point, it is not the end of learning, and a key contribution to learning in these cases was the informal and action-based learning that occurred outside the classroom. Part 3 introduces a series of chapters which are fairly diverse, but have the common aim of enabling reflective learning, while choosing a variety of means to this end. None of the cases is an exemplar of a learning organization, but perhaps because of this they have interesting 'real world' problems and solutions, steps forwards and backwards which may hold insights for others engaged in reflective learning. Our conclusion in Chapter 22 summarizes the role of reflective learning in organizational learning.

Clearly a learning organization not only enables the individuals within it to learn as individuals, very much in the traditional Human Resources way, but additionally develops intellectual capital through organizational learning. The potential effects of such learning are increased performance through shared knowledge and skills. In addition, where organizations understand the learning process itself, then they are likely to achieve transformation through creative and innovative differentiation. This book addresses possibilities about how such learning can be, or is being achieved, explicitly and implicitly. Conditions for intentional learning are given as well as what is needed for less explicit learning for individuals, groups and organizations.

We do not assume that the learning environment is neutral in organizations. Our definitions of learning emphasize the social context and therefore the power nexus experienced by learners. The individual's responsibility for learning is accepted, as well as the organization's responsibility for their learning, without assuming that learning takes place within a neutral context. The factors of class, race, gender, status and relative opportunity are real elements in a learning environment. In this respect the book offers no easy solutions, preferring to grapple with the uncomfortable realities about learning in organizations, and our contributors reflect this position.

2 The Nature and Context of Learning

Anne Brockbank, Ian McGill and Nic Beech

The nature of learning

There is no science or theory of learning which embraces all the activities involved in human learning. Most of what we do, think, feel and believe is learned so the field of activities is wide and varied. There is little agreement among researchers about what learning is, for example the behavioural psychologist tends to identify learning in changed behaviour, while cognitive psychologists seek for change *inside* the learner as evidence that learning has taken place. Traditional academic learning has tended to emphasize learning as exclusively a mental process, whereas progressive approaches to learning insist that learners must be active and learn by doing. Recent progressive ideas include emotional elements in learning and we recommend that all three domains are attended to – that is, doing, thinking and feeling – for deep and significant learning.

Early research on learning, dominated by behaviourism and cognitive psychology, limited itself to measurable, observable behavioural outcomes. These early 'testing' methodologies paved the way for categorization and inventories from which educationalists, trainers and indeed recruiters, could interpolate the intellectual/personal capacity of the learner. The testing methods of these early researchers reveal their model of the human learner as passive receptacles. The previous learning, past experience and expectations of learners were largely ignored, as only what was ostensibly being measured was relevant.

Researchers have tried to redress the balance by exploring the impact on learning of individual differences, giving taxonomies of learning styles which recognize that individuals may vary in their response to learning opportunities (Kolb 1984; Honey and Mumford 1992). Such typologies have left the actual learning process as mysterious as ever, but the acknowledgement that individuals learn differently has alerted trainers to the danger of an approach which assumes that learners are all the same. We return to learning typologies below.

New research has taken into account *how* people learn as well as *what* they learn, by using 'asking' methodologies known as phenomenography (Mann 1987). Such studies revealed a variety of orientations, approaches and strategies, suggesting that deep holistic learning is preferable to surface serialist learning, and is likely to be achieved by learners who take responsibility for their own learning, and are motivated by their own learning ambitions. The move from 'testing' to 'asking' uncovered the importance of context in the learning process, revealing that learners 'play' the system of learning, by compliance with powerful forces, often against their own instincts and best interests (Marton 1981; Saljo 1988; Pines and West 1986). The importance of the sequencing of learning, and the possibilities for inter-

active reflections has been stressed both in the emergent themes drawn from the cases, and in the detail of several of the cases in Parts II and III.

The move towards asking learners builds on the ideas of personal construct psychology, allowing the learner to create their own constructs and meanings in describing their learning (Kelly 1955), as well as recognizing that learning and knowledge is created within a social context. When learners themselves are consulted about their learning they are revealed as active responsible adults who are capable of sharing their meanings and justifying their understandings. The socially constructed nature of knowledge has been explored at length elsewhere (Berger and Luckmann 1966), and we note below the power of the social context in learning. The social systems in which a learner is embedded will dominate much of her learning, as 'no human thought is immune to the ideologizing influence of its social context' (Burr 1995, p. 21). The workplace has its own ideology, often invisible to learners. However, the power of the learning context can be used to enable development towards a more general concept of ideology, through recognition of other and self as sources of knowledge, and reflective learning offers a method for doing this. The value, cultural, emotional and interactive contexts of learning can be seen to vary considerably in the cases presented, and this highlights the importance of raising such issues for consideration both in learning design, and explicitly with learners.

Most modern theories promote the concept of reflection as essential for deep and significant learning. We summarize below the theory underpinning our approach to learning and, in particular, reflective learning, in organizations which seek development and growth. A detailed discussion of the requirements for reflective learning can be found in *Facilitating Reflective Learning in Higher Education* (Brockbank and McGill 1998).

We define reflective learning as an intentional process, where social context and experience are acknowledged, in which learners are active individuals, wholly present, engaging with others, and open to challenge, and the outcome involves transformation as well as improvement for both individuals and their organization.

This type of learning process is inherently complicated, and it takes place in complicated situations. It is therefore inappropriate to prescribe one best way of doing reflective learning. The approach taken here is to raise a series of questions and issues that are intended to help others make their own journey. To coin a phrase: *the only real path is the one you see after walking across the desert when you look back and see your own footsteps.* In Chapter 5, on emerging themes, we extract some of the main questions that reflect the paths that others have trodden.

Learning as a social activity

We start from the value that people are abundant in their resources. They bring their experience to learning situations. This contrasts crudely with the view that people are 'empty vessels' to be filled. This metaphor is discussed in detail in Chapter 20 on knowledge management and learning. But learning does not occur in a vacuum. The context in which learning may happen is crucial. Learning is a social process, which will influence the degree of 'agency' (autonomy) experienced by the learner. Hence the learning context will affect how autonomous the learner feels. The social process is critical to learning. By social process we mean the context and conditions in which learning takes place, which will influence how intentional learning situations are created and undertaken.

A social constructionist stance, drawing on the work of Berger and Luckmann (1966),

holds that our realities are deeply influenced by our life experience. So learning contexts are themselves socially constructed. In addition the social constructivists tell us that 'we create rather than discover ourselves' and we do this through engagement-with-others, using language in discourse (Burr 1995, p. 28). For reflective learning, the recognition that 'the self' may take an infinite variety of forms (Gergen 1989), that our conceptual space is created through our language (Potter and Wetherell 1987), and that our context is defined by the prevailing discourse (Grant et-al. 1998), enables learners to access their potential and challenge what constrains their learning.

The prevailing discourse is defined as 'a set of meanings, metaphors, representations, images, stories, statements and so on that, in some way together produce a particular version' (Burr 1995, p. 48) of events, person, or class of person. So examples of how discourse prevails are given by terms like 'attitude problem', down-sizing, on-message, globalization, unionized, eco-warrior. Identities are constructed through discourse – for example, how intelligent someone is judged to be may relate to their physical appearance and to how they are allowed to talk without interruption. These factors are differentiated between the genders. The operation of discourses is not power-neutral, but rather is imbued with power relations which impact on how people are defined and granted or not granted voice, resources and decision-making powers. The individual is not a given, as the self is continuously constructed through the social relationships, discourse and practices of the organizational culture in which he or she is embedded (Townley 1994).

Hence as learners we enter a system that is not value free, where power is exercised that can influence our progress and affect our learning context. These contexts exist across a whole spectrum of organizations, from formal educational institutions to public companies and voluntary organizations. In-house learning is explicitly aimed at fulfilling the purposes of the organization and these are generated by 'leaders' within the organization, who ideally will be the designers of learning. The reality is rather different in our current corporate world, where the legal rights of proprietors take precedence over those of the employee, let alone the client or customer.

In addition, there will be implicit learning which takes place informally as individuals come to grips with the culture and 'ways of doing or saying things around here', that is, the learning climate and the dominant discourse.

The social nature of learning offers opportunities for the learner to reflect upon her learning not only by herself, but with others. Being able to undertake reflection alone is necessary but not sufficient. The tendency to self-deceive, collude and be unaware is ever present. When others are present the learner has potentiality for challenge which may not be available alone. As meaning is created in relation to others, then reflection and the creation of meaning is inevitably a social process. The context in which such reflection occurs is the learning relationship.

The learning relationship is one that can occur formally or informally, explicitly or implicitly. When people in an organization find themselves in an enabling learning role, the stance they create with the learner(s) is crucial. Without explicit recognition of the interaction as embodying a relationship, then in working with these conditions we may be less effective. There is a tendency for knowledge to be treated as static, disembodied, as a product rather than process where learners may be detached from the knowledge being imparted. Moreover the enabler may also treat the learner as detached, disembodied, object, passive. This is a very limited form of relationship inhibiting learning for the learner. Similar hierarchies can occur in line relationships in organizational contexts.

In recognizing the interaction as constituting a relationship between enabler and learner and between learners, we are saying that the outcome of the interaction, that is, the knowledge, comes through communication. As one writer has expressed it: 'and what is implicit in communication is the sense that the other person can understand and make sense of what is being said. Where this sense is absent, what is ostensibly being offered is unlikely to be assimilated' (Salmon 1980, p. 14). We will examine the form of the interaction in more detail in Chapter 4 in relation to dialogue and reflection.

Power and passivity in learning

If learning takes place in a social context then we must examine the issue of power. Many writings on the learning organization and materials relating to development, particularly management development, treat that development in an individualistic and decontextualized manner. In other words the idea that the individual manager is responsible for their own development suggests that their progress is a product of their own motivation, commitment and drive. Some of the tools for enabling managers to determine their progress, for example, learning styles, assume a neutral context, as if the manager was somehow the same gender, class, and race and that the notions of diversity, status and relative opportunity did not exist. There is also a tendency to ignore the impact of discourse, culture and ideology on learners.

For effective organizational learning, there is a need to recognize power relations rather than power as a 'given' commodity, which leaves the individual feeling helpless. All social and personal relationships, including work relationships, have a power element. Where learning procedures recognize such power relations this can lead to a political agenda for change if desired (Townley 1994). We note here our use of the term political, often perceived as negative, and consciously wish to draw attention to the way that discourse itself promotes particular power relations. Where the learner becomes aware of the reality of such discourse and identifies practices which dominate relationships in the workplace, there is hope of personal and organizational transformation.

Class, race, gender, role, identity and relative opportunity all impact on learning. In addition, the organization is not neutral territory. Organizations have their formal and informal power structures and relationships in which employees are actors, as well as organizational agents and respondents. Engaging in reflective learning and development will impact upon those structures and relationships, particularly if development is related to promotion as well as operational effectiveness. The organization will learn to the degree that 'it can reconcile individual and organizational needs to release and support the inherent energy and creativity of its individual members' (Pedler et al. 1991, p. 172). The assumption that individual and organizational learning goals are compatible has been questioned and the complexity of negotiating within the tension explored. Antonacopoulou (1999) has identified the positive and negative attitudes of managers towards the need to learn. Her findings illustrate how the interaction of personal and organizational factors create conditions that affect the individual's receptivity to learning, and are situation-specific, making the concept of 'styles' nothing more than an excuse for resistance.

This brings us to the essential tension which exists between organizational purpose and self-development. How the organization generates its purpose may influence the commitment of its members. There will be difference and conflict in any organization, particularly about its purpose and chances of survival. The inevitable conflict between individual need

and corporate purpose has been noted by John Heron: 'what makes an organization enlightened is that it has built-in procedures for acknowledging such conflict and working constructively with it' (Heron 1977, p. 7).

The political process of learning from difference, challenge and conflict is unfortunately dubbed as 'politicking' and viewed negatively, an example of how discourse can silence voices. The power of discourse lies in its connection to how an organization is run. A discourse is so embedded in our discursive culture that it is invisible and hidden from us. Therein lies its power: 'Power is tolerable only on condition that it masks a substantial part of itself from us' (Foucault 1976, p. 86). The challenge of embedded discourse is the 'uncovering' of its taken-for-granted status, often by drawing on alternative discourses, considering multiple meanings, a variety of metaphors, other's stories, and so on. This may be based around an enquiring management style focused on 'coping'. It will require managers (and others) to hold multiple conceptions of reality at any one time, in other words to develop a Janusian perception (Rothenberg 1979).

Where the embedded discourse is resistant to challenge, the organization will be unaware of its culture, convinced of the 'truth' or validity of its position, and this ideological belief will be enjoyed by many of its members. Organizations which seek culture change and transformation are seeking to dislodge the prevailing discourse and generate a new 'view of the world'. The difficulty is that the very structures and procedures which maintain the prevailing discourse may work against the prospect of transformation. For example, judgemental appraisals and a blame culture will resist openness and honest debriefing as too risky. Additionally, it can be argued that discourses are really powerful when they are not perceived especially not perceived as a problem. Under these circumstances there would be no intention to change them, and hence they continue to be 'natural' or 'the only way to do things'. Reflective learning opens a Pandora's Box for organizations. If individuals and groups are encouraged to challenge existing ideologies then they may become aware of some of the other realities of their corporate system. Those enlightened organizations which have the courage to open up their culture to reflective learning will be taking a risky step towards transformation and future survival.

Aspects of such enlightened organizations include the need for development programmes likely to deliver managers and others with the high-level skills needed to support reflective learning, and we say more about these skills in Chapter 4. Whilst emphasizing the need for taking organizational responsibilities seriously, it is important that the responsibility of the learner remains just that, the individual's responsibility to manage their own learning, whilst keeping in sight 'the greater good' that is, the needs of the organization as a whole (Adlam and Plumridge 1990).

If the learner feels a lack of power in a potential learning relationship, then there will be a lack of trust: the learner will not feel able to trust the learning context, others in that context, and any enabler of learning. Given that reflective learning will involve feelings or emotions in addition to thinking and action, a lack of trust will inhibit any display of emotion or vulnerability and therefore openness to learning. When we really learn, particularly that which is potentially transformative, we lay ourselves open to uncertainty and can be (temporarily) unstable. Uncertainty can engender emotions and we need conditions of safety that ensure those expressed feelings are not taken advantage of. Determining who is part of the learning relationship will be important depending upon the nature of the learning task. For example, it may be inappropriate to organize development groups or learning partners where there are line relationships between members of the group.

Levels of learning in organizations

When individuals learn they may improve their performance and they may also transform themselves. When organizations learn they are likely to transform themselves. This has been described as not only doing things right, but also, more challenging, doing the right things. In addition, an organization which is capable of reflecting on the learning process – that is, learn about learning – is likely to develop, prosper and survive. We can identify these three levels as improvement, transformation and learning about learning:

- Improvement: Reflective learning will deliver improvement, as learners process their work, assessing and reconsidering for improved performance, that is, 'doing things right'. This we identify as reflective learning for improvement.
- Transformation: Reflective learning for transformation offers the potential for learners to move one step further and reconsider their work in strategic terms, questioning and challenging existing patterns, thereby opening the door to creativity and innovation, that is, 'doing the right things'. This we identify as reflective learning for transformation.
- Learn about learning: We also offer the idea of a further level of reflection, which can only occur as a consequence of the first two, and that is reflective learning about learning. This entails an individual or organization standing back from their improvements and transformations and seeking to identify 'how we did that' so that this knowledge can be transferred to future situations.

Reflective learning for improvement is a necessary component for organizational success but it is no longer sufficient for organizations, which hope to survive in the world continually subject to change. The ever-changing market environment demands learning that can develop and create ever new ideas and products, whilst keeping in mind the organization's responsibilities to its stakeholders and not just its shareholders. The increasingly globalized economy impacts, along with the rapidity of social change, upon the public and voluntary sectors. In order to keep in the race, the organization needs to collectively stop and reflect, critically, on the organization's purpose. Reflective learning for transformation occurs when learners are enabled to pause and reconsider, preferably with others, the nature of what they are doing. This means more than re-examining the task in hand. It means re-examining the rationale behind what is being done. When such a dialogue with others is enabled throughout a system, the organization collectively reflects, reconsiders and ultimately transforms itself from within.

We need to define reflective learning for improvement, reflective learning for transformation, and learning about learning. This can be usefully elaborated by recourse to notions of single- and double-loop learning.

Single- and double-loop learning

The terms single- and double-loop learning were first used by Argyris and Schon in 1974 to distinguish between learning for improving the way things are done, and learning which transforms the situation. Single-loop 'instrumental' learning, whilst it achieves immediate improvement, leaves underlying values and ways of seeing things unchanged. Improvement learning may involve reflection on the given task but is not likely to change it. Double-loop

learning takes place when assumptions about ways of seeing things are challenged and underlying values are changed (Brockbank and McGill 1998). Double-loop learning, in questioning 'givens' or 'taken for granteds' (tfgs) has the potential to bring about a profound shift in underlying values by cracking their paradigms or 'ways of seeing the world' ('world' here denotes the realities of an individual, group or organization). Thus we are defining double-loop learning as reflective learning for transformation.

Moreover, in organizations, double-loop learning must be seen in the context of non-static systems, communities, societies and the world where change and uncertainty is increasingly the norm. A recent development of the double-loop model recognizes the significance of the socio-political context, where 'Discontinuities and uncertainty are rife ... generating needs for new forms of social learning' (Weil 1997a, p. 124).

Single-loop learning or day-to-day maintenance learning for improvement, meeting goals and altering practice on the basis of experience, enables progress to be made. The concept of effective single-loop learning has been described graphically in a well-known diagram by Kolb (1984), where goals are set on the basis of theory, action is taken, and, on the basis of this experience and reflection, a new action or plan is devised. For day-to-day learning the loop is productive and the learner gains competence and confidence, that is, this is reflective learning for improvement. The process is illustrated in Figure 2.1 below.

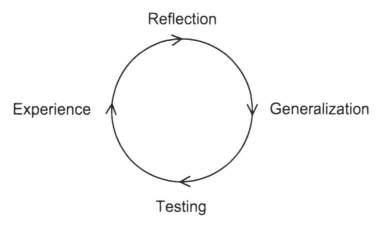

Source: Brockbank and McGill 1998.

Figure 2.1 Single-loop learning

The cyclical nature of learning illustrated here is rarely realized in practice as typical training and development programmes talk about the cycle but are actually an engagement in a linear process *with the ends joined up* (Hawkins 1994). Hence even single-loop learning with a reflective element is not always achieved.

We refer now, with permission, to Peter Hawkins' original diagram to illustrate double-loop learning in Figure 2.2 (Garratt's egg-timer *c*. 1987, cited in Hawkins 1994).

The arrows in the lower circle indicate day-to-day functioning in single-loop learning. When conditions are favourable, assumptions or taken-for-granteds (tfgs) are questioned, and the learner may swing out of lower circle orbit and begins to traverse the upper circle in double-loop learning mode. The learner has 'come outside of their box'. The option remains

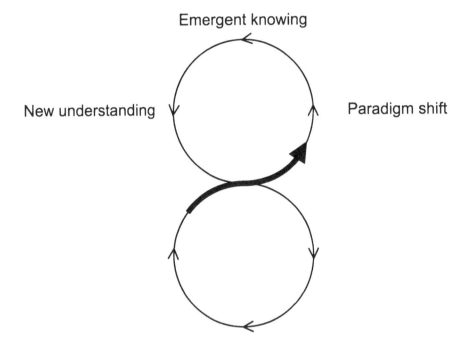

Source: Adapted from an original idea by P. Hawkins 1997, in Brockbank and McGill 1998.

Figure 2.2 Double-loop learning

of returning to the single loop when appropriate, perhaps to test a new theory in the time-honoured way, and continue to achieve improvement with a new understanding. The single-loop orbit is contained and can be traversed within, say, a project or programme, setting goals within a given cycle of activity or achieving a level of understanding within a professional field. The double-loop orbit would occur when reconsidering the whole project or programme with a view to major change, or even reconsidering an organization's purpose, structure or culture, that is, learning for transformation.

What is needed to enable the learner to shoot out of the single orbit, and traverse the exciting and potentially disturbing orbit of double-loop learning? If we were to pursue our analogy of orbits and rocket science the answer suggests that what is required is *energy* to fuel the 'burn' of a changed trajectory. Where is the source of this energy to come from?

The evidence suggests that emotion and motivation are connected and that double-loop or transformative learning can be triggered by strong emotion, through trauma or 'peak' experiences (Brookfield 1987, p. 7). In addition the process of questioning and challenging the taken-for-granteds (tfgs) can stimulate strong emotions, disturbance, distress and also joy and exhilaration (ibid., p. 8). We are told that a certain degree of energy or excitement is necessary for learning to occur, so that a crisis may generate organizational learning. However, research suggests that stress is a major block to learning, and an organization where fear is rife and staff are operating under pressure is unlikely to engage in transformatory learning (Brundage and Mackeracher 1980). So there is a fine line here between reflective learning that stimulates emotional energy and transformation, and stressful situations which inhibit

learning. The individual learner may judge where their own fine line exists – this will be different for everyone. Boredom is a sign that no learning is taking place and it has been said that 'all progress in business life comes from kicking a habit, from doing something new and refreshingly different. Because if you do what you've always done, you'll get what you've always got' (Browning 1998).

Single-loop learning and double-loop paradigm shifts or different ways of seeing the world have effect at the level of the individual. However, for organizations there will be a need for transformative shifts amongst significant numbers of personnel if the organization is to meet emerging challenges, because of continuing fundamental change surrounding any organization. It may be that there is individual, collective and/or sectional resistance or myopia to change, in which case the organization may become increasingly obsolescent. Alternatively, opportunities can be made for double-loop learning alongside the maintenance of single-loop learning, offering hope for organizational learning, transformation and survival. Such opportunities, which we define as reflective-learning-with-others, that is, reflective dialogue, are described in Chapter 4.

Double-loop learning

The tendency to overlook the obvious, the taken-for-granteds (tfgs) is supremely human. Some of the tfgs form quite powerful defences, known as defensive reasoning, which are difficult and painful to dislodge.

As learners, the prospect of analysing our defensive reasoning (Argyris 1991) is threatening on four counts:

- We may lose control.
- We may not win.
- We may not be able to suppress negative feelings.
- We may not be rational.

For chief executives, senior managers and directors, trained in the Western rational system, such threats are real and powerful, notwithstanding external pressure from their shareholders. Their continued defensive reasoning maintains comfort and clones another generation of managers in their own image. This brings us to another aspect of the learning organization which has been noted: the leadership issue. Organizations which learn are likely to be led, not by 'heroes' but by designers. Leaders in aspiring learning organizations need to be designers of the learning process for their organization, stewards of the vision, managers of creative tension (Senge 1990). How can this happen in a legal framework in private enterprise and global industry where the rights of proprietors routinely take precedence over those of employees? Where conflicts arise the political process in organizations rarely offers facilitation for resolving differences. On the contrary, politics is perceived as pernicious and informal activity like 'politicking' as pejorative. We discuss how 'politicking' and informal dialogue may promote reflective learning in Chapter 4. For leaders to engage in reflection they need to be confident in themselves, and able to tolerate doubt and uncertainty about their decisions. Leaders are traditionally insecure, power-hungry and not prone to self-analysis, and this works against them engaging in reflective learning (Coopey 1995, quoting Kets de Vries 1991). To engage in double-loop learning calls for a degree of vulnerability in those

at the top of the organization which seeks to learn: learning will be nurtured in organizations where leaders are not seen as heroes and where defensive reasoning is undermined, with the CEO in the lead.

The importance of reflection for individual learning is understood at all levels of learning, from reflective learning for improvement (single-loop or maintenance learning), through reflective learning for transformation (double-loop or evolutionary learning), to our third level of learning, where the learner goes one step further to consider and reflect upon how the single- and double-loop learning was achieved, in other words, reflective learning about learning (Argyris and Schon 1996, p. 20). How does this apply to organizational learning? Donald Schon makes this clear: 'Productive organizational learning … is the organizational counterpart of what an individual does when s(he) engages in reflective practice or reflective inquiry. A learning organization could be an organization that creates the conditions for individual reflective practice' (Schon 1994, p. 11).

Conclusion

Learning can be perceived in a variety of ways: new knowledge and understanding, a change in behaviour, or a revision of attitude. In addition, learning may lead to improvement in performance, a necessary component of successful business and service in any organization, or it may lead to transformation, both individual and organizational. When learners dare to traverse the double-loop by confronting their taken-for-granteds (tfgs) they may transform their view of the world and therefore their organization. A clever organization builds on such individual transformation, and indeed will encourage and enable it to happen. The complex power of discourse and culture is recognized by such an organization and development programmes are likely to reflect this. A learning environment, which nurtures single- and double-loop learning, and offers learners a chance to reflect on their learning, demands high-level skills in those enabling learning, either formally or informally. We look now at how we can make learning reflective.

3 Reflective Learning and Organizations

Anne Brockbank, Ian McGill and Nic Beech

The rapidly changing environment for organizations, the global marketplace, and sweeping social and political change make organizational learning essential for survival. The Chief Executive of a company which has experienced decline and renewal in a stormy environment is definite about how the company has achieved its growth: 'Learning is at the heart of a company's ability to adapt to a rapidly changing environment' (Prokesch 1997).

Pettigrew and Whipp (1991) identified a number of variables which differentiated organizations that were effective in managing change and those that were not. These variables included:

- environmental assessment – the availability of key people, the character of the organization, the organizational and external environment
- leading change – building and legitimating a receptive context for change, creating the necessary capabilities and constructing and directing the nature of change
- linking strategic and operational change – justifying the need for change, supplying vision and building capacity
- seeing human resources as assets and liabilities – demonstrating the need for change, cumulative supportive activities, linking human resource management (HRM) action to business needs
- achieving coherence – consistency and integrity

Such an approach may represent significant structural and systems change, but each variable, if it is to be successfully enacted, requires individual and organizational learning. For example, data on the environment must be gathered, analysed and communicated to decision makers, and if there is to be increased coherency, interaction between different functions so that they are 'pulling together rather than pulling apart' needs to be developed. Typically this would require developing greater understanding of each others' roles, abilities and limitations, and how the parts contribute to the whole.

Salaman (1995) offers an analysis of six factors of learning which he argues could contribute to an ability to manage change in the way implied by Pettigrew and Whipp (1991):

1. The structure of the organization needs to encourage learning and include openness which subjects top decisions to scrutiny from throughout the organization.
2. Learning needs to be rewarded, both financially and socially, for example, through role modelling.

3. A culture which supports relationships through acceptance of intimacy, trust and affection, rather than being based on individualism, needs to be in place.
4. The style of leadership, counter to the predominant norm in Western cultures, needs to be one which fosters egalitarianism, connections between people and identifying and correcting performance.
5. Open and productive relationships between various stakeholder groups (such as workers, clients, suppliers, managers, shareholders and so on) need to be created.
6. There is an impact from the macro/societal culture in which the organization exists. Where that culture is characterized by distance, formality and anxiety, non-learning is more likely than learning.

One aspiration that gained currency in the managerial discourse was to become a 'learning organization'. Such an organization would be able to manage change such that all the variables cited by Pettigrew and Whipp were successfully dealt with, and also fulfil the requirements specified by Salaman. The Learning Organization has been defined as 'an organization which facilitates the learning of all its members and continuously transforms itself' (Pedler et al. 1991), as 'an organization that is continually expanding its capacity to create its future' (Senge 1990, p. 14), 'and where people are continually learning how to learn' (ibid., p. 3).

Individual learning and organizational learning are part of both definitions and one or other alone is insufficient for *organizational* transformation. Clearly the individual may transform their orientation to work, and make changes to personal behaviour and goals. But if this is not accompanied by organizational activities of a transformative nature, the organization itself remains unchanged, and this is likely to affect its survival in the marketplace. Although the Learning Organization is an attractive idea, many questions have been raised about its practical viability. For example, how can an organization learn? Some experts say that only individuals learn and an organization will learn by stimulating and encouraging the individuals within it to engage in real and significant learning. Who is to judge what is real and significant? What if the individual's learning is counter-productive to the organization's aims, explicit or implicit? How would organizational learning be recognized? In addition, as Salaman (1995) has argued, in order to transform into a learning organization, typically major cultural, structural and systems change is necessary. This is problematic, not least because, as Argyris (1986) has pointed out, many organizations have established routines and norms that reinforce non-learning. These norms focus on defence, control and the avoidance of (potentially creative) conflict and risk-taking: 'Protect yourself unilaterally – by avoiding direct interpersonal confrontation and public discussion of sensitive issues that might expose you to blame. Control the situation and the task – by making up your own mind about the problem and acting on your view, by keeping your view private and by avoiding the public enquiry which might refute your view' (Argyris 1986, p. 40, cited in Salaman 1995, p. 105).

If the organization and its members become dominated by such norms, problems will result because effective change becomes less likely. It may be that the goal of being a Learning Organization which is transformational as a whole and for all its members is unachievable in practical reality. We would argue that reflective learning offers an alternative that is both achievable and able to engage with the social complexities discussed by Argyris and Salaman.

Reflective learning has the advantage of focusing on activity rather than claiming a state of being, and learning is always likely to be a state of 'becoming' (Chia 1996) rather than static. Change and learning are intrinsically linked as it is through perceiving, adapting and

making sense of circumstances, and one's potential for action in those circumstances, that people are able to cope with change. Within the complexity of change it is unlikely that a unified frame of sense-making (Goffman 1961) will be accepted as true by all actors in the situation. What is more likely is that there will be some diversity of understandings. It is fully possible for different groups of actors to perceive what is ostensibly one set of 'facts' as a good change, a bad change or no change at all. Similarly, it is not unusual for the leaders and recipients of change to view things differently. For example, the problems currently being experienced are evidence for the recipients that things are, as they expected, getting worse. And the same problems are evidence for the leaders of 'teething problems' on the way to the expected better future (Beech 2000). From a logical standpoint, both perceptions cannot be right. However, in the socially complex setting of organizations, 'reality is what we take to be true' (Zukov 1980; quoted in Keenoy and Anthony 1992, p. 236). Both realities can coexist, and the groups that express them may or may not be cognisant of the 'reality' of the other group.

The question is, what can managers do in such circumstances? One answer is that the role of managers is not to achieve perfection, certainty or singular clear direction. Rather their role is to cope, and to enable others to cope (Beech and Cairns 2001). Coping is typically used in a pejorative way in the discourse of management – indeed, if someone says they are 'coping' it can be taken to mean the opposite. However, in the positive sense, coping is about seeking to make the differences between different realities overt and understandable to others. This is not done with the aim of resolving them to one stance, or to impose a dominant view. Rather the point is to understand how others think, and why they think like that, and on the basis of this understanding to decide how to engage with them in terms that are meaningful to them, however foreign they seem to one's own reality. This approach is different to Pettigrew and Whipp's proposition about achieving coherence, because it envisages divergence being maintained and used, and it regards conflict, as long as it remains impersonal, as potentially useful in generating new solutions.

Clearly, this links closely to learning. Developing a genuinely open mind, able to 'read' the discourses of others and take their realities as if they make sense when they do not from one's own perspective, is a learning skill. It is an essentially social skill, and dialoguing and questioning are its prime virtues. These stand in contrast to the virtues of traditional conceptions of management – those of giving clear vision and direction, and of inspiring and transforming others. The reflective learning approach is less heroic, and offers an alternative which, we would argue, is beneficial in times and social circumstances of change. (Here a note of caution: we are not suggesting that there is no role for vision, leadership and direction, but we are asserting that these styles of managing may not in and of themselves be sufficient to stimulate learning and effective change in (post)modern complex change situations.)

Rather than seeking to achieve a solid state of being, reflective learning is active – a continuous process of 'becoming', in changing circumstances. It can operate in a localized and micro fashion. Being a Learning Organization implies major structural and cultural change. Reflective learning can be achieved by small groups and individual managers can seek to inspire it within their locus of influence even if the overall organizational culture is not sufficiently supportive to be a Learning Organization. For these reasons we believe that it is a fruitful way forward in current organizational realities.

The next chapter will explore the nature of reflective learning and how it can be achieved in practice.

4 *Reflective Learning in Practice*
Anne Brockbank, Ian McGill and Nic Beech

In this chapter we address the 'how' of reflective learning by describing it in practical terms, indicating what it is, what it looks like in practice, and what is needed to enable it to take place in an organization. The nature of reflection is explored, and reflective dialogue-with-others is recommended as a key method of reflection if individual or organizational transformation is desired. We discuss reflective dialogue and the skills needed for effective double-loop learning, and complete the chapter with some ideas which link the content of dialogue with the levels of learning described in Chapter 2.

How can we make learning reflective?

LEARNING IS ACTIVE RATHER THAN PASSIVE

The idea of an active learner requires real and voluntary participation, quite unlike the passivity of lectures and 'up-front' training. The importance of doing and action is critical for organizations where tangible outcomes are sought from learning. However, modern enterprises seek informed action for future survival. Behavioural change can be achieved through focused training, and this may be adequate in certain situations, but activities which exclude thought and emotion are unlikely to deliver reflective learning. Real participation by the learner can be limited by location, resources, the learning context and the quality of the learning relationship. Developing the use of multi-media for learning can address some of these issues, for example, IT and distance learning can be used to enable learners to either carry out effective learning on their own, or prepare for attendance at interactive sessions. In the cases reported here an increasing use of multi-media was detected, and in the modern world of restricted resources (particularly time) such an approach can be beneficial. Where employees are perceived as passive self-limiting learners, apparently lacking initiative, social and cultural factors are likely to be present. Where learners, for whatever reason, are or feel powerless to influence their working life this affects their stance toward learning, for example, when a line manager discourages junior staff development by blocking opportunity and limiting freedom to act. Where learners have the opportunity to act they have immediate and relevant material available for reflective learning.

Interactive on-line learning satisfies the need to construct knowledge actively, where the learner participates in gleaning the facts and material desired. However, on-line learners, although interacting with the click button, often remain passive as far as learning is concerned, although the Web conference/chat room may provide the opportunity to reflect with others, if the process is well facilitated. The development of reflective learning on-line is still in its infancy just as it is in the face-to-face learning situation (Brown et al. 1999).

LEARNERS USE THEIR EXPERIENCE FOR LEARNING

Experiential learning in its 'active learning' interpretation (Weil and McGill 1989) offers learners recognition and a role in the learning process. This enables learners to place what they are learning within the context of their work, whilst recognizing their life experience. The value of experience as a starting-point for learning has been ignored in traditional settings where the learner is assumed to be an 'empty vessel' to be filled with knowledge. Chapter 20, on CELT, explores some of these issues from the perspectives of alternative metaphors – those of 'transfer' and 'travel', and the view held is that active travel is a more functional perspective to hold when engaging with learning processes. Formal training may have the limitations implicit in the 'transfer' metaphor in which knowledge is 'loaded into' the learners. For many employees life experience may include unhappy learning events, such as school days where they suffered put-downs from teachers and bullying from fellow pupils. A history of academic failure is a starting-point for many learners at work. On the other hand many individuals rise above the unfortunate school experiences and become successful and mature adults in non-academic arenas. Hence, replicating traditional academic approaches when conducting reflective learning in practice may be predisposed to failure. In addition many learners experience oppressive and discriminatory practices in the present. For many, the realities of race, gender and class issues are a day-to-day pressure. Reflective learning includes all such experience as significant material for learning and offers space and place for acknowledging and contextualizing experience.

LEARNERS CONSTRUCT THEIR OWN LEARNING WITHIN A SOCIAL CONTEXT

The idea of a socially constructed world, where each individual contributes to their experienced reality and meaning is created in relation to others, can be recognized in reflective learning. In addition, the power of the learning context to control meaning is recognized in reflective learning through dialogue. The social context of learning has been the invisible 'black box' of the learning process, with the power imbalance implicit in formal training being taken for granted. For reflective learning the social context is part of the learning process itself and the social context provides the facilities for dialogue with others. Interactive learning on line offers some opportunity for learners to construct their own learning and this can become reflective learning if conditions for dialogue are present. Much of the social context relates to the identities and roles people associate with themselves. For many of the organizations explored in Parts 2 and 3, breaking down such conceptualizations was important. This could take the form of team managers changing to a more facilitative and developmental style of management, development of values and vision in a particular setting, or increasing cross-functional working. Any such changes require alterations to attitudes and expectations, and when these alterations impact on the conception one holds of 'the other', there is inevitably a knock-on effect for the conception of 'the self'. These changes are emotionally powered and are hard to predict or control. Lessem describes some of the phases of such transitions in Chapter 21.

REFLECTIVE LEARNING IS NOT A 'STYLE'

The idea that human beings have one set way of learning, stamped on them from birth is the most disturbing outcome of the 'styles' movement. The success of learning styles in management development tells more of the need in organizations to categorize people than the

creation of an objective way of measuring people. It can also be criticized for simplifying what is actually a very complex process. Developments of the Kolb model which focus on observable behaviour are more reliable guides to learning 'orientation' but rely on accuracy of self-report. The *process* of completing these inventories is itself reflective and this may account for their success, as learners are given the time and space to reflect on their learning, discuss it with others and, perhaps consider potential actions. Recent commentaries have identified the weaknesses of stand-alone styles and inventories of learning (Reynolds 1997) as diagnostics, and alerted us again to the danger of de-contextualizing the individual learner, and potentially ignoring the social reality in which learning takes place. For most people, styles, content and significance of learning will vary over time, place, function and personal orientation. What is needed is a way of dealing with such complexities, rather than trying to eliminate them (or at least exclude them by use of a tightly focused model).

REFLECTIVE LEARNING IS HOLISTIC

Traditional approaches to learning have emphasized mental processes; some training concentrates on behavioural change and action while personal development recognizes emotional and social factors in learning. The reflective process values learning which comes from every part of a learner's experience, be it familial, personal or practical. Reflective learning draws on all aspects of the learner, recognizing the significance of a diversity of experience. Recent research suggests that there is not one form of human intelligence, but multiple forms, including visual, musical, kinaesthetic, logical, inter/intra personal and so on (Gardner 1985). The concept of emotional intelligence has emerged as a topic of focus in the UK in the last ten years, offering the prospect of including feelings as part of the learn-ing process (Goleman 1995; Cooper and Sawaf 1997). Emotional factors have been underplayed in the learning literature, where the mental capacities of a person were considered superior to their actions. Western education, and particularly management education, embedded in rationalism, has systematically downgraded the emotion in learning, another instance of management development which denies the context in which individuals learn and the emotional impact of power issues in the workplace. This rationalist tradition in British management resists including emotional elements in learning, and this impacts seriously on learning in organizations. The emotional content of learning is essential for energizing the learner, as well as being a critical component of deeply reflective learning.

REFLECTIVE LEARNING ENRICHES KNOWLEDGE

The acquisition of facts is a familiar model of learning, but remains what it is, surface learning, and many learning environments may limit learning to facts without enriching knowledge. Recent research has enlarged our understanding of how the brain learns. Neuroscience and cognitive psychology have identified how the brain processes material in a self-organizing way, using existing knowledge to generate new meaning from new information (Rose and Nicholl 1997). For deep and significant learning, new knowledge needs to be processed and made sense of within a reflective process, and reflective learning provides this. In the postmodern condition (Lyotard 1984) it cannot be assumed that 'facts' exist in the way that they have been traditionally conceived. Outside the physical sciences (and even within that field), there are few statements that can be entirely unequivocal. Given the global and multi-cultural nature of our socio-economic context, what is good practice in one place may be bad

in another, and assumptions that underlie our taken-for-granteds (tfgs), which may be unconsciously held, may vary considerably in different social settings. The result is that differences may exist between such settings as to what constitutes a 'fact'.

REFLECTIVE LEARNING INCLUDES DOUBLE-LOOP LEARNING

Almost any learning experience offers the potential for improvement where an existing procedure is fine-tuned for improved performance – this is known as single-loop learning. Such learning is the day-to-day achievement which maintains quality and continuously improves existing practice and product in organizations. In addition, reflection, under certain conditions, may lead to transformation where existing ideas, the tfgs are questioned, challenged and reconsidered and this is known as double-loop learning. When the tfgs, the assumptions which are so often the barrier to organizational change and development, can be realized, then, if conditions are right, transformative learning results. Again the danger of assuming that reflection automatically results in creativity and innovation neglects the power of context on the learner. For many, the learning environment restricts potential learning to single-loop learning, for example, the improved performance which emerges form successful coaching. An organization which seeks to nurture double-loop learning and achieve transformation, would need to be aware of its hierarchies and recognize their power.

REFLECTIVE LEARNING USES DIALOGUE

Self-reflection is a familiar concept to us, a private affair, internally conducted, having the advantage of preserving the confidentiality of our struggles as well as the potential for self-delusion! Reflection-with-others, or dialogue, offers the power of challenge and different perspectives to the learner, and ultimately the potential for double-loop learning. Dialogue is an important element in recognizing the cultural power of an organization, allowing issues of influence, authority and status to emerge, as well as class, race and gender issues which affect learning and development at work. Experience and knowledge without reflection is limited and organizations which seek to stimulate creativity and innovation will need to make space for reflection to occur.

Reflection

The idea of reflection as an individual activity, pursued in private, in isolation, is a persistent one. It belongs to the rational model of learning which suggests that the cognitive mind alone can solve any problem, sort out any confusion, because the mind is all-powerful and any contribution from anywhere else is dismissed. Some will say that cognition includes emotional elements and if so then such reflection will be the richer for it. We propose a radical definition of reflective activity for transformation, by agreeing that intrapersonal reflection is effective, and may offer opportunities for deep learning, which may or may not be shared with others, *but is ultimately not enough to promote transformative learning especially for organizations*. On the other hand, providing for interpersonal reflection in reflective dialogue with others guarantees that learners are challenged, that double-loop learning is an option, and that the transformative learning which results from dialogue

is spread across the organization. How possible is it for organizations to make such provision?

In particular, Easterby-Smith identifies the lack of time for reflection as a major hindrance to learning in organizations: 'It is the obsession with activity which is probably one of the biggest hindrances to organizational learning. Even Kolb recommends a *separate* period of reflection' (1990, p. 28; emphasis added). Another hindrance to learning is the difficulty in discerning what activities are 'useful' in organizational life: 'In a world where action rather than reflection is valued, even the reflective learning organization apparently has to race at a pace that leaves little room for deliberation' (Thatchenkery 1996, p. 5).

But there is no simple procedure to guarantee organizational learning: 'Innovation ... is a process through which uncertainty is intentionally increased' (Nonaka 1988, p. 12). People may be required to work in ways that do not seem entirely rational, that is, they may need to use intuition rather than traditional deductive reasoning.

The obstacles to learning in organizations have been summarized on numerous occasions by Argyris: 'Openness and risk taking seem to be limited to those discussions and problems where emotions and interpersonal problems are not involved' (1986, p. 194). The avoidance of conflict or confrontation, and the taboo on discussing either is the outcome of such limitations on discourse and we return to this theme in Chapter 5. A recent study confirmed that organizational culture and structure, and what have been called 'soft' issues are key factors in organizational learning. Successful organizations like Nokia and General Motors set about creating a learning culture by appointing 'knowledge champions' and making learning activity a required competency, in attempts to capture 'learning-in-action' (Mayo 1998).

In addition, the experts agree that structural change (revising patterns of power and prestige) and cultural change (revision of rules and values which are anti-learning) will give the learning organization a chance of success. We suggest that a culture change towards pro-learning can be effected through reflective dialogue procedures, providing that power relations in the organization structure do not mitigate against such dialogue. By this we mean that chief officers and senior managers who model reflective dialogue themselves offer examples of the openness and risk-taking that transformative learning require. In addition a no-blame agreement (common in service debriefings) enables their staff, in their turn, to take risks and be open to double-loop learning, with all the potential of transformative learning for the organization which this brings. We will look now at the detail of reflective dialogue and its potential for transformative learning.

WHAT IS REFLECTIVE DIALOGUE?

Reflective dialogue or reflection-with-others is distinguished from internal dialogue, where reflection is limited to the insights of the individual. The detachment required to look critically at the self is difficult to achieve and there is a danger of self-deception. Individualistic learning isolates the learner and leaves her to her own view of the world, a view that is mediated by personal biography, social and economic forces, and these give rise to 'assumptions, beliefs, perceptions and ways of construing and acting on experience' (Weil and McGill 1989, p. 247). Such assumptions, beliefs, etc., tend to remain untouched by internal dialogue, but may be challenged by reflective dialogue-with-others. So dialogue-with-others offers opportunities for reflective learning at all three levels:

1. Reflective dialogue-with-others may lead to a reconsideration of how things are being done, and how things can be improved. We call this reflective learning for improvement.
2. Reflective dialogue-with-others also offers the possibility of engaging at the edge of those assumptions and beliefs, reconsidering the tfgs and we have identified this as reflective learning for transformation.
3. Reflective dialogue-with-others, when improvement or transformation has occurred, can take learning one step further, so those learners learn about learning itself, from their experience as reflective learners. For example, the realization that a particular method of production is economically sound but environmentally damaging may lead to altered methods, a transformation perhaps. In addition, those involved may choose to identify what factors enabled the realization to emerge and the change to be implemented, that is, the learners reflect upon their reflective learning. Consideration of what issues were considered in dialogue and how they were processed would enable learners to pinpoint the key elements of their learning for future reference, and this also applies to organizations.

WHAT IS DIALOGUE-WITH-OTHERS?

Dialogue does occur naturally between people, but for effective reflective learning, intentional dialogue is necessary. Naturally occurring dialogue may reflect the power differences in a situation and this inhibits learning. So the senior member of staff whose dialogue with juniors takes the form of a monologue about how things should be done, with which they are obliged to agree, is unlikely to promote reflective learning for improvement or transformation! Intentional dialogue takes account of hierarchies, recognizes them and makes them explicit so that where line management relationships exist these are openly admitted and may well be avoided. However, with the demise of the tea trolley (a tradition soon to be revived), the potential for informal transactions to embrace reflective dialogue is largely discounted in organizations.

There is a tendency for formal transactions, in the form of information transfer and learning centres, to be seen as genuine learning opportunities as against informal transactions where the process is not under surveillance – the latter are often dismissed or suppressed. Formal transactions do not accommodate what have been called the 'peculiar characteristics' of information (its distinction from physical goods for instance), and are unlikely to stimulate innovation (McDonald 1999). On the other hand an organization which supports informal networks, peer support groups, mentors and simply social events, are promoting 'an essential part of managing change from an information perspective' (Millar 1999).

We noted previously the bad press which 'politicking' receives and this view of politics as negative may reflect the need to control all transactions within organizations. Such control dictates not only what can be said, but also what can be seen in order to be articulated, so that language is itself a control mechanism. The Foucauldian idea of discourse as the set of rules which determine what is known or indeed learned, identify such rules as limitations on learning and knowledge (Townley 1994). For instance, there is no language for emotion in management-speak, it is dominated by the rational tradition which denies or suppresses uncertainty, chaos, emotionality, humour, grief, sexuality and the boundary between work and non-work (Fineman and Gabriel 1994). This can be seen in the case of Sterling Bank (see Chapter 6). We discuss two different forms of discourse below.

The social context of learning has been discussed in Chapter 2 and we confirm here that

for organizational learning to occur an 'I-space' must be created for dialogue in order to promote the 'social learning cycle' and reveal some of the tacit knowledge within the organization (Boisot 1999). The significance of social contact for real learning is confirmed by the experience of learners at Lloyds TSB's learning centres, which showed increased 'hits' where administrators provided 'a welcoming face'. Facilitators spoke to users during learning sessions, and *at the end* because 'they all needed to talk afterwards' (Hills and Francis 1999, p. 48, emphasis added).

The Post Office's use of the knowledge interview for after-action reviews is an example of good project management. The interviews can take one-and-a-half to several hours, offering learners a chance to reflect and are found to be more effective than interactive computer packages (Whitehead 1999). The interviews enabled learners 'to get below the bald facts about how things were done and discover why they were done' (ibid., p. 71).

Dialogue is not limited to two people, but of course there must be more than one, because meaning and new understanding comes 'through us and between us' (Bohm 1996, p. 6). Intentional dialogue has a purpose, which is clear to the dialogue partners. Hence the process is agreed from the start. Reflective dialogue engages the learner's realities and subjective experience, giving space for the learner to consider and reconsider, without haste. This form of discourse has been entitled 'connected knowing' as against 'separated knowing' where the dialogue seeks to analyse and itemize rather than to understand and connect with the learner (Goldberger et al. 1996). We discuss the skills needed to conduct a connected dialogue below.

Definitions of reflective practice venerate the process of reflection, urging professionals to indulge in it before, during and after their practice, with a view to improvement, transformation and, hopefully, learning about the learning process (Schon 1987). Such definitions imply self-reflection, and this, we suggest, seriously limits the quality of learning achieved. We noted above the limitations of self-reflection, and recommend that any system of reflective practice should include reflective dialogue-with-others, in order to optimise potential transformation through challenging the assumptions, the tfgs, the embedded beliefs which constrain the learner who is not 'connected' to others through dialogue.

WHAT DO WE CONDUCT DIALOGUES ABOUT?

The material for conducting dialogues in the workplace is the content of work, the tasks and processes which form the work we do. Task is a description of what is being done or going to be done. Process is a description of how the task is being done or is going to be done. Thereafter the dialogue is reflective, taking the form of questions and comments about what has been described. Reflection can occur at three levels:

1. For reflection for improvement, dialoguers will analyse and discourse with the learner about what has been described and this process mirrors a learning review, often found in good project management or thoughtful coaching.
2. For reflection for transformation, dialoguers need to proceed with care, and here the learning relationship and trust is crucial. Examining the tfgs in a process uncovers material which may be uncomfortable and destabilizing, so dialoguers need to have skills in the emotional arena, be comfortable in it, and have a clear grasp of appropriate boundaries in the workplace. Examples of reflection for transformation can be found in highly effective mentoring and in some types of supervision.
3. Where reflection for understanding the learning process is the aim, a step back from the

two earlier processes is required, and consideration given to how the reflective learning was achieved, whether it was for improvement or transformation. Reflection for understanding may occur, for example, in learning sets, or through the medium of a learning journal (see Rigano and Edwards 1998).

The content of dialogue is dictated by the learner, who brings material from a current, past or future project, and it is likely to cover the three domains of learning:

- doing
- feeling
- thinking.

Doing and thinking are familiar areas for modern organizations. The commitment to emotional literacy is less significant and here lies what we maintain is the key to effective learning. A dialogue which gets 'below the surface' is likely to stimulate double-loop learning and enable the tfgs to be questioned and challenged. In so doing, defensive reactions may be provoked and emotion may be stimulated for learners and those engaged in dialogue. Where learning partnerships are established the dialogue is encapsulated within a learning review process and learning partners are reviewers.

The capacity to deal with emotion appropriately has been dubbed 'EQ' and, together with IQ is a predictor of future success in business (Dulewicz and Higgs 1998, pp. 42–5). EQ has been defined as: 'the ability to understand and reflectively manage one's own and other people's feelings' (Mayer 1999, p. 49) and those who are emotionally adept are those who 'know and manage their own feelings well and who read and deal effectively with other people's feelings' (Goleman 1995, p. 36).

The overemphasis on action and thinking has left a gap in our understanding of organizational life and some seek to redress this conspiracy of silence: 'Our objective is to convey human experiences ... We believe that emotions play a central role in organizational dynamics, a role that has not been appreciated fully by organizational theorists' (Frost et al. 1992, p. ix).

The idea that transformative learning can occur where emotional material is ignored, whilst favoured in the rationalist organization, fails to appreciate the nature of the changes which take place when a meaning structure is transformed through reflection. Jack Mezirow clarifies how our meaning *schemes* or patterns may be refined, elaborated, replaced and transformed by reflecting on the content and process of what we do. However he maintains that meaning *perspectives*, which grow from psychological, sociolinguistic and epistemic codes, are not nearly so responsive to simple or self-reflection. What is needed for transformation of perspectives, based as they are on cultural codes, is what he calls 'critical premise reflection'. This is defined as a process involving 'a critique of assumptions to determine whether the belief, often acquired through cultural assimilation in childhood, remains functional for us as adults. We do this by critically examining its origins, nature and consequences' (Mezirow 1994, p. 223). The recommended method for such learning to occur is dialogue as 'dialogue is central to human communication and learning' (ibid., p. 225). The chances of such a critique being achieved without generating emotion are low, and, where emotion is denied or suppressed, transformative learning is unlikely. Other no-go areas in organizational discourse have been identified by Fineman and Gabriel as, chaos, uncertainty, emotionality, humour, grief, sexuality and the boundary between work and non-work (1994, p. 376).

WHO SHOULD BE INVOLVED IN THE DIALOGUE?

The opportunity to conduct dialogues is open to everyone, informally at least and an organization which nurtures dialogue in its workforce will benefit (Zuboff 1989). However, we recommend that dialogue be formalized for maximum effect. Clearly a system which gives space and place for dialogue will promote reflective learning, by formalizing the process and making the dialogues intentional. The workplace is full of opportunities for learning. Making space for reflective learning is the challenge for organizations which seek to develop and grow.

The idea that only qualified people can dialogue is not sustainable. Informal dialogue relies on the person available at the time. The same people can be encouraged to engage in formal dialogue, structured for the organization's purpose, and dialogue skills can be learnt through the process itself, that is, engaging in dialogue is an easy way to learn the skills. For example, all staff involved in a particular project may be offered 'briefing' and 'debriefing' sessions where people can operate in twos or threes to unpack potential or realized issues. Formal training and education programmes should include learning reviews as a matter of course, and these should occur before, during and after the formal input. Programmes which run without the provision for reflective dialogue are a potential waste of resources, as the learning is limited to surface material and the opportunity for reflective learning is lost.

There are corners in organizations where men (and sometimes women) hide from their emotions and avoid anyone else's, and these characteristics have been valued by the rational organization. For tomorrow's learning organization, which seeks to transform itself, the avoidance of emotive matters is not an option. For some people such learning will be a step too far, and they may choose to leave. On the other hand, when emotional material becomes part of the permitted discourse, many people in the organization will find themselves comfortable with such an approach to learning. Finally, those engaged in dialogue will need to have a sensitivity to the emotional and political issues in the workplace.

The reflective dialogue process demands structured time, space, clear boundaries, tolerance of uncertainty, competence in dealing with emotional material, and managers/developers with high-level skills. The habit of referring to such high-level skills as 'soft' is one of the ways that organizations shoot themselves in the foot, denying the very aspects of their work that will stimulate transformative learning.

SKILLS OF CONDUCTING DIALOGUE

Obviously a reviewer needs to be prepared to listen, as well as taking a turn as speaker. The dialogue should be structured to ensure that there is no monologue. Action learning is a good example of such structured dialogue (see McGill and Beaty 2001). One-to-one examples of structured dialogue include coaching and mentoring. In addition, colleagues conducting learning reviews should structure the process to ensure that issue(s) are contained. Those conducting a dialogue, as learner or reviewer, will need to understand containment and boundaries so that the process is not intrusive but remains challenging, particularly when reflecting for transformation. The key aspect of dialogue for learners is a space for them which is protected and will not be overrun by others or other matters.

The skills needed for effective reflective dialogue can be identified by reference to the three levels of learning identified above:

1. Dialogue for improvement
2. Dialogue for transformation
3. Dialogue for reflecting on the learning process.

DIALOGUE FOR IMPROVEMENT

Where the learning sought (by the learner) is instrumental, that is, reflective learning for improvement, then Kolb's loop provides a good model. The key skill for the learning partner here is questioning, and for the learner it is accurate recall, as well as a propensity to think laterally, considering all possibilities and factors which may influence or have influenced the outcome. This model conforms to what has been called preview and review coaching or modelling scenarios as predictors of future reality (de Geus 1992).

DIALOGUE FOR TRANSFORMATION

Where the learning sought is significant and likely to challenge assumptions and tfgs, that is, reflective learning for transformation, skills are needed which address the learner's defensive reasoning and which can reveal systemic characteristics for the learner. Let us look at the skills needed for both.

Following Argyris and Schon's approach to unravelling the theories-in-use concealed by defensive reasoning, the dialogue may follow the procedure whereby the learner is invited to parallel the factual account of a task/problem/issue/event with the unsaid thoughts and feelings which accompanied the facts (Argyris and Schon 1996, p. 78). In order to accept such an invitation, learners will need to trust their reviewer and feel safe enough to discuss the 'hidden' material. We assume that the power relationships inherent in the dialogue couple are explicit here. According to Egan (1990), the most powerful skill for building this kind of trust and rapport is that of empathy which has been defined as 'the ability to understand the world of the other, their thoughts, feelings and experience ... and to communicate that understanding in full' (Brockbank and McGill 1998, p. 195). This corresponds to the 'connected knowing' described earlier as an alternative to 'separated knowing' and calls for a willingness to enter the other's world, and live in it long enough to connect with the other's reality (Goldberger et al. 1996).

The realization of one's part in the recursive loops of a circular system begins with the recognition that organizations are like living biological systems, with feedback loops which enable learning so that elements in the organization can regenerate themselves. The process of realization calls for an adult-to-adult interaction, a respect for the learner's experience, acceptance of the recursive nature of organizations, and recognition of the limits of power in the system (McCaughan and Palmer 1994).

The process of realization is an uncovering of subconscious processes within individual learners and their colleagues, which have become established as a pattern through culture, beliefs and language, offering short-term benefits. When such processes are scrutinized consciously, they are often revealed as counterproductive to the organization's purpose, and, because they are largely subconscious, persist in day-to-day practice (Senge 1990). We are told that if the conscious mind can be 'kept in a quiet non-judgemental state of observation and playfulness' the subconscious is released for new learning (Gallwey 1979).

The key skill here is a quality not frequently found in organizations, that is, being non-judgemental. The temptation to blame is omnipresent in organizational life. For this reason

the reflective dialogue activity should be a structured, intentional process, protected from organizational pressures, where those in dialogue agree that 'blame' will have no place here, as well as the other boundary issues mentioned above. The no-blame technique works well in particular contexts, for example, debriefing active service units after manoeuvres, recording near-misses by pilots for air traffic control, and debriefing emergency services. So the no-blame technique can be used if the advantages are recognized and the time and space is allocated. This can be enabled through adopting a structured procedure for workgroups which requires members to allow space for each other to speak, to avoid evaluating the comments of each other, and to be willing to speak out on their own views (Easterby-Smith et al. 1999).

DIALOGUE FOR REFLECTING UPON THE LEARNING PROCESS

Where reflection on the whole learning process in either 1 or 2 above is sought, there are a variety of approaches. We noted above the action learning structure, which includes such a reflective process on learning as an integral part of effective action learning programmes. Reflective models of mentoring, professional supervision and some executive coaching include a review of the process itself. Where programmes include learning reviews, an additional reflective review is valuable if the resource for it can be found, where learners are given time and space to dialogue about their learning process in earlier dialogues. An alternative to such a reflective review is the use of a reflective learning journal, where the learner draws on material from earlier dialogues to arrive at conclusions about the learning process. We note that learning journals as a substitute for dialogue are unlikely to provide the deep reflection needed for transformation.

The need for ownership of the reflective process is vital for reflection on the learning process itself, particularly when moving towards the solitary practice of journal writing. We recommend that learners are encouraged to use the dialogue process as the basis for journal compilation, and that support from a variety of sources such as colleagues, peers, mentors and managers, is essential for learners to reflect upon their learning (Rigano and Edwards 1998, p. 444).

Within the dialogue process, which demands the suspension of self and a focusing on the other's world-view as relevant and real, the beginnings of organizational learning occur; the potential for realization is not limited to the learner in dialogue, as Daloz maintains: 'In order to see how ideas different from ours exist in their own legitimate framework, it is necessary to leap out from our shell of absolute certainty and construct a whole new world based on some other person's ideas of reality, other assumptions of truth' (Daloz 1986, p. 228, quoted in Brookfield 1987, p. 113).

Conclusion

In this chapter we have described reflective learning and summarized the requirements for it to take place in an organizational setting. We recommend a deliberate and formal allowance of space and time, as well as recognition of the skills needed for effective dialogue. For transformative reflective learning, the issue of trust is crucial with a no-blame agreement in position, as well as care where learners may be confronting their taken-for-granteds (tfgs). Additional reflection, possibly using a journal method or set, enables learners to realize how they have achieved their transformation or improvement.

5 *Themes of Reflective Learning*

Anne Brockbank, Ian McGill and Nic Beech

The contributing authors of the chapters in this collection of cases were prompted by some 'starting-point' questions for contemplating the learning process they would report on: What process or intervention happened? What were the reasons for it? What actually happened? To what extent was the process effective, and why? What learning did you derive from the experience? These questions were deliberately posed only as starting-points and in the process of reflection the stories told were diverse and followed their own structures and logics. The editors obviously had their own ideas about reflective learning and a perspective on the relevant theory, but in preparing this analysis of themes we have attempted to suspend our preconceptions as far as possible and to delve into the stories of learning as data. The approach taken was broadly based on grounded theory (Strauss and Corbin 1998; Glaser 1992). Key themes were identified in the learning narratives, and the data and emerging themes were revisited until there was 'saturation' in that no new themes emerged. From an initial long list of themes, dominant ones (those with repeated references from the data) were selected and these are presented below. The intention in presenting these themes is not to close the mind of the reader, but rather to stimulate the reader to ask questions of the narratives themselves, and it should be emphasized that the themes are one possible analysis out of many. To this end, the themes are presented as questions rather than outcomes. The chapter closes with a summary of general learning points which emerged from this process of analysis, but again we hope that the reader will draw their own conclusions and not feel limited by ours.

Emergent themes

SHOULD TIME AND SPACE FOR LEARNING BE 'CARVED OUT' AND GIVEN EXCLUSIVE PRIORITY?

Traditionally, in systematic approaches to learning, it was regarded as important to isolate time specifically dedicated to learning, and to carry this out away from the interruptions of normal work. Frequently this led to a degree of formality in arrangements for learning, and there was often a compartmentalization of training into courses of various types. This was regarded as superior to 'learning on the job' because it allowed for effective analysis of needs and training design. It also allowed for trial and error without major negative impacts on the work outcomes. However, it did introduce potential problems of transference of learning back into the workplace. In some environments the value of time away from work and of lengthy courses has been questioned. In other settings, organizations have sought to maintain a degree of separation with the aim that people should dedicate themselves to learning

as their central task when they are learning. In the cases presented in this volume a variety of approaches are adopted, each of which has pros and cons.

In some commercial organizations it was difficult to carve out time for learning. Similarly, in the case of the Cathedral Centre, Salford (see Chapter 16), learning sessions had to be arranged within the normal facilities and at times when clients typically might expect access to centre workers. During development sessions, clients would knock on the door, and the response of managers was to attend to the clients' needs. This interrupted the learning processes, but it also had a positive impact of highlighting the culture of being client-led, and this shared value was important for the performance of the organization.

In other cases, such as Thus (Chapter 11) and Novartis (Chapter 9), modular programmes combined dedicated time away from the workplace with project work back at work. The aim was to achieve periods of concentration in which there would be learning focused on new knowledge and input as well as reflection on actions taken since the last meeting, with project work in between sessions.

A number of examples are concerned with action learning and this approach also seeks a balance. The action learning sets occur away from the normal time and space of work and during sessions each individual has dedicated time on their focal issue (see, for example, Chapter 8). In Chapter 15, Binns and McGill discuss the way that action learning has a direct impact on the way that learners performed their jobs subsequently.

In each of these cases a balance is sought. On the basis of the evidence presented here it would be wrong to conclude that it is either right or wrong to carve out special time and space for learning. More typically, organizational decisions are made that reflect the culture and expectation of the stakeholders. In all cases there was a concern to make sure that the learning would 'make a difference' rather than being for its own sake. And therefore, pertinence to issues in the workplace was as important as stretching minds and extending skills. Learning with a purpose often started in the workplace with an awareness of things needing to be done differently, but social and reflective phases of learning were often best achieved away from the job. These issues relate to the concepts discussed by Lessem in Chapter 21, particularly in the phase of transferring from 'knowing to becoming'. Learning, thinking and acting are intrinsically linked, and they occur in the context of the history, culture, relationships, technologies and processes of the organization. Given the complexity of the context, it is likely that finding the balance between being embedded in it, and standing outside it temporarily to practise and reflect, will be difficult and will require ongoing trial and error.

IS TIME CONCEIVED AS PROGRESSIVE AND LINEAR IN REFLECTIVE LEARNING?

Some approaches to learning and training are linear. The classic model is to analyse training needs, design the training and decide on what methods to use, implement the training and subsequently review to assess the learning achievements of the participants and the impact on the organization. Such a systematic model is in evidence in some of our cases, for example the Pearl Assurance story (Chapter 10) and Norwich Union (Chapter 19). However, it is not necessary that this should always be the case. In some instances, the progression is not linear. For example, in the case of Thus (Chapter 11), the original design had to be altered during implementation when it was found that some parts of the applied action learning approach that were tried with the first cohorts were not working in that context. The new project-based approach was jointly developed on the basis of participant feedback and was more successful. In some instances, learning is not straight-line progressive over time. For some, learning can

be discontinuous and occasional. For example, the GPs learning through the use of the CELT system (Chapter 20) directed their own learning as and when they experienced a need or an interest, and used the system to marshal information, explore resources and reflect on their learning. They fitted these activities into busy work schedules, rather than having to realign their work in order to fit in with a programme of learning. In the action learning cases there was a blend between planned interactions with the learning set and self-directed work between sets. The sets provided a time when there was both backwards reflection and forward planning.

WHAT MEDIA SHOULD BE USED FOR REFLECTIVE LEARNING?

The short answer to this is 'all media'! In the cases presented here there are examples of almost every form of media for learning. Some are based on IT, for example, CELT (Chapter 20), others have paper-based distance learning, for example, Sainsbury's (Chapter 7). In Sterling Bank (Chapter 6) the 'preparation for learning' component included audio tapes and activities based on the scenarios in the tapes, computerized self-testing and 360-degree feedback. In the Northwestern Health Board (Chapter 8), projects, personal development plans, workshops and self-managed action learning sets were used.

In almost all cases, however, face-to-face interaction, either in the shape of learner-to-learner groups or learner-developer sessions were highly significant. For example, in Norwich Union (Chapter 19) although the issues were centred around IT, there was an identified need for the 'people touch' and behavioural skills. In the Sterling Bank case (Chapter 6) the multi-media approach was not a substitute, but a preparation for interactive learning. As with the action learning examples, some activity away from the learning group was regarded as important, and such activity could be individual and entirely task-focused. However, in order to capitalize on such activities, interaction was still seen as important.

This being the case, we might ask why it is so. Reasons which emerge in these cases include the need for leadership and peer-group motivation, the need for the input of other people in questioning and analysing the actions and issues, the need for emotional support, the need for theoretical input that can be questioned and engaged with as it is happening, and the need for periods in which learning is the key focus of activity.

WHO 'OWNS' THE LEARNING?

Almost all cases state that top-level support in the organization is a requirement for reflective learning to take place. In this sense, ownership needs to come from the top. In several instances it is the head of personnel or human resource management (HRM) who is the key leader. This may be expected as training and development is likely to fall within their remit. The case of Sainsbury's (Chapter 7) is a good example of how the consistency of support from this level is vital to the continuance of the programme. In other cases, whilst the head of HR was centrally involved, it was also important to have the backing of the Chief Executive. In the case of Allied Distillers (Chapter 13), learning was central to, and embedded in, a change process which was driven by the top executives, but which over the years involved other grades as participants. This was reflected in phases of learning which were top-down designed at the outset, but which have subsequently involved the learners and 'users' in design and modification of courses.

In addition to top-level support and commitment, ownership by the learners themselves

is identified as a necessary requirement throughout these cases. Action learning (for example in Chapters 8 and 15) focuses on issues that are both real and important for the learners. The learners focus on analysing the issue, deciding on a course of action and implementing it, before returning to the action learning set for further reflection. The personal attachment to the issue is what ultimately drives the action, and the quality of the action underpins the quality of the reflection.

In other cases the learning was focused around programmes which had been designed by a combination of training providers and HRM staff of the organization. In such cases there can be a danger of lack of ownership by the learners. Several of the approaches reported here seek to address this in two ways. First, the programmes were typically tailor-made for the client, reflecting concerns and learning needs that they had. Second, the formalized parts of the programmes were interspersed with activity in the workplace. This could take the form of project groups which identified issues related to the topic of the module they had just taken, and which they would then conduct self-managed activity to be reported at the next module. Alternatively, in some cases, project groups were formed with tasks that would run through the whole programme, building in new knowledge and foci as the programme progressed. In either case, the design idea was to make the ideas, issues and skills important and applicable to the real lives of the participants, and so to enhance their ownership.

WHAT ARE THE IMPLICATIONS FOR MANAGEMENT PRACTICE?

There is a range of implications for managerial practice, but two that are highlighted in these cases are the role of managers in developing others and the need to break down traditional 'silos' of organizational practice. It would seem that managers are increasingly being expected to develop others. In the case of the London Borough of Ealing (Chapter 15), the aim was to enable managers to reflect on their practice and explore new ways of managing ('seeing the wood for the trees') as part of extensive organizational and cultural change. The transferable skills were beyond level-one (or single-loop) problem solving, and enabled them to work in a more developmental way with those that reported to them. For example, for one action learner the skills of questioning were developed and there was a move away from 'spoon-feeding' others towards facilitating them to become problem-solvers. In both Novartis (Chapter 9) and Allied Distillers (Chapter 13), the development of team leaders explicitly required them to be able to develop others and this entailed interpersonal, communication and analytic skills along with the technical skills of their function.

Another common feature is seeking to inspire managers to develop beyond the confines of their functional specialism. This can be difficult because, as Lessem points out in Chapter 21, this entails some degree of change in personal identity. It also entails people moving outside their arena of certainty and status into areas where they are novices. However, in modern organizations, breaking down the 'silo mentality' – in which certain skills, problems and solutions are owned by a single group of specialists – is vital in order to achieve more flexible and efficient performance. In Novartis (Chapter 9) the cross-functional make-up of participants had been influential in encouraging managers to understand more about other parts of the business, and to think beyond their normal issues and problems. In Thus (Chapter 11), part of the design of the project teams was to bring together people from different parts of the business, who were functionally and geographically remote from each other, and had come from former companies that had quite different cultures. In both cases it was through getting groups to work together (in addition to meeting and talking) that assumptions about each

other started to be broken down. Following this, a number of projects delivered process and product changes which had an integrative impact on the organization.

Management is about dealing with change, the unexpected and the problematic, and about getting others to have the confidence and ability to do likewise. Increasingly it is also about breaking down traditional barriers to flexible and speedy operation. As a result, reflective learning and effective managerial practice can never be far away from each other.

WHAT ARE THE IMPLICATIONS FOR ORGANIZATIONAL SUCCESS?

Given the time, financial and energy investment that reflective learning requires, it is only likely to be regarded as justifiable in most organizational contexts when it can be seen to have an impact on the aim and objectives of the organization. In the case of Pearl (Chapter 10) there was a strong business driver in that they were in such difficulties that radical change had to be made if they were to survive. In Allied Distillers (Chapter 20), the extremely competitive environment also meant that 'staying the same' was not a realistic option as they would be under threat from the competition if they could not improve flexibility, productivity and performance. Similarly, in Sterling Bank (Chapter 6), there were strong business imperatives to change as the whole retail banking sector altered its approach to customers, the use of technology and the speed of change. Traditionally, some businesses when faced with pressures have responded by seeking to cut costs, and as a result have reduced their training budgets. This approach is short-sighted, as it is unlikely to deliver flexibility, creativity in solving problems and enhanced quality, which are typically required to overcome business pressures. Research has shown that business success is correlated with investment in people, rather than merely cutting short-term costs.

Walton (1985) established a model of management in which performance was achieved not through seeking to control and constrain employee activities, but through establishing a shared understanding of what needed to be done, and then enabling employees to carry out their activities through training amongst other HRM practices. Walton cited a number of case studies, and since that time a stream of research has explored the linkage between progressive human resource management practices and organizational performance. The contribution of 'enhancing the quality of people' has been stressed by Delaney and Huselid (1996) who offer a useful analysis emphasizing the logical flow of, and connection between, HRM practices. Effective recruitment and selection should be complemented by improving quality and contribution of current employees through training and development. A sharing of personal and corporate objectives should be fostered through reward systems and performance management and employees need to believe that they will be treated fairly. Where this occurs performance has been shown to increase (Pfeffer and Veiga 1999). Becker and Huselid (1999), surveying research findings, state that bundles of good practice in HRM, incorporating effective training and development, have now become a source of competitive advantage. In a major study in the US covering more than 2400 firms, Becker and Huselid (1998) found that considerable differences in organizational performance were attributable to high-performance HRM practices. In particular, organizations placed one standard deviation higher than the norm on the HRM system index showed differences in performance measures as follows:

Market value	+ 24%
Accounting profits	+ 25%

Gross rate of return on assets	+ 25%
Sales per employee	+ 4.8%
Staff turnover	– 7.6%

This research has been supported in the UK, where Patterson et al. (1997) found strong linkages between the acquisition and development of skilled people, job design stressing autonomy, flexible problem solving, and positive employee attitudes and performance. They found that HRM practices correlated with an 18–19 per cent variation in productivity and profitability. It is clear that in organizational contexts typified by change, continuous development of the workforce will be necessary to maintain such competitive advantage.

In our cases, transfer of learning to the workplace in a way that it would impact on performance was the key issue. In Chapter 21, Lessem discusses innovative ways of assessing transformation using collective storytelling in Anglian Water. Such an approach is useful in filling some of the detail behind the macro statistics used by Becker and Huselid (1999). Many of the modular programmes entailed work-based projects, sometimes assessed, that would directly transfer new learning into the workplace. Pearl Assurance (Chapter 10) was one example of this, where measures of success were also established at the beginning of the programme. Similarly in Thus (Chapter 11) projects were designed to have definite, and often measurable, outcomes in the workplace. Sometimes tension arises when deciding whether or not to invest in learning concerning how far corporate performance is attributable to the learning and development of individuals and groups within the organization. The quantitative work referred to above is helpful in this regard, but for many it is the real-life stories that are more convincing. Hence, it is important to substantiate the generic research with qualitative research that can provide a view of what has (and has not) worked within specific contexts.

WHAT ISSUES DO RELATIONSHIPS RAISE FOR REFLECTIVE LEARNING, AND VICE VERSA?

So much of reflective learning is about relationships that the theme is almost ubiquitous. The learners normally have important relationships with each other, with facilitators or trainers and with those who will be affected by the outcomes of their learning, such as clients or customers. However, there are some aspects of relationships that are worthy of highlighting. In Chapter 21, Lessem introduces the concepts and practice of a 'community of practice'. Such a community is important for the practice and development of professional practice and for the continual development of an area of specialism. Normally this is thought of as a grouping that can interact face-to-face, but in the case of CELT (Chapter 20) such a community is facilitated to operate remotely through the use of IT. The case of Sainsbury's (Chapter 7) raises a number of relationship issues. There are questions of trust between the 'purchaser' and 'supplier' of training. A contractual form of relationship involving money has connotations for the way that people can work together, and it is important that such relationships can be maintained over time. Changing the people at the point of interface in the relationship is one potential problem faced by more than one case presented here, and it is something that must be managed carefully. In the case of the Northwestern Health Board (Chapter 8) there was an intention that the purchaser would increase their own skills to the point where they could take over the supply themselves. Clearly this could introduce problems, but if it is an overt intention it can be managed successfully.

The real issue is how the various relationships involved in learning can be established, reasonable expectations set, and the progress of the relationship be monitored and managed. Sterling Bank (Chapter 6) provides an example where effort was put into building the relationship at the outset, and this is repaid during the operation of the project. The one assumption that should be questioned is that relationships will be satisfactory without being worked on. Normally it is an area where trust and fluidity will only really emerge over time and with sustained effort.

HOW DO EMOTIONS RELATE TO REFLECTIVE LEARNING?

Learning is not an emotion-free activity. Lessem in Chapter 21 stresses that learning is part of our nature, involves crossing boundaries, changes our identities and is part of our personal 'becoming'. In addition, learning happens in a communal setting. In view of this, one should expect emotional attachment to such changes. Clearly, emotions can be both a positive and a negative force for learning. For example, Wanless in Chapter 16 talks about the frustrations staff had felt in their roles, and how this could become a block to creative thinking about changing the situation, but was also a motivating force when it came to developing new ways of working. She is clear that for learning to happen, the learners need to be open to pain as well as fun. In the CELT example, in Chapter 20 the significance of emotional attachment to perceived success and failure is stressed. In this case, professional workers are reflecting on incidents that have gone well and badly, and their self-expectation, and that of the public, is that failure will not/should not happen. Therefore, finding ways in which they can express and explore failure is important for learning. In this case, an IT system provided the means for confidential, and yet communal exploration of both success and failure in learning, including the emotional aspects of this. Where trust can be established, learners in reflective dialogue may be able to access the emotional energy to confront their taken-for-granted view of the world, and engage in the sometimes scary double-loop journey to transformation.

There is no straight answer to the question of how emotions relate to reflective learning. However, it is clear from the cases that emotions and reflective learning are intrinsically linked. One should be prepared for this linkage to act both positively and negatively with fluctuations over time and circumstance. The situations in which this issue has been made overt are those where it has been most successfully dealt with.

WHAT ARE THE IMPACTS OF NARRATIVES AND SYMBOLS ON LEARNING?

An issue which often arises in the planning of training and development is the nature of the organizational culture. For example, where a culture is typified as being a 'blame culture' the likelihood of learning through experimentation is remote. Experiments go wrong, and the question in the learner's mind is 'what happens if this goes wrong?' If the expectation is that they will be blamed for the consequences, then they are likely to adopt a risk-averse posture, which will impact on the potential learning outcomes.

Whilst an argument in this form makes sense, there are problems with considering culture as an 'undigested whole'. Some would argue that organizations do not own cultures that they can manipulate and change at will. Culture is embedded in society as a whole and does not stop or start at the boundaries of the workplace. Attitudes, assumptions and values held by the workforce will represent those of the society from which they are drawn, and will be influenced by longitudinal factors such as family, religion, language, socio-economic group-

ings, education and so on. What happens in the workplace may influence the way that people behave and may impact on some of their attitudes but efforts to manage culture are ranged against the macro forces listed above. If this argument is accepted it becomes more difficult to typify organizational cultures as 'blame' or 'macho' or 'creative' and so on. The reality is likely to be far more complicated, and if the conception of the culture is simplified excessively, then decisions based on that simplification are likely to be flawed. However, this argument does not remove the need to deal with cultural factors in learning. One solution is to examine some of the localized elements of culture, rather than trying to develop a holistic perception of it. So, for example, there may be a concentration on particular symbols and narratives which have an impact on perceptions and sensemaking amongst the learners.

Narratives can be thought of as storylines that people use in making sense of their experiences. For example, an heroic narrative normally entails the hero going through a trial of some type, often involving a villain, and prevailing by maintaining the integrity of special skills/identity (Beech 2000). Heroic accounts of leadership are not uncommon, and leaders are pictured as intervening in situations that the followers were unable to deal with and making a clear and firm decision which solves the problems. The potential difficulty with such narratives is that they can reduce learning to imitation of the hero, which is, at best, single-loop learning. In many tasks, particularly professional and managerial ones, there is little chance of exactly the same circumstances arising again in which directly imitated behaviour can be applied.

Narratives that may be more effective for learning are those which include openness to change and development from errors. In Chapter 16, Wanless tells the story of the 'mushroom crisis' in which the Cathedral Centre was overwhelmed by a donation of mushrooms. Apart from the problems of storing the vast volume of mushrooms and discovering a sufficient variety of recipes to use them in meals for the clients, there was a problem of having to focus the staff resource on dealing with the mushrooms. Whilst this was happening, the reduced number of staff working with the clients had to deal with a violent incident that nearly went very wrong. Things worked out in the end, but, importantly, learning was successfully derived from the simple story which impacted on the policy for dealing with donations and staff resourcing. In a 'blame culture' the problem would probably have been explained as being someone's fault, and the implied learning from this form of explanation is that the 'someone' is the problem. However, in the Cathedral Centre, several levels of learning were derived. We cannot tell what the culture is like in the Cathedral Centre as a result of this story, but it is practical as a vehicle for learning.

Another example, provided in Chapter 14, shows how simple narratives can be used to challenge predominant assumptions. A GP had been seeing a patient who was at high risk of coronary heart disease. The patient had been advised to take up suitable exercise and to attend a dietary clinic. Although three appointments had been made for the patient to attend the dietician's clinic, he had not shown up. The GP went to a local community centre on a different matter and coincidently found the patient cycling on an exercise bike. Surprised by this, the GP asked the patient what he was doing. Surprised by the GP's surprise, the patient replied that he was exercising. The GP challenged the patient about his non-attendance at the dietician's clinics. The patient was amazed – why should he go to the dietician? It was his wife who did all the cooking! This is a story of a simple encounter in which the assumptions held by different people suddenly became revealed to each other, and the source of the problem became obvious. At a single-loop level of learning this led to changed behaviour for this

particular patient, but at the double-loop level it was seen as a critical incident that impacted on the approach being taken to coronary heart disease risk.

Like narratives, symbols can have a high impact on learning. Narratives are entwined with sensemaking in a dynamic way – they tell a story involving different characters over a period of time. Symbols tend to be 'one-offs', but they carry weight because of the meaning that is attached to them. Leadership is a function that is heavily symbolized. Lessem explores in Chapter 21 how an effective leader can reify the desires and aims of followers through a phrase or a practice in such a way as to galvanize support. Dives shows in Chapter 19 that celebrating success was important in establishing a learning dialogue in Norwich Union. The actions and commitment of the Personnel Director in Sainsbury's is shown by Muskett in Chapter 7 to be vital to the course and learning processes getting off the ground and maintaining movement thereafter. In Novartis, leadership was both the content and involved in the process of learning, and Ritchie reports in Chapter 9 on the impact of people listening to a leader who stresses his own ongoing learning, and who, as a result, becomes a role model for others. In the case of Thus, McInnes et al. in Chapter 11 report the significance of presentations to high-ranking members of the board. When these were well attended by the senior people, they had a strong positive impact. On occasions where there was a problem with attendance (due to business pressures) there was still a strong impact, but not a positive one. Being there, and being a role model seem to be important aspects of leading for learning. But it should not be assumed that the role model is an heroic one in which the hero has never made a mistake. Actually, the greater effect seems to occur when the leader is open about their own learning and issues they have encountered.

HOW DOES REFLECTIVE LEARNING IMPACT ON PEOPLE BEING DIFFERENT?

When reflective learning works, it leaves people changed. At a basic level, it can change the skills we have, but more importantly it is likely to change the assumptions we make and the approach we take to solving problems. Sang in Chapter 17 focuses on the issues of values, and how they change. He points out that we inhabit an inherently contradictory world in which people's behaviour and attitude constantly impact on others. Both reflective learning and high performance take people outside their normal states of being, and it is in such new contexts that visions and values may be challenged.

In Chapter 21, Lessem covers in detail some of the transformations that can be expected. It is, as he says, a hit-and-miss affair, difficult to predict and probably impossible to control. When such learning is taking place some of the real value-adding outcomes are those which are not predicted, and if people are to make significant contributions to developing organizational performance, then being open to the unexpected differences in them, and the unexpected differences they can make is vital.

General learning points

COMPLEXITY

When one is dealing with learning, it seems that almost everything is related to everything else in ways that are not always predictable. This complexity can be considered on a number of levels. One is exemplified by Lyon's 'life in five chapters' (Chapter 18) in which the facts

remain (apparently) the same, but the learner's orientation to, and perception of, them is fundamentally altered through experience. Another is highlighted by Sang in Chapter 17 where the interplay of values and systems of sense making such as the political, organizational, managerial, professional and personal interact at the point of decision making. The application to practice introduces a further level of complexity. As Weil et al. point out in Chapter 14, focusing on evidence-based approaches is functional in some disciplines, but when seeking to reduce concepts and processes to simple competences, recordable evidence and so on, will not capture the complex uncertainties and dilemmas that we face in the field of practice. In this field there are no simple and incontrovertible facts, and perceptions change with values, time, experience and the social context of understanding. Knowledge and understanding cannot be thought of as fixed or decontextualized.

If we accept that these levels of complexity are in evidence when learning is occurring, the ensuing question is: how do we cope with such complexity? The danger of populist approaches and 'quick fixes' is that they cope by disguising at least some aspects of the complexity. However, on the basis of the cases presented here our argument is that this complexity should be engaged with head-on, and this can be addressed through the challenge of reflective learning.

CHALLENGE

The central challenge that lies within each of the cases presented is the undoing of 'taken-for-granteds'. This issue is emphasized by Bourner et al. in Chapter 8. Following the work of Megginson (1994), they discuss both planned and emergent learning. Planned learning has been the dominant paradigm and is associated with needs analysis, programme planning, delivery and review. In short, it is the way that expenditure on training and development is typically justified. However, a considerable amount of learning simply does not fit in with the intentions of training designers. Rather, individuals and groups will derive learning from unexpected sources, will take divergent meanings from experiences, and will create their own way of understanding and coping with complexity. Reflective learning must be open to these possibilities, and foster them. In order to do this, learners must be aware of the values they hold and their 'taken-for-granteds', and typically it is through experience that they are able to develop their own challenges. This can be supported through structured learning, such as action learning which provides a social setting for challenge, or can be facilitated privately, as in the case of CELT discussed in Chapter 20, in which the learner can explore their emotions, lack of knowledge and informational needs supported through an interactive IT system.

CRITICAL INCIDENTS

Challenge and motivation to undertake depth learning often relates to critical incidents. At the organizational level this can relate to strong business imperatives, as was the case with Pearl Assurance, discussed in Chapter 10. On the other hand, it can be a personal realization which facilitates a break-through in understanding. Weil's example of the coronary risk patient and GP showed how assumptions can be challenged through 'high-impact narratives' as long as the 'readers' of the narratives maintain an open mind in exploring the underlying causes of behaviour. To the team involved this was a critical incident in helping them to conceptualize the problem in a more holistic way incorporating medical and social issues,

neither of which could be neglected, and either of which could foil endeavour in the other. Other examples appear in the Cathedral 'mushroom' incident, and the formal process of demands analysis at National Children's Homes given by Lyon in Chapter 18.

Such critical incidents will not always be predictable or controllable. For those engaging in reflective learning the point is to be able to recognize them when they happen.

COLLABORATION

The cases presented here are a tapestry of collaborative relationships which were vital to learning processes. Some are between learners, for example, those operating in cohorts on organized programmes or in action learning sets. Others are at the organizational level. One example is the joint work between Sainsbury's and Manchester Metropolitan University discussed by Muskett in Chapter 7. This relationship developed over time, and there were periods when it was distinctly uncomfortable, and when each side had *unrealistic but reasonable* expectations of what should be delivered by the other. So, for example, Sainsbury's had a reasonable expectation of a lead-time for developing a course, which in the context of the university system was not deliverable, and the university staff had assumed that because they had not heard from Sainsbury's by the deadline that they did not want to run the course this year – again both reasonable and unrealistic. In another instance, this time between providers is described by Ritchie in Chapter 9, the leadership programme at Novartis was delivered jointly by the Oxford Group and Ashridge Management College.

Collaboration, whether at organizational or individual level, introduces many problems as well as possibilities. In many cases, however, it is inescapable if effective learning is to be achieved. The reason for this is not simply that more knowledge and skill will be required than a single organization will have at its disposal. In addition, the involvement of others often plays a symbolic and facilitative role, without which critical incidents and challenges to the tfgs will not be realized.

PRAGMATISM

For reflective learning to be embedded and valued, it needs to make a difference to behaviour and performance. For many organizations there will not be an investment in development unless there is a belief that it will yield returns, and such judgements are made not only on the basis of proposals but in view of previous investments and whether or not they are perceived to have been effective. Hence issues of deliverables, measurement, transfer of learning into the workplace and impact are important. There is a tension here in that if the situation is as complicated as we are arguing it is, it is unlikely that changes in performance can be identified with isolated causes such as changes in skill level. However, coping with the complexities involves being able to present evidence to decision makers in terms that are meaningful to them. For some of the cases covered here, for example, Allied Distillers (Chapter 13) and Sainsburys (Chapter 7) this means evidence of cost/benefit. For others, such as the Salford Cathedral Centre (Chapter 16), effectiveness in implementing their values is paramount. Action learning, for example as carried out in Ealing local authority (Chapter 15) focuses very strongly on transfer of learning into practice, and this must be a focus for all forms of reflective learning.

2 *On the Journey – Learning Through and Around Development Programmes*

6 Learning and Performance Management at Sterling Bank

Anne Brockbank and James Hill

The relationship

We are senior consultants with The Company, a people strategy and training consultancy – our relationship with Sterling goes back ten years. The relationship, which was primarily with the Corporate Banking Division, began in quite a small way in 1991, and ultimately Sterling became one of our biggest clients. Sterling responded to our 'Behavioural Specialists' advertisement, with a request for training in their centralized recruitment function in Group Human Resources. The first offer from The Company was a one-day competency interviewing course in 1991–92 for senior executives; the course ran 19 times.

These interventions formed the foundation for the ongoing relationship with Sterling as they gave us access to senior people in the organization who, over the years, have championed our approach and seen its value in the development of the business.

Sterling has been involved in banking for over three hundred years and operates worldwide, including all the major financial centres. The group is one of the main providers of coordinated global services to multinational corporations and financial institutions. Sterling has five divisions, employing 100 000 staff, that are managed as international businesses:

- Retail Financial Services
- The Sterling Card
- Corporate Banking
- Capital Markets
- Worldwide Investors.

For two years, our relationship with Sterling served to establish our reputation as behavioural specialists, and enabled us to understand the business issues faced by the organization, how Sterling wanted to develop itself, and what competencies were needed for its new focus on customers. This enabled us to respond when a plan emerged at Sterling to introduce Performance Management. Although it was too early for us to compete for the business, that is, the actual training work in Performance Management, we were able to persuade our contacts at Sterling that our expertise could make a difference.

We set out to consciously target Performance Management as potential business, starting from the question 'How can we help them?' and allocated time and resources to the relationships with key people in the organization. Using the balanced scorecard approach,[1] we offered free time: seminars, journal papers, write-up notes of meetings, shared insights and so on, prioritizing our offer against dimensions on the scorecard like income, margins,

consultant days, quality of life and values. We systematized the process, using a contact sheet at quarterly team meetings, so that we could evaluate how much time to spend with people for returns and even turn down work if we considered the client would not benefit. We routinely gave free coaching, listening and challenging, with follow-up notes to communicate our understanding. We also invited our Sterling contacts to our hospitality events, as a thank you to our clients for working with us. Our work with Sterling was restricted to the retail division and corporate banking (including off-shore). Because Sterling consists of over thirty separate businesses, it is necessary to relate to them individually.

In addition, The Company's team of 30 consultants were offered Sterling briefings, covering details of the business, key issues, how people found working with Sterling staff, learning so far, and the way forward, using our scanning of Reuters and financial news. We created a Sterling newsletter, internal to The Company, and a Sterling telephone directory.

So what exactly was Sterling hoping to achieve with the introduction of Performance Management? Defined as 'a systematic approach to improving individual and team performance in order to achieve organizational goals' (Hendry et al. 1997), Performance Management (PM) was the starting-point for the Sterling plan. However, the significance of Performance Management in an organization depends on its culture, its relationship with employees, and the types of job they do, hence the usefulness of establishing a link between behavioural and business objectives. Such a link is problematic in any business, but Sterling began from a strong position here. Because Sterling's business is money, employees could quickly relate their own potential monetary reward to business outcomes. However the traditional culture at Sterling, based as it was on the 'cheque mentality', that is, 'do the words and figures match up?', did not make it easy for senior managers to adopt a process which focuses on growth and development rather than assessment, on relationship rather than a sanction or decline approach. In order to maximize the impact of Performance Management, Sterling's cultural tendency towards blame, where the only options were right or wrong, needed to develop into a relationship-based process with strong behavioural competences.

In addition there was a need to 'open up' the organization and question 'taken for granted' ways of doing things: 'We are told that the difficulties and conflicts traditionally associated with the determination of rewards can be overcome in a learning organization by opening up assumptions which govern reward policies so that they can be shared and examined, enabling alternatives to be discussed and tried out' (Coopey 1995, p. 200, quoting Pedler et al. 1991).

Sterling's limited amount of in-house expertise in Performance Management meant the company had to look outside the business for support, and because of our reputation, we were offered the initial work with the off-shore banking section. The Company does business with people not organizations, and the Sterling team of consultants at The Company were able to persuade contacts in the organization that we could help to shape their thinking about PM, build on existing ideas, and design an effective intervention, based on sound Performance Management principles.

The off-shore section work established the reputation of The Company in PM development at Sterling. Through our contacts Corporate Banking then asked for training in Performance Management skills for managers, team leaders and directors based on the work in the off-shore section – training on the skills needed to manage performance in the way that would maximize learning and autonomy. However, this was complicated by the culture change that was taking place at the time. The existing style in Corporate Banking was strongly competitive, and independent research had established that Sterling was far behind

external competitors in how they were perceived by their customers. There was a need to move towards a relationship style for corporate customers and this, together with the introduction of IT, devolved budgets and structural implications, led to an emphasis on how team leaders manage their people and run the Performance Management process. We came in to help give team leaders the skills to help them perform these tasks. There was a shift from a focus on task to a relationship emphasis, with managers seeking to improve their performance through their teams in order to please their corporate clients.

Meetings with senior managers in the corporate banking division, together with invitations to seminars and social events, enabled us to maintain a network with key people in Sterling, and led to a meeting with the director for senior executive development for the whole organization. He was keen to pursue the relationship between The Company and Sterling and encouraged us to tender for the Performance Management programme in corporate banking. We competed with four other suppliers and were awarded the contract after presenting to a panel consisting of senior HR development personnel. The design and delivery of our programme are given in detail below. Why did The Company get the work against stiff competition? On the basis of feedback, the reason given was our ability to really listen and understand Sterling's needs, and our ability to formulate a solution, using our learning principles. Our approach differentiated us from other contenders in that we offered a balance between prescription and freedom, depth as well as breadth, using The Company's learning principles, while still giving a possible solution to the problem in concrete and specific terms.

The programme

The purpose of Performance Management for Sterling was identified in consultation with our client as the need 'to differentiate performance in order to reward or not reward'. Sterling was seeking to 'flatten out' their reward curve for employees, so that high performance would be recognized appropriately, as would poor performance. The existing system tended to 'bunch' rewards for employees within one narrow middle band. The new Performance Management system is designed to enable managers to take more responsibility for decisions about rewarding their team. Managers who found it difficult to give feedback, either negative or positive, to their people, had tended to shelve the responsibility by opting for the narrow band or passing it up to their superior. Sterling wished to devolve pay budgets to each team leader, and give each manager responsibility for making the decisions within it, rewarding their team, from a limited pot, in proportion to their performance. In order to be able to do this, managers needed to have the confidence to make a good case for decisions and communicate them clearly. The behavioural skills for Performance Management include coaching skills, dialogue skills and quality feedback.

The programme was a mixture of assessment and development and its purpose, identified in discussion with our client, was 'to give managers the intellectual framework to make reward decisions and some practice in the behavioural implications of making those decisions' and 'to differentiate performance within a Performance Management process'.

The programme, using The Company's learning principles, had a major 'preparation for learning' component. Each participant received an audio tape dealing with Sterling's pay policy and discipline policy, as well as four sample scenarios. Each manager would listen to the tape privately (mostly during car journeys) and then make judgements about salary

increment and bonus for each character, within a finite salary pot. When ready, a test distributed on disk enabled participants to self-test their knowledge. In addition, each participant received 360-degree feedback, based on the Sterling leadership competences.

The actual workshop focused on behavioural assessment and feedback. In small groups, managers reviewed their tape decisions and discussed their rationale. There were no right answers, but sometimes ways forward emerged from the workshops, with the implementation of policy developing dynamically. Participants at the workshop were assessed through their test results and observation of their performance in dealing with the actor-driven scenarios.

Accreditation was a key element in the programme. The test result and behavioural analysis of participants' interactive scenarios were the basis for accreditation and this was clear and transparent from the start, another key learning principle used by The Company. Throughout the programme participants were reminded that their behaviour was subject to assessment and accreditation was a key driver for successful learning.

Learning reviews were undertaken by the HR department, who met with managers, to discuss how they would implement what they had learned with their teams. This operationalized a key learning principle for The Company – that learning should be transferable – hence the importance of a review process. Learning reviews were undertaken both with Sterling and within The Company and we discuss these below. The work we did in the early days designing the above programme helped us win the contract to design and deliver Performance Management introductory training for Sterling Bank's operations in Africa.

Reflective learning from the project

We consider here the potential for reflective learning which our intervention offered to, first Sterling as our client, and second, ourselves as providers.

LEARNING BY STERLING

Sterling is difficult to describe as a learning organization. Because of its size, some parts of it show learning organization characteristics and other parts do not. When we have worked with the organization, we have seen big improvements, from one intervention to the next, where our ideas have been taken on board by managers, incorporated with their own, and real progress has been made. In other interventions we solve the problem together in a way which requires lots of energy and input though sometimes the same problem re-emerges later.

What about the programme we have described above? Has the organization been able to use it for reflective learning either for improvement (single loop) or transformation (double loop) as described in Part 1 of this book? And has the organization benefited by learning about the learning process it has been through?

The qualitative programme evaluation was 99 per cent positive, with comments such as:

- 'Glad that Sterling is taking this approach to accreditation.'
- 'This was the most worthwhile two days I've spent in the bank in a long time.'
- 'We need this kind of professionalism in people management.'
- 'Overall very constructive and confidence building.'

The additional business won as a result of our success indicates a level of satisfaction which is coincident with a positive learning experience, where people feel they have gained something worthwhile which can make a difference to their professional lives. Because the programme we offered tied in with the Chief Executive's message to employees, and his first 'Dear Colleague' letter mentioned the programme, this provided a focus for managers, and gave them the confidence that their learning was coincident with organizational objectives. Senior staff in the group attended the programme, putting themselves under pressure of accreditation, and they became important role models. This made a clear link between behaviours and strategy, as the participants were the people who would implement the strategy, showing evidence of reflective learning for improvement in the organizational context. The organization began to consider how to accredit their employees on their competence in managing people in the same way as this programme accredits their management of money.

The quantitative evaluation is still in progress, and answers the question 'Has this programme had an effect on the distribution curve of salaries?' When the measure is available it is likely that the programme has impacted on the distribution curve, but not perhaps as much as Sterling hoped. They recognized that the change required, from a salary matrix system to team leaders making highly responsible tough decisions, could not be achieved overnight. They accept that the process could take two to three years. In reviews with Sterling we discussed what we achieved in a short space of time and it is likely that the design will be adopted as a model programme across other divisions in the group.

The Performance Management activity in Africa showed significant success, we think partly because of their skill in learning from the UK experience, partly because of their ability to persuade, and also because of the geographical distance from the centre, where cultural factors are much more powerful. In Africa it has been possible to create an enclave where Performance Management has thrived. In terms of individual learning the groups in Africa also exhibited a thirst for learning which we rarely see in the UK. We recall growing up in a society where education was the route to advancement, to change social standing or monetary prospects. We found that the people in Africa share that view and see learning in the job as the way to improve themselves, their families and their lot in life; this ethos is evident in their work. Such motivation to learn is less apparent in the more affluent UK. So again we found evidence of reflective learning for improvement.

The organization had been forced to learn from negative press comments on branch closures, ATM charging and chief executive salaries. The change of chief executive coincided with a new strategic direction with Sterling prepared to learn from customers. The traditional style of banking, where processes were carried out by people – for example, cheques processed manually – has gone, with increasing automation, so the need for large numbers of people has dwindled. Sterling went for natural wastage, fair routes out for those who chose to leave, and many did, taking a wealth of experience with them. The managers' work remaining has become stretched, because there are still managerial jobs to do but less people to do them so less time for learning and reflection. In addition, because of the contraction there has been no outside recruitment, so infusion of new ideas is not strong. New blood has come mainly from graduate recruitment, bringing a particular kind of academic learning, largely frowned on by old-stagers.

There are signs of a learning environment developing in Sterling. A recent example of intentional corporate learning was the project to revise their method of compiling data on corporate customers, to include the costs of developing material for clients, servicing the

account and so on. This has altered the configuration of the sales force, where portfolios which were highly profitable under the old system are now middle ranking in importance to the organization. Pilot results show unexpected implications for the business processes in that division and questions are being asked about learning from the pilot and how that learning can be spread out, a sign that employees are ready to learn about the learning process. We have encouraged Sterling to use its pilot projects in a learning way, that is, using the process consciously to note how things are changing and how this affects the business. In fact we are recommending that projects provide space for reflective learning, so that the benefits can be passed on.

For Sterling, like other financial institutions, the commercial environment in which it exists predisposes it to move quickly and this makes reflective learning difficult. Shareholder pressure discourages Sterling from taking the long view, preparing to learn, learning and reviewing – so that it's packed like your parachute, securing maximal learning from the project. As consultants and developers, we rail against this, but it is too easy to stand outside and criticize. It may be that banking employees do not desire to withstand those tough commercial pressures; after all, they chose to work in this sector, with all its traditional emphasis on short-termism. New start-up banks are now threatening market share and Sterling is becoming more thoughtful about its evolution, within a pressured environment. The key point to stress as developers is that expensive programmes without some element of reflection are inefficient for learning. So for large corporate spends there is less quality learning than there could be and this may ultimately lead to a change of stance on reflective learning.

In terms of formal learning, Sterling is beginning to set up a corporate university, offering accredited learning for its employees. The environment is a friendly one, so informal learning takes place through networking and relationship exchange. Although this tends to be career-focused, it also operates for individuals in terms like 'how can I make this job easier, do my job better or get this project signed off?' When Sterling employees are offered the chance to network informally, they take it, and these events could include intentional reflective learning. Like any organization, key information is not found in a set of procedures but discovered in transactional exchange and genuine willingness to help. Sterling is good at that. Also, with structural changes taking place so rapidly at present, the informal network is a source of stability as it takes much longer to change, and may offer a way in to spreading culture change initiatives. We found that the Performance Management programme tutors were acting as change agents, communicating the culture change desired as well as conducting the training. We had evidence of informal exchanges as described above: people who had enjoyed the programme told others, influencing their mind-set before they came to the workshop, so although it was semi-compulsory there was no sense of people arriving as prisoners of the event. Our contact procedure (phoning delegates before workshops) helped with this, as did the distance learning assignment.

The learning initiatives and opportunities in Sterling come from particular networks and workable projects. This bottom-up approach is being encouraged by the new Chief Executive who has expressed a desire to set up projects in an action learning way. At present projects are set up and reviewed, but the review focuses on the task, rather than the learning process, so that those projects are limited to reflective learning for improvement. Unfortunately, the tendency to move swiftly on to the next project means that reflective learning for transformation is unlikely and even the first-level learning is not passed on. Projects designed with a reflective dialogue element (as in action learning)[2] offer a huge opportunity for transformational learning especially in the management of people. For instance, the new system for

assessing the value of a corporate client will yield improvement in profit, and offer the opportunity to radically change the way Sterling looks at these customers. The Performance Management programme may have led to transformational learning for individuals – we saw signs of this at the workshops – but we have not been able to track that back into the workplace so we have no proof of it happening in the organizational context. The realization that there is another way to manage employees and customers can be potentially transformational, and Sterling was setting out to promote such a transformation. Only time will tell if they have succeeded.

For Sterling to be able to take time and space for reflective learning that will lead to transformation, there needs to be a consistently healthy share price, giving the Chief Executive the chance to position learning and for role models to emerge. The Chief Executive is actively spreading a learning message through informal road shows, tapping into the informal network, being open to employee concerns and offering transparency, not easy in a big organization. At present, employees take the space for reflection and reflective dialogue, informally, in their own time, or, as with the Performance Management cassette, in time (while travelling by car) which is neither the employee's or the organization's. The investment in space and time for reflection as an organizational strategy would be a big departure for Sterling in the financial environment of today.

Learning by The Company

The particular learning from our work with Sterling in the design and implementation of the Performance Management programme, relates to how The Company managed the project and how the project affected our relationship with Sterling.

In terms of the management of the project, given its size and scope, our stakeholder approach paid off, in that the team who managed the programme spent time in setting up what became a machine to process over a thousand delegates, distance learning packs, 360-degree results, accreditation and consultant liaison. The stakeholder approach enabled every member of the team to contextualize their part in the process, with a full understanding of the other parts, as well as a joint vision of the project. Our team manager took responsibility for quality control, testing and checking our suppliers, and liaising with Sterling, again using the stakeholder approach to define responsibilities. To ensure consistency the same venue was used so that all delegates experienced the same learning environment, a must for accreditation.

We learnt from the project that we need to be more assertive earlier in order to ensure that our *client* has the necessary capability in whatever field they elect to take responsibility. As this affects our success, we need to be more pro-active, taking the role of customer, as Sterling became our supplier in terms of administrative support for the programme. In future, we will check out our client's capability in terms of their resources and previous experience of the activity concerned, just as we would with our suppliers. In this way we can have complete faith in our client's part of the programme.

We learnt that more interim learning reviews allow early warning of difficulties as well as providing the space for reflective dialogue. The resource base was underpowered for the size of the project, and its complexity demanded a more sophisticated support system. We learnt that slim profit margins stimulate creativity, so quality need not always imply higher costs, but it's a fine line which relies on early discipline and clear project architecture.

One significant learning from our work with Sterling has been the value that we offer an organization, and the importance of being clear about what we will or will not contemplate as a commercial proposition. We have adopted learning principles and they form part of the package we offer clients. Our value lies in our understanding of how people learn, and setting up the conditions in which they can learn most effectively, at team, organizational and individual level. Our approach is transparent and transferable, enabling people to continue without us, a real added value. We leave a learning heritage with our clients.

Notes

1. The Balanced Scorecard is a method of analysing any activity in relation to its important dimensions.
2. An account of action learning is given in Chapters 8 and 15.

7 *Learning with Sainsbury's during the 1990s*

David Muskett

This chapter recounts the collaboration between an academic institution and a commercial enterprise: the university (formerly Manchester Polytechnic) was Manchester Metropolitan University (MMU) and the commercial enterprise was J Sainsbury plc. The Department of Retailing and Marketing at Manchester Metropolitan University mounted and ran an exclusive Distance/Open Learning version of the BA (Hons) Retail Marketing Degree for Sainsburys' junior management. Essentially it explores organizational learning and cross-cultural learning between two organizations that perceived each other to be very different yet ultimately were able to work together very effectively. It certainly proved a steep learning curve for the university, particularly in terms of formalizing our course planning and shortening our time-scales for achieving goals. Lessons learned by the department have been applied to relations with other retail and business clients through the new programme of commercial courses since developed.

The most senior manager involved, the Personnel Director, has remained a constant positive factor for the ultimate oversight of the relationship. This has enabled evaluation of learning at company level. However, it is harder to evaluate what individuals have learned, as most of the middle managers over the years of the programme have either left the company or moved on to other work. Writing in 2000, they now seem more able to appreciate what we can offer them than in 1990 and also to a lesser extent what are the limitations of process that we face in an academic environment. There must have been some level of reflective learning to cause this transformation albeit under the constant pressure of the market on Sainsbury's part.

The chapter uses a chronological approach with most evaluation in the text and various phases of the developing relationships are described. There are broader reflections at the end.

Enquiry phase: development – demands – compromise – support

Sainsbury's approached Manchester Polytechnic's Department of Retail Marketing in the summer of 1989. They had been a supporter of our Sandwich Degree[1] in Retail Marketing since before its launch in 1984 and have taken placement students and graduates from the programme. They approached us because they faced a particular problem. The south-east region of J. Sainsbury's had linked up to a London-based polytechnic seeking some level of validation of their in-house training programme for junior managers. In order for them to obtain a Certificate in Management, extra work set by the polytechnic was to be undertaken

by the junior managers and accreditation given for their already completed in-house training with Sainsbury's. This neat arrangement had apparently foundered and no work had been set for the 30-odd student/managers signed up to the scheme.

It is worth setting in perspective Sainsbury's position in 1989. They were the leading UK grocery multiple with the largest market share and were highly profitable in the booming late 1980s. It had also led them to a culture of some level of arrogance and complacency in how they operated – we were to come across this repeatedly over the following years. They were used to getting their own way.

As author I became involved with a meeting in the late summer of 1989 and was asked to be 'Course Leader' for the putative programme. Polytechnics were constrained in what they could do at that time because the majority of their courses were validated by external bodies, most notably the Council for National Academic Awards (CNAA and B-TEC). Any course we might offer Sainsbury's would have to fit within what was feasible with the validating body. At this meeting the dimensions of what they were seeking were discussed with their senior training people and from our side we outlined what we saw might be feasible, the sort of time-scales we needed and the constraints we faced. We agreed to work on a proposal for them and sought some up-front money to release a member of staff (the author) to do this. It was clear they felt under time pressure and said they needed to have something implemented in 1990 and so agreed to this initial financing.

During the autumn of 1989 we worked on our course proposal and Sainsbury's seconded a member of their Retail Training Department to assist us in this and she came to Manchester to work for three weeks. It became clear we faced a number of physical constraints. There was not a suitable design of a retailing-based Certificate in Management at that time. We were the only UK provider of an undergraduate degree in Retailing so had no other body of expertise to draw upon. Second, the cycle time for new course validations under the CNAA process was relatively long and had to be booked well ahead. Third, it was clear that Sainsburys were not seeking a conventionally taught part-time programme but more something that was based around student-centred distance learning.

We worked out that the only structure that might be feasible for us within likely time constraints was a parallel design to our existing Sandwich Degree in Retail Marketing. A degree by open and distance learning was devised which would take five years to complete to honours level. It also had Certificate and Diploma in Higher Education awards built in for students who might drop out at level one and level two of the programme, and it validated the Sainsbury's training material at level one of the programme which comprised just over half of the credits.

We realized that this design required us to write our own in-house distance learning material in Retailing over the next five years followed by annual updates – an expensive operation. We also felt that dedicated taught residential periods were needed to teach 'hands-on' skills and to give students that vital contact to build confidence and team spirit, so two weeks residential per cohort, per annum were also built in.

In terms of costing, as this was not to be an open public course, the full costs were to be met by Sainsbury's. Our proposal to them included both dedicated administrative and academic staff for the programme for which we sought full cost funding as a separate item. Then a sliding scale of per capita fees for student tuition were to be added.

The outline concept and costings were then put to Sainsbury's at a difficult meeting in early 1990. The company had clearly underestimated the likely scale of the proposal and also the costs that might be involved. In a now infamous phrase one training manager said to us 'I

thought academics came cheaper than that.' It was not guaranteed to improve the atmosphere between us and betrayed a certain arrogance about their attitude towards us. A final detailed proposal was put to them for submission to their Directors' Board Committee in late January 1990 and Sainsbury's promised us a decision within two to three weeks.

Eventually for reasons which the author never could quite understand, no decision was taken until late March 1990. By then we felt that they had missed the deadline for course design and validation. We deliberately had done no further work on the programme because of the possibility of their rejecting the proposal. Sainsbury's were very unhappy about this and by turns threatened and cajoled us that they must have the programme by the autumn of 1990 at the latest. They did not, could not and perhaps would not understand why a 'supplier' would refuse to deal with them on their terms. In one particular conversation, the author pointed out to people in JS Retail Training that ultimately we did not need them and resented being treated as a 'baked bean supplier' when we were a strong independent organization.

Compromise was reached and we began to work on what might be feasible in the timescale. Our initial intention was, provided we received CNAA validation (the date for the event was fixed for July 1990), and as we would have insufficient time to write the needed distance-learning material for an autumn start, we would generate what teaching we could and teach more directly via three intensive residential weeks during the coming academic year. Sainsbury's even offered us more money to bring in outside help to write material but we pointed out that this was not feasible as we were virtually the sole leading UK experts in undergraduate retail teaching at that time. Their initial position could be described as 'why do these awkward academics not want to do it our way?', as they were impatient with our procedures. Over time they came to understand that our validation processes were designed to ensure the quality of our output and guarantee national recognition. In short they recognized it could not be a straightforward buyer–supplier relationship which comprised the basis of their relationships with the vast majority of other organizations. We stressed the value of our independence to them in terms of the credibility such national recognition of qualifications brought to their staff. At this early stage the organization was being challenged about its taken-for-granted assumptions and, to their credit, they transformed their attitude.

From the university's perspective we learned that our usually relaxed style for preparing teaching material in general terms, then honing at the last minute, would not do if we were to have fixed residential dates and to assemble distance-learning material. This was quite a shock to the system in 1990, which relied on informal procedures, student feedback, backed up exceptionally by the intervention of external examiners. Quality was presumed to be controlled by the CNAA review system but this did not encourage staff to reflect on their practice directly and regularly. We had to set up systems for planning, preparing and monitoring material which were more rigorous and formal than hitherto. This practice has stood the university in good stead for later commercial client relationships and also the more rigorous quality control procedures which now apply to higher education, principally through the Quality Assurance Agency.

Having made the decision to go ahead, Sainsbury's showed great commitment to the project and there was extensive liaison between us and their Retail Training Department. For the validation event their Personnel Director attended in person to lend his support (having arrived by helicopter!). After searching questions, the CNAA panel gave its approval with limited conditions about monitoring results and both the teams from Manchester and Sainsbury's felt rightly in a mood for self-congratulation.

First phase: first cohorts

As the university insisted on keeping academic control of the programme, although Sainsbury's organized the recruitment, we had the final say in whom to accept or reject. We gave a 'favourable expectation' to those who had already been signed on for the defunct programme in London and then recruited on the basis of standard university minimum requirements of two A Levels and five GCSEs including English and Maths. Some candidates fell short of the standard minimum and were interviewed by the course leader to evaluate their commitment and ability. A small number were rejected as the result of the interview. A cohort of 60 was eventually assembled and this was to be the target for immediate future years. Formal teaching began in November 1990 at Sainsbury's Training HQ Fanhams Hall in Hertfordshire, whose comfortable accommodation has been the centre of the overwhelming majority of residentials since. The pattern was set in that a number of academic and administrative staff travelled from Manchester in rented cars loaded down with printed materials to pass on to the students. What we found was a cohort of enthusiastic and largely extrovert students with a 'can do' mentality which contrasted sharply with some of our full-time students. They were fun to teach.

Sainsbury's Retail Training were however initially cautious if not suspicious and insisted on a member of their staff being there all week to help/take part in some sessions just to make sure everything was OK. With hindsight, we probably overpacked the first week with activity and left our students tired out with study and presentations. Formal feedback was sought and was overwhelmingly positive at the end of the week including one student claiming that his brain hurt! Sainsbury's seemed happy that we could be relied upon to deliver what we said.

The pattern was now set with students' assignments being sent into Manchester and returned with a formal feedback sheet. Staff prepared distance-learning material and it was sent out regularly to the students. In our formal relationship with Sainsburys, they always delivered what we asked and always paid our invoices promptly. In the autumn of 1991, we recruited for a second level-one cohort as the first cohort moved into level two. In our own parlance they became JS1, JS2, JS3, etc. depending on which year they were studying. Exams were taken in Manchester with as far as possible the open learning students taking the same papers as full-time students, for both economy and to establish exactly equal academic standards.

In evaluating the first phase of the Sainsbury–MMU relationship, there was a mismatch of understanding on both sides. MMU's Department of Retailing and Marketing received the Sainsbury's degree as a new challenge and an opportunity to earn extra funds outside of government funding. We knew we would have to learn to manage the client relationship. We did not appreciate that we would have to ask serious questions about our way of working and to amend them rapidly as we learned from the process. For example, this affected administrative staff as well as academics who were expected to work off-site for the first time. Adapting standard administrative contracts to do this proved surprisingly difficult. In learning terms we were forced into double-loop learning and questioning the whole set of assumptions we carried. There was pain attached to this process, a classic condition in transformative learning, and the presence of a relationship in which the transformation occurred.

Sainsbury's were forced to adapt too. Their wishes were straightforward, to be able to offer a nationally recognized qualification to their junior managers. Their liaison team in Retail Training and Development were used to being in control of their own training courses which were well thought-out but highly prescriptive in content. Our material made them a little

uncomfortable because it was less formal and stressed experiential learning broadly based on the Kolb (1984) model. When they saw that students could learn independently and saw the positive feedback, they were able to loosen up their initially strict supervision of our residentials and the training officers responsible no longer felt obliged to stay with the students for the duration of the residential as they had initially. We later found that a number of their people-based training programmes sought to use a more reflective style so clearly double-loop learning had begun for them as individuals. We believe that training personnel witnessed in our programme for the first time a successful example of experiential learning. Time constraints plus a lack of continuity in Retail Training staff may have proved a damper on better corporate learning, as there was no provision for reflective review.

Middle phase: pursuing the programme

Retail Training at Sainsbury's tended to allocate one officer to manage the 'Manchester' project, as they called it. From our perspective the problem we had was that this responsibility passed from person to person too frequently with an average period of incumbency being about 12–18 months. We found this lack of continuity a particular bugbear and the new person coming in was rarely briefed adequately. The Course Leader and Course Organizer often had to brief the incoming person about the programme and its operation. The Retail Training Department eventually developed confidence in us and did not feel the need to supervise the residentials directly. This led to student complaining that no one from Sainsbury's was bothering to take an interest in them. This was far from true, as Sainsbury's regularly organized celebratory dinners at Fanhams Hall during residentials to mark each significant milestone for each cohort, for example, Certificate in Higher Education, Diploma in Higher Education and Ordinary Degree. Senior managers were invited to the events and mingled with the students often gaining a better understanding of their situation and what they were studying with us. It was a useful learning exercise as managers were tackled on the practical aspects of learning/study, for example, time off, the essential nature of residentials and the need for managers' support. We actively encouraged students to lobby senior managers at the social events. The senior managers also learned wider things about the company's operations at these events and amongst the inevitable trivial complaints they did seem to get some useful suggestions from the students. The better managers made a point of asking questions and listening, so that a real reflective dialogue took place. The students were then able to feel empowered to make comments directly to senior managers without the usual threat of the strict hierarchical information flows which usually applied. Subsequent events suggest that some of the communication had positive effects, as students experienced more practical support in the company. Poorer managers used it as an exercise to demonstrate their company status and to hector the students about company policy so the transformational learning was far from universal. We also made a point of listening and learning from the senior managers too, so the university could adapt better in future to the needs of other corporate clients. We used these occasions as opportunities to demonstrate that we were firmly connected to the 'real world' of business as they perceived it.

As we gradually built up to the maximum of five cohorts running together, it was a major operation for us in managing the student work, the distance-learning material, tracking assignments, planning and staffing the eleven cohort weeks of residentials annually. The first cohort reached honours degree in 1995 and had shrunk from 60 to 32 by this time. Student

wastage seemed quite high initially but given the pressure of work on them at Sainsburys and the demands of university work over five years, the outcome was not unrealistic. Virtually all students who left part way through the course, left with a stage qualification, not empty handed. The staff involved were particularly proud that we awarded a first-class honours degree to a student from the first cohort. In five hectic years we had learned much and were able to test directly how successful our learning was, partly because we could use student experiences in the company to frame the exercises, assessments and the written distance-learning material that the students worked with. The assumption that a degree course anchored in practice is likely to lead to reflective learning confirms the contention that learners must have some active material to reflect upon. However activity and practice alone are insufficient. Our programme offered JS students the opportunity to reflect upon their work with others and transform their approach to it.

Sainsbury's were generous in their provision for the new graduates and laid on a lunch at one of Manchester's top hotels for graduates, partners and parents. The chairman, David Sainsbury, personally attended and spoke at the lunch and presented prizes for the best overall student project. Much good publicity was generated for Manchester Metropolitan University as it was called by then and for Sainsbury's. Our own Deputy Vice-Chancellor attended the same lunch. The department was rightly seen as achieving explicitly the final aspect of the university's four-part mission statement 'To meet the needs of industry, business, the professions and the wider community'.

Later phase: querying costs and querying outputs

The situation gradually began to change as Sainsbury's faced a number of pressures by the late 1990s. There was a high wastage rate amongst the graduates of the first two cohorts as many former students left Sainsbury's with their degrees to seek pastures new elsewhere. We argued that a proportion of these might have left earlier had it not been for the degree but it cut little ice. A project was instigated by Retail Training to investigate why graduates were leaving and came broadly to the conclusion that the company had no structures in place to recognize and reward with an enhanced career path these now-experienced graduates who were generally in their mid/late 20s. There seemed to be a philosophical problem attached to the culture at Sainsbury's. Try as I might, the author argued for some recognition even as a token of their graduating and received a blank refusal from the senior manager in Retail Training and Development. His view was that promotion was achieved on merit, not just because someone had recently graduated even on such a focused course as the BA (Hons) in Retail Marketing and we could not shift him. This mirrored a cultural attitude that many students had suffered from line managers during the course of the programme summarized by the attitude 'I worked my way up, why shouldn't he/she?', an instance of the kind of defensive reasoning cited by Argyris (1991). Some store managers went out of their way to make life difficult for their trainee manager/students even though this was expressly against the wishes of the Personnel Director. When we discovered this happening we intervened discreetly on their behalf and on the odd occasion more directly.

The high wastage rate made Sainsbury's begin to query the costs involved in the programme, which were indeed substantial. To make matters worse, they were under increased trading pressures and had lost market leadership to their major rival Tesco. There was a round of redundancies amongst managers in an effort to cut costs and clearly the degree pro-

gramme began to look more vulnerable. During 1997 and 1998, discussions were held between Sainsbury's and MMU as to the possible future of the programme. It was concluded that although they acknowledged the course as a quality educational experience, demonstrated by graduation success rates, it should not be pursued further. The reason for this was that it was not achieving the corporate goals they now had in mind, which was to offer continuing education and training opportunities widely throughout the company. They saw the focus as being too narrow with too small a group of students benefiting. The cohort recruited in autumn 1997 were to be the last on the degree, gaining their honours degrees in summer 2002.

Our proposals to Sainsbury's offered a number of alternative ways of meeting their needs as expressed to us although their needs were partly unclear to us and were perhaps not fully formed. We proposed as an interim a certificate in Higher Education only, in effect year one of the programme, for the group of A-level entry junior managers who had been the original target group and one cohort was recruited on this basis in the autumn of 1998. As the degree had progressed, we had attracted a group of older, more experienced managers and most had done very well indeed. The university and the Department of Retailing and Marketing had by this time developed a suite of courses at post-graduate and post-experience level designed exactly for this group of more experienced managers. The department had a number of clients up and running with the Retail Management Development Programme (RMDP) as it was called. We made an outline proposal based around these two-tier arrangements and put a more specific proposal on paper in late 1998 as a follow-up with indicative costings. There was no cohort intake of any sort in the autumn of 1998.

Discussions continued through 1999 and we were declared educational supplier of first choice by Sainsburys after the proposal was put to the Sainsbury's board. No clear decision was taken and the company became more preoccupied with its commercial and trading situation and its market difficulties. No cohort was recruited in the autumn of 1999 either.

By February 2000 we had still no definite commitment for any go-ahead with the RMDP proposal. The existing programme is managed day-to-day by a former graduate. The company requested another report from us on the RMDP proposal, as they were unclear as to what we could do for them. The corporate goals for such a programme remain unclear to us as potential providers. However the new MMU Course Leader pursued this proposal and an experimental intake began in the autumn of 2000 under the new design. We hope that having responded to Sainsbury's requests for greater flexibility, they will feel able to continue with the new design.

Reflections

The open learning degree has been by most standards a terrific success academically as virtually all students have left with either a stage award or a degree. Our external examiners have commended the standards achieved including a number of first-class honours degrees. We have also had as far as we can tell the longest working relationship between a major retailer and a university in the UK. Both sides have learned from each other. We have gained much hands-on experience about organizing distance-learning material and the organizing of residential teaching whilst operating with a customer who faces real time and financial business pressures. We have also sharpened up our act in terms of planning for the future and being systematic about our scheduling. Virtually all the academic staff have business experience

and have brought this to bear on our relations with Sainsbury's and subsequently with other clients.

Sainsbury's have learned about and perhaps confirmed that new less directive teaching and learning methods offer wider scope for staff development, and also about the constraints which apply to the obtaining of nationally recognized qualifications. They have also retained some of their graduates and most have been promoted and are making a real contribution to their business. From my perspective, the weakness in the relationship has come from their not finding ways of transferring learning effectively within the organization. This would have required a meaningful briefing of incoming 'Manchester project' managers and a handover which included a proper list of required activities throughout the year which could be updated regularly. What was missing was any real history of the relationship which would have prevented the same questions being asked over and over again by new project managers. This gap was probably caused by the fact that the business tends to be focused in the relatively short term. This is driven in part by the trading pressures put upon UK-based public limited companies to perform and achieve satisfactory returns for City investors and Sainsbury's are hardly unique in facing these pressures. We have observed across a number of retailers that there is also a pernicious focus on week-to-week results in each store driven by the availability of mountains of Electronic Point of Sale data even though some fluctuations are quite random. The result is that the organization from our perspective tends to run on 'dipped headlights', as it must be said do other retailers. As a result they never get into the second loop to learn about learning and the process. There is a strong task-driven focus throughout the organization which has proved difficult to shake out of students to make them think laterally about problems. Sainsbury's organization is driven by hierarchy, although this has been addressed in recent times when management layers have been flattened out in stores. This hierarchy had tended in the past to make them slower in decision making, as each layer sought the approval of the next before making decisions. We have felt the victim of slow decision making on a number of occasions over the years.

We have also been more convinced that vocationally focused academic study does have a contribution to make to the effective operations of business organizations. Our JS graduates are financially and computer literate, have knowledge of how to seek effective information, have enhanced people skills and also a strategic focus when required. This is vital whilst the business is under stress in its core grocery markets with both Tesco and the cash-rich Walmart who now own ASDA threatening their market share daily. A group of in-house lateral thinkers can do no harm under these circumstances. Above all we have taught them to think independently in an environment that had not always encouraged this. We hope that the lessons both sides have drawn will enable us to have a fruitful continuing relationship.

Note

1. 'Sandwich' being descriptive of a programme, degree or course which incorporates a placement element within it, usually 'sandwiched' between traditional attendance at college or university.

8 Learning to Manage Change in the Health Service

Tom Bourner, Sue O'Hara and Trix Webber

This chapter is based on recent work undertaken for a large public sector health care organization by the University of Brighton's Management Development Research Unit. In the first part of this chapter we provide an overview of the programme, the second part looks at the 'story behind the story', that is, the story of the development of the programme, and the third part contains reflections on the journey we took.

The programme

The challenge facing a large public sector health care provider in 1998 had elements that will be familiar to many public service organizations: increasing demands of government initiatives, new legislation and the need to recruit trained staff. These factors, together with a substantial number of new jobs, created a situation in which some of the organization's traditional management practices felt increasingly inadequate.

Rather than 'tinkering at the edges', the organization's directors wanted a significant strategic development intervention. Their aim was to create a style of management which would allow managers at all levels to innovate and find new ways of crossing traditional boundaries. They wanted a programme which combined management development and organizational development and one that they could run in partnership with the programme's developers and eventually take over and run themselves.

The programme created by the University of Brighton for this public sector health care service, comprised a combination of projects, personal development plans (PDPs), workshops and self-managed action-learning set meetings; it lasted for one year, coming on stream in June 1999. Managers who signed up committed themselves to (1) carrying out a change project that would fulfil some element of their service plan and bring about an improvement in the workplace and (2) engage in programme of personal and professional development.

An initial five-day residential course aimed at enabling participants to develop the skills required to manage their own sets, identify potential change projects and elements of a personal development plan. The action-learning sets then met monthly for a full day throughout the year. Over the year, one-day workshops were provided on change management, project management, performance management and basic research skills to support the participants in their change projects and the implementation of their personal development plans. A mid-year process review workshop enabled managers to reflect on how the sets

were working and to develop action plans to address any problems. The final element was an end-of-year review and evaluation workshop.

SELF-MANAGED ACTION LEARNING (SMAL) IN PRACTICE

Past experience indicated that the high cost of facilitating action-learning sets was a barrier to the extensive use of action learning in organizations. Self-management of the sets was therefore the key element in providing a programme that could be sustained by the organization internally.

In the SMAL model the first two action-learning set meetings were facilitated by an experienced set adviser, who modelled good practice. Thereafter, set members took turns in taking responsibility for managing the set to ensure that the set meeting took place and achieved its purpose. Adopting the name 'Self-managed action learning' was intended to empower managers; it communicated the fact that they already had relevant skills to manage the set meetings without the need to rely on an external facilitator.

To avoid the sets feeling isolated, as well as providing a means for review and evaluation, the role of 'Set process adviser' (abbreviated by the term 'Set PA') was created – a role that was taken by members of the organization's own team. Set process advisers attended the whole of the first two facilitated set meetings. At subsequent meetings they joined the set for the final 30 minutes of the day in order to conduct a review of learning, including learning about the self-management of the set. This was intended to *support* the process of self-management – it ensured that the set members would feel that there was always help available should they need it.

The programme was designed to be delivered to cohorts of about forty managers at a time. It was intended that subsequent cohorts of managers would be attracted to join by recommendation from members of earlier cohorts. The aim was that eventually about four hundred managers would choose to take the programme. Only a programme on this scale, it was thought, could alter the culture of management within the organization and have the level of impact required.

OUTCOMES

The final review and evaluation workshop for the first cohort in June 2000 included a 'conference' attended by the Chief Executive and other members of the organization's senior management team. Change projects and a review of the learning achieved were presented via group presentations and individual poster displays. The change projects included initiatives such as developing support frameworks for general practitioners, setting up quality circles, establishing a pre-admission assessment clinic for orthopaedic patients and a scheme to reduce patient waiting lists for dietary advice following heart attacks by replacing one-to-one sessions with action-learning sets. This last project succeeded in cutting the waiting lists from nine months to seven weeks.

DID SMAL WORK?

As far as the organization is concerned, the answer is certainly, *yes*. To date, over 330 managers from a broad range of professional backgrounds and disciplines have completed or are at various stages within the programme, the eighth group having started in October 2001. Participant feedback has been consistently positive. Here are a few examples:

- 'My practice is more reflective and I am learning to assert myself. I feel that I have become a change management agent. Being on the management development programme is like being continually woken up by an alarm clock with a snooze button.'
- 'The most important skills I have learnt are active listening, questioning, saying "no" more often and using creative methods such as brainstorming. I network more and I have more confidence. Being on the programme has been an uncharted voyage of discovery both for me and the organization – the destination is in my hands with their support and commitment.'
- 'I had plans and ideas before the course but I kept the lid on them at all times. Now I have the confidence to take a risk and put forward a plan or idea to senior management. Because of the support the management development programme provides, I can voice my thoughts and fears.'
- 'Because of the programme I think differently – I feel I have a licence to be creative. I take more risks. I also give more feedback and involve staff as an integral part of the service.'

Recruitment is healthy. We were clear from the outset that a programme like this must be based on voluntary participation so we depended on personal recommendation of participants for recruitment of each new cohort. That participants, past and present, are recommending the programme to colleagues is one measure of its success.

Another measure of the programme's success is the result of an independent evaluation by the Institute of Employment Studies (IES) when the first cohort completed the programme in 2000. The IES 'found excellent managerial learning, visible from both the individual set members, their line managers and their subordinates'.

None of the self-managed action-learning sets has collapsed so far and only one manager has left the programme without completing it. From this evaluation, managers believe they have developed their skills in managing change, assertiveness, confidence, reflecting, planning, delegating, problem solving, listening, networking, time management and managing working relationships. Ongoing evaluation by the organization's team has enabled improvements to be introduced with each new cohort of managers.

The story behind the story

The first contact we received from the organization was a letter from someone who had completed a Masters course in the Centre for Management Development at the university. Since that course he had subsequently been promoted to head up the Personnel section of the organization. The Masters course, which was based on action learning and reflective practice, had been a good experience for him and he wanted to talk with us about developing a programme, based on similar principles, within his own organization. He wanted the programme to involve sufficient managers that it would impact on the whole organization's management culture.

When we met to discuss the project we discovered two main stumbling blocks. From his perspective the main obstacle was the likely cost of the programme on the scale he had in mind. From our perspective the main barrier was that our relatively new Management Development Research Unit (MDRU) was intended to undertake work which had a *research* focus rather than replicate courses that we had previously developed. The MDRU mission was as follows:

To be a centre of excellence in management development research. We intend to be internationally known and respected for our research and practice in action learning. We intend also to have a strong reputation for developing innovative approaches to management and management development.

Our research will be informed by, and give direction to, management practice. It will be valued and used by managers and contribute to the success and development of themselves and their organizations. We will apply our research to our teaching and learning practice within the university and the wider community.

What the mission did not say is that we were, and are, at least as keen on research through *innovation* as research through *discovery* and that we are especially enthusiastic about integrating research and *development*.

Probably every research unit has a range of projects that it would like to undertake should the opportunity arise and it was through reviewing such projects that we found a way round the obstacles. Some years before we had looked at what it takes to participate effectively in an action-learning set (Bourner et al. 1997). We had also looked at the pitfalls encountered in action learning (Bourner and Weinstein 1996). This work led us to ask the question, what does it take for sets to self-facilitate successfully?

We were aware that self-facilitating action-learning sets were not new, and that some had been very successful (see for example, McGill et al. 1989) but we were also aware that, more generally, the reputation of self-facilitated sets was not good. In practice, it has proved desirable or necessary for action-learning sets to be facilitated by set advisers.

The record of self-facilitated sets goes some way to explain why most action-learning sets have been provided with an external set facilitator. Allowing for the fact that action-learning programmes that *fail* get spoken and written about *less* than ones that are successful, our impression was that the success rate for self-facilitating action-learning sets was substantially lower than for action-learning sets with a dedicated facilitator. Some of the leading writers on action learning (for example Weinstein 1995; Pedler 1996) stress the importance of good facilitation for successful action-learning sets.

On the basis of our earlier experience and research into action learning, we had come to believe that self-facilitating sets could be successful only if the set members happened to contain enough people with skills of group facilitation.

This line of reasoning led us to the idea of consciously developing facilitation skills in a workshop for participants before they began a programme of self-facilitated action learning. Consequently, we had a research project 'on the shelf' along these lines. The core idea was that we should develop a programme that started with an extensive workshop aimed at developing skills of facilitation of group learning to *precede* a programme of self-facilitated action learning. We were able to develop this idea to meet the needs of the client for an extensive but affordable programme of action learning and our own need for a programme that would involve research and development rather than the simple application of a known 'formula'.

After considerable discussion we identified the following skills and understanding as the prerequisites for successful membership of a self-facilitated action-learning set:

- *Questioning skills* – to help people to learn how to find solutions to their own problems
- *Active listening* – to communicate to people that they are being understood; to help them clarify their situation, their thoughts, and their feelings; to help them work out their own solutions; to hear without judging or evaluating

- *Giving and receiving feedback* – to help people learn and develop; to enable them to feel valued
- *Understanding group processes* – to appreciate the difference between task and process and between facilitative and sabotaging behaviours
- *Creative problem solving* – to provide a range of tools to help people when they ran out of options
- *Reflection* – to help distil the learning from experience and distil learning from the outcomes of actions
- *Understanding learning processes* – to enable people to appreciate the variety of ways in which people can learn.

As we were honing down an initial list of skills towards the above list, we had a meeting with the client and colleagues and realized that this set of skills overlapped hugely with the skills required for the participative management style which the organization wished to encourage. Increasingly, we began to use the term 'facilitative management' as the style of management that the organization wished to move towards.

In one of our development meetings, we decided to brainstorm all the things we could think of that could go wrong with an action-learning set. Our intention, at that stage, was to provide a manual of guidance for the action-learning sets. We envisaged a sort of 'troubleshooting manual' along the lines of 'If that is going wrong then try this'. Soon our brainstormed list contained over a hundred items and we were still going strong; at that point we realized that this approach was not viable. The 'car repair manual' was clearly not a useful model for helping the sets overcome the potential difficulties in facilitating their own sets.

Instead, we concluded that it was more important to communicate clearly to prospective programme participants the core values and beliefs that we saw as underpinning our own facilitation of action learning. We believed that with an understanding and commitment to these values and beliefs, set participants could come up with their own creative solutions to problems they might encounter with the action-learning process – that they could learn their way out of problems that they encountered. This approach would also allow participants understand the implications of joining an action-learning set and so make an informed decision if they wished to participate. We therefore set about identifying what we saw as our core values and beliefs in facilitating action-learning sets and it was these (shown in the appendix to this chapter) that we decided to communicate as clearly as we could at the foundation workshop. Our commitment to being explicit about our values and beliefs in the dissemination of professional practice was influenced by work we had been undertaking on 'practitioner-centred research' (Bourner et al. 2000).

That was the general way that we approached the potential pitfalls in the implementation of action learning. However, our experience with action learning also suggested that there are two specific pitfalls that are most commonly encountered by action-learning sets. On the one hand, set meetings can become 'talking shops' with little action; on the other hand, they can become simply a means of 'progress-chasing' with little reflection and hence little learning. These pitfalls can be summed up as 'all talk and no action or all action and no reflection'.

Our response to this danger was to offer the action-learning sets a modified action-learning process. In our experience, most action-learning sets divide the available time at each set meeting equally amongst the set members. In each person's 'time-slot' (that is, share of the total time), the attention of the whole set is focused on helping that person make progress

with the challenges that they are encountering in managing their change project and learning from so doing. Ideally, this takes the form of reviewing and reflecting on the actions that the person has taken since the last set meeting and then helping the person find actions that will enable them to maximize progress by the next set meeting. For the SMAL sets, we decided to make this sequence *explicit* in the process of the set meetings. The first part of a SMAL set meeting would be devoted to *looking back* to learn the lessons of participants' experience since the last set meeting. The second part of the meeting would be devoted to *looking forward* to identifying the actions that help the participants make progress with their change projects and PDPs (personal development plans). In other words there would be two 'rounds' in each set meeting – the first devoted to reflection and the second devoted to moving forward. We felt that, in addition to avoiding both pitfalls mentioned above, this more structured process would be less daunting to people who were new to action learning and would have to manage the process on their own.

Finally, our brainstorm of possible pitfalls led us to conclude that most of the pitfalls were associated with 'managing' an action-learning set rather 'facilitating' *per se*. We were familiar with Tom Reeves' statement that 'Managers basically have to do two overlapping things. They have to keep the existing show on the road – that is to say manage the routine or recurring activities for which they are responsible. They also have to innovate and make improvements – that is to say change the way things are done or which things are done' (Reeves 1994).

It seemed to us that a major part of the role of the set facilitator was very similar: first, making sure that the set happened and achieved its objectives, and second, helping the set find ways of improving its process. For this reason, we urged set members to establish the role of 'set manager' on a rotating basis. This meant that for every set meeting someone in the set took responsibility for ensuring that it 'worked', that is, achieved its purpose. It also meant that the set meeting provided a forum to try out and practise the skills of 'facilitative management'. At the end of the set meeting the set process review provided an opportunity for the set manager for that meeting to get feedback on their facilitative management of the day's proceedings.

At the same time as we were developing this programme we were conducting a review of action learning across the university (Bourner et al. 2000). This was prompted by our awareness that the University of Brighton probably has more courses based on action learning than any other university in the world. We found 27 courses across the university claiming to use action learning, with at least one such course in each of the six faculties. In studying this phenomenon, we discovered that action-learning sets were being used with two main tasks: to complete projects and to assemble portfolios of evidence of learning. We interpreted this as the use of action learning to support *emergent* learning and *planned* learning respectively (see Megginson 1994, for a discussion of these terms). We decided that we could develop the programme for the health care organization to include both emergent *and* planned learning. Consequently, each participant would not only work on a change project (to bring about some change in the organization that they thought would be desirable) but would also work on implementing a personal development plan.

Whilst we (the programme designers in the MDRU) were confident about the concept of self-managed action-learning sets, we were also aware of the need to provide reassurance to the client that we had built in sufficient support for the self-managed sets to ensure that they would not fail. When we collated all the elements that we had built into the programme to support the self-managed sets they amounted to the following list:

1. The opening workshop contained an intensive training in the skills of effective set participation and of managing a set effectively.
2. Each set would be provided with support materials to help them to self-manage.
3. Each set meeting would end with a half-hour process review with a Set Process Adviser (Set PA).
4. A set could request a session of intervention by an external set adviser if they encountered problems that they could not (yet) manage.
5. The programme contained a full-day workshop to review the action-learning set process approximately four months after the start of the programme.
6. The first two set meetings would be externally facilitated.
7. The values and beliefs we saw as underpinning action learning were to be made explicit. This would provide a set of 'operating values' to work from when managing the action-learning sets. It also would make it easier, at the outset, for people to either commit to action learning as participants or decide not to get involved.
8. The set meetings would be managed by individual members of the action-learning set on a rotating basis
9. The Set PAs would be mentored by University of Brighton staff.
10. A structured process for set meetings (with a 'round' for reflection followed by a second 'round' for planning next actions) would be provided.
11. Adoption of the name 'Self-managed action learning' (SMAL) rather than 'self-facilitated' action learning would help to empower managers, because it would enable them to bring their management skills to managing the process of the set meetings, and it would help to demystify the process by avoiding the use of the less familiar term 'facilitation'.

Reflections

What lessons have we learned from developing and operating the programme? We often use the following tool to support reflective learning: 'three things we like best about an experience and three things that, with hindsight, we would have done differently'. Applying this tool to the development of self-managed action learning provides a first trawl of lessons.

The three best aspects were:

1. We have found a way of making possible the much more extensive use of action learning by making it more affordable.
2. We did a good job for our client – who has increasingly become our friend.
3. We have moved the MDRU closer to its mission.

Three things we would have done differently were:

1. We would have probably started the programme with a 360-degree feedback exercise.
2. We would have included support for mentoring as an additional form of reflective learning.
3. We would have given more explicit consideration to the issues facing internal change agents.

The remainder of this chapter will record other reflections on the experience of developing and operating the programme.

First, we have found it valuable to make explicit the values and beliefs that we see as underpinning self-managed action learning (please see the appendix). The way that we identified these values and beliefs was to ask all those people involved in the delivery of the first programme to write down what they individually believed to be the core values and beliefs underpinning their own practice of action learning. We then worked with the combined lists to produce a prioritized list short enough to be useful to the participants. Although the purpose of this exercise was to produce material for the programme, it proved to be a valuable learning experience for the programme team. It provided each member of the team with insight into where each other member of the team is coming from, which made working together more enjoyable and enabled us to work more effectively as a team.

Second, we learned a lot about the facilitation of action learning. We learned that the set of skills needed to facilitate an action-learning set is a restricted set of the skills needed for more general group facilitation. For example, the skills of managing conflict are needed less because conflict is much rarer in an action-learning set than in a work-group (where interdependence of group members' contributions are usually crucial to the level of outcome achieved). We learned that the skills of effective participation in an action-learning set and the skills of managing an action-learning set are to a very large extent substitutable for the skills of facilitating an action-learning set.

Third, we learned that the skills of managing an action-learning set are very similar to the skills of facilitative management and similar again to the soft skills of managing change needed by internal change agents. This was a very important lesson in the context of the client's organization as one senior member of the management team expressed concern that if some managers were prevented from using a 'command and control' style of management they would be left with no method of managing at all. By acquiring the skills of facilitative management such managers acquired a real choice about how to manage.

Fourth, we learned from the *surprises* that the programme brought us. For example, in designing the programme we drew attention to its potential benefits, but one benefit we did not anticipate was that of 'networking'. The organization provides a wide range of functions across a large rural area and when we evaluated the programme with participants one of the benefits that was frequently mentioned and rated highly was the opportunities that it provided for networking across this dispersed organization. This benefit was unintentionally enhanced by our decision to work with relatively large cohorts of 40 participants.

Fifth, we recognized that the form of the programme changed during the process of its design, development and implementation. It was not simply a matter of us designing a programme to the client's specification and then implementing it. Rather, we had numerous meetings with the client and their colleagues and, as we hit obstacles to what we had planned, we modified the plans. With hindsight, we now see this as a 'learning approach' to programme development and implementation. We see a parallel here to the distinction between a 'programmed approach' to managing change (Cummings 1995) and 'learning approaches' to managing change. The great danger with programmed change is that when there are unintended consequences of actions taken, and when pitfalls appear, it can derail the plan, whereas *learning* approaches to managing change treat unintended consequences and pitfalls as opportunities for reflective learning.

Sixth, again with hindsight, we could recognize the benefit of working with a client who had completed one of our programmes before. It meant that he was familiar with our values

and beliefs having experienced them in action. This meant that there were no shocks in terms of core values and beliefs embodied in the programme. Indeed, it was probably a desire to bring these beliefs and values into the organization that contributed to the client's wish to have us work with their organization. This smoothed the development process and makes us want to do more work with people who have previous experience of our work.

Finally, we hear much nowadays of *evidence-based practice*. Our experience of developing this programme has impressed us with the need to make provision for *practice-based evidence*. It is important for us to be aware not only of the flow of knowledge from research to practice but also to be aware of the flow of knowledge from practice to research. This emphasizes the need for people to record the lessons that emerge from professional practice so that they can be shared with other practitioners.

APPENDIX: OUR VALUES AND BELIEFS UNDERPINNING SELF-MANAGED ACTION LEARNING

VALUES

1. Personal responsibility and proactivity
2. The ultimate purpose of learning is to make a difference
3. Learning from action – and action informed by learning
4. Support and challenge of peers
5. Encouraging feedback
6. Collaboration, giving and receiving
7. Learning as a lifelong process.

BELIEFS UNDERPINNING THE PROGRAMME

1. Management learning and development is about developing the ability to get something done rather than developing the ability to *talk* about getting something done.
2. Two basic components of learning are P and Q where P is 'pre-packed knowledge', already set out in books or known to expert authorities, and Q is 'questioning insight', the capacity to identify illuminating questions and fresh lines of enquiry.
3. In a context of rapid change today's problems tend to be different to yesterday's problems. P, pre-packaged knowledge, is the product of solving yesterday's problems. As the rate of change rises the value of Q in learning rises relative to the value of P.
4. Lasting behavioural change is more likely to follow the reinterpretation of past experience than the acquisition of fresh knowledge.
5. In order to learn from experience it is necessary to make the time to reflect on that experience.
6. We get more learning from experience if we try new things.
7. There is much that we can learn with and from other people that we cannot learn alone. We can learn from other people when they ask us questions that are different from the ones that we ask ourselves.
8. Feedback is necessary for learning. Feedback can come from the consequences of our actions as well as from the responses of other people.
9. The desire to learn is stimulated by the need to deal with real problems or engage with real opportunities.
10. In a changing environment learning is a survival condition: '(1) When the rate of change is faster than that of learning, the organism fails. (2) When the rate of learning is as fast as (or faster than) that of change, the organism is likely to adapt, survive or even grow' (Revans 1984).

9 Leadership Learning at Novartis

Ian Ritchie

This chapter is the story of a successful collaboration between the Oxford Group, Ashridge and Novartis, to design and run an imaginative programme to develop a cohort of new first-line leaders. The programme involved the participants, the tutors and the companies in significant personal and organizational learning.

The Oxford Group is an international consultancy and training organization that works on all the people dimensions of business. Its main capabilities are in the fields of people assessment, communication, leadership and management development, and organizational change. Ashridge is a private college which offers a variety of management development programmes.

Novartis is a world-class life sciences organization, created in 1996 from the integration of two Swiss giants, CIBA and Sandoz. At the time this was one of the largest corporate mergers in history, valued at $63 billion. The two companies shared over three hundred years of life sciences research and experience, in the fields of pharmaceuticals, crop protection and nutrition. They came together to form the world's fourth largest company in their sector. The organization employs 14 800 people world-wide.

The relationship

As is often the case, the relatively recent relationship between the Oxford Group and Novartis as companies is founded on a long-term relationship between people. Richard Nicholson, the Management Development Manager of Novartis in the UK, worked previously for Hoechst, the German chemical and pharmaceutical company. Back in 1989, the Oxford Group was appointed to run an executive development programme for Hoechst UK, based around customer service and total quality management. Ian Ritchie of the Oxford Group led that programme and worked with Richard and his colleagues on what turned out to be a highly successful leadership development initiative. Richard progressed to become the Management Development Manager of Hoechst Marion Roussel, the pharmaceutical division of Hoechst, before leaving to join Novartis in 1999. Over the intervening years, Richard and Ian kept in touch, although they did relatively little work together. However, Ian and the Oxford Group believe that relationship development is a serious business – it's all about making time to have a dialogue about what each party is doing, the issues they are facing and the solutions they are devising. Ian keeps a database of all the close business contacts he has built up over the years and ensures he creates those dialogue opportunities through invitations to seminars and workshops, invitations to breakfast meetings and social

events and just making the occasional phone call or visit. The whole focus is on trying to add value for both organizations through sharing knowledge and learning. So when Richard was looking for someone to work with on a Leadership Development programme for Novartis, it was natural that the Oxford Group was on the list of the organizations he contacted.

The need

Richard was looking to run a programme which eventually became known as Leadership 2000, the main subject of this chapter. Richard and his colleagues were putting together a comprehensive and integrated leadership development programme covering all levels of leaders in the Novartis UK operations. Leadership 2000 was targeted at first-line leaders and those about to be appointed to such positions.

Novartis is a very innovative enterprise. In 2000 they achieved approval on 11 new drugs and have a further 13 applications under consideration. They are introducing drugs in the next two or three years at a faster rate than the industry norm and this was one of the main drivers for the programme. They are expanding their product portfolio so rapidly that they need a bigger and more effective sales force to sell the drugs. In the main, the sales force consists of graduates, employed because they must be able to go into GPs' surgeries or hospitals to sell a technical product to experts. Novartis UK forecast that they would not have enough people in their organization to meet this rising demand and external recruitment would be difficult, expensive and risky. They decided that they must develop some of the people already inside the business to become leaders of teams, at the same time as they hired in more new graduates to work for them. The Leadership 2000 programme aimed to develop the skills of leading a team and developing team members.

Richard approached a number of possible providers to design and run the programme and followed a conventional process of getting each potential provider to respond to a written brief. The Oxford Group was included in the bidding process and took time to visit Richard and try to understand the real needs of the programme and the measures of success that would indicate that it had worked. The measures of success identified for the programme included the hard quantifiable statistics of how many of the participants would be promoted to team-leader level within 12 months and how many of the participants would still be working for Novartis at the end of 12 months.

Most unusually, having completed the selection process, Novartis did not pick one organization to work with them, but two. Ashridge was the other and this has proved to be an inspired solution. The collaboration between the Oxford Group and Ashridge has worked very well in spite of some early misgivings by both parties. Clearly the organizations are competitors, so there was a risk in sharing information and being very open. However as the four tutors involved (two from the Oxford Group and two from Ashridge) got to know and respect each other, the initial misgivings soon disappeared.

Naturally there were budget and logistical constraints within which the programme had to be designed. A five-module programme, with two days per module, spread over nine months was the chosen format. Two of the modules would be run by Ashridge, two by the Oxford Group, and one would be delivered jointly.

The programme

The programme was designed around a set of Novartis competencies, adopted by the organization world-wide, reflecting the acknowledged skills, behaviours and knowledge required to be a successful leader in Novartis. The team of tutors, Claire Foster and Ian Ritchie from the Oxford Group and Fiona Dent and Tony Montes from Ashridge, met together to formulate some ideas for the programme. These were then discussed and refined in meetings with Richard Nicholson and his colleagues. It was decided that the programme would open at Ashridge with a module on Leadership, followed by a module on Customer and Results Focus, run by the Oxford Group at a venue yet to be decided. The participants would return to Ashridge for the third module, on Collaboration, before venturing off-site again for a module focused on Innovation and Communication run by the Oxford Group. The formal element of the programme would be concluded with a final module on Change Orientation at Ashridge, run jointly by the two faculties.

The programme would be residential, with the participants staying at Ashridge for three of the modules and at venues to be decided by the Oxford Group for the other two. It was also decided that the participants would gather together the evening before the start of each module.

A brief summary of the material covered in each of the modules is probably helpful here.

- **Module 1: Leadership** examined the theory of leadership, looked at leadership styles and used diagnostics to help the participants understand their own leadership strengths. The importance of self-managed learning was emphasized and the participants were encouraged to use the Ashridge Learning Resource Centre, a facility that they would be able to access remotely throughout the programme. A series of outdoor activities brought to life the messages from the classroom and solidified the personal learning. A guest speaker, Angela Bacon, who had competed in the BT Round the World Challenge yacht race, concluded the module, bringing to life much of the learning through her dramatic real-life examples. The Oxford Group liaised with Ashridge to create a 'bridge' to the next module, meeting the participants and giving them some pre-work to complete before the next module. A key element of the module was a presentation from the Chief Executive of Novartis UK, Adrian Adams, a point that will be returned to later.

- **Module 2: Customer and results focus** concentrated on understanding the importance of customer relationships and the need to deliver on commitments to get results. The module started from the Novartis Vision, cascading down to the personal contributions needed to help to achieve it. The participants were given techniques for analysing the needs of their customers and assisted in devising measures of success to ensure that they delivered what their customers really valued. The Commercial Director, Ian Clarke, gave a hard-hitting presentation on the issues facing the company and challenged the participants to develop their own personal styles in their relationships with their customers. The second day of the module was mainly dedicated to the technique of coaching team members to achieve results, through role playing real life-based examples. The Williams Formula One Centre proved an ideal choice of venue, with its clear results focus, and the module was rounded off with a fun session on the racing car simulator!

- **Module 3: Collaboration** was a wide-ranging module aimed at developing and understanding the processes and skills necessary for fostering effective collaboration in business. It

helped raise the awareness of the participants' interpersonal styles and how they influence others and work in teams. It encompassed the value of working with and understanding diversity. There was the customary mix of theory, practical exercises, diagnostics and reflection. The module finished on a high by involving everyone (including the tutors!) in a percussion workshop. A team of professional drummers led a session in which the whole group was taught to collaborate to produce some very creditable and exciting musical results!

- **Module 4: Innovation and communication** was designed to address two of the Novartis competencies. The importance of innovation in a life sciences company is perhaps obvious in terms of products but this module looked at how innovation is a necessary part of every leader's job. The participants were given some techniques for generating creative ideas and (most importantly) getting them into action. There was a strong link here to communication, in that new ideas must be presented to others who have to be persuaded of their value. The participants spent much time on developing innovative solutions to issues drawn from their own working lives. The module was run at the Granada Studios in Manchester, and the final task of the two days was to produce a TV programme summarizing all the learning from the whole programme to date, that is, Modules 1 to 4. This was an excellent opportunity for reflective learning that seemed to work well for most of the group.

- **Module 5: Change orientation** was effectively only one day long, as the second day was taken up with a major presentation by the group to the Executive Management Team of Novartis UK. The first day followed the pattern of previous modules, with tutor input on organizational change theory, individual and group working on real-life examples, and personal reflection and action planning. In the evening, Simon Scott, the Oxford Group's Director of Organizational Change, gave an entertaining presentation on the challenges facing all businesses in the coming years. The second day was dominated by the major presentation, for which the group had prepared exceptionally well in their own time. They devised a complex and high-risk 'production' and carried it off superbly. It was very well received by the Executive Team and all the participants must have enhanced their standing in the eyes of their managers as a result. The process of presenting learning in this way is an example of reflective practice in action and this was seen as a key success by both Ashridge and the Oxford Group.

The programme kicked off with 16 individuals, 11 men and 5 women, who were either doing a front-line sales job or an equivalent job in head office, such as a marketing role at the same level. They were all graduate calibre individuals, mainly in their twenties, with an exceptional one or two who came up different routes in their forties and thirties. Maturity and mixed experience in the group was useful – when considering and sharing learning, this variety of backgrounds gave added dimensions to the processes of dialogue and reflection.

Is Novartis a learning organization?

Ian Ritchie says, 'I think it is. When I listened to Adrian Adams kicking off the programme, I knew that he believes that they are working in a high-tech organization, an organization that is evolving rapidly that has to learn better and faster than its competitors. He stresses how

much he personally is still learning and how much he wants everybody to be learning in the organization. He gave an inspirational opening address to the Leadership 2000 programme. He gave high-level personal support to the programme and was an excellent role model. Adrian comes from a humble background in a northern mill town, and has risen up through the organization. The Leadership 2000 group is very ambitious and they can relate to someone who has achieved success as he has. The organizational culture is "you need to be developing and growing yourself in order that the business can grow." It's a very positive message. Of course there is another side of most organizations and in Novartis it is true that the drive for growth puts stress and pressure on people. This in turn works against having time for reflection. Participants would go back to their jobs after two days on a module to find 97 emails and hours of voice-mail messages. It's difficult to shield people from this in the flat structures that exist in Novartis, as in most of our clients. However, against this background, the way the Chief Executive behaves is crucial. Adrian talked about his own learning. It was very good anecdotal stuff about how he learnt and the opportunities he grabbed. For example, he encouraged them all to develop their own "trademark". He argued that you need to be known for something in the organization and talked about the reputation he got for some very specific things that he did. He was promoting the idea that you're all Novartis employees, but if you wish to progress you have a responsibility to develop yourself, develop your trademark, sell yourself internally. Good developmental stuff with a hard edge and a great start to the programme.'

When looking more broadly at the company and the industry in which it operates, Ian sees a number of factors that support the view that this is as good an example of a learning company as he knows. He comments, ' Novartis is growing rapidly, bringing new drugs into a dramatically changing market. Organizations such as pharmaceutical companies that are reliant for their success on leading-edge technology don't have a problem with persuading people to learn. In some other industries there is often a resistance, because there isn't the academic foundation to the industry. In a pharmaceutical company the place is full of PhDs and people who are heavily involved in continuous professional development. They have to keep up with their science. It pervades the culture of the organization and so going on training is not a dirty thing and doesn't attract the kind of the disparaging remarks that are sometimes made in other organizations. Going off to a symposium on the latest cancer drug, say, is just seen as what you've got to do in order to keep up with the pace in this fast-moving industry. In my experience this open-minded approach to scientific and product learning extends itself to marketing, finance and people skills learning, including leadership. Novartis comes as close to epitomizing a learning organization as any I know.'

Did it work?

After the successful completion of Leadership 2000, Leadership 2001 was launched with a new group of 18 participants. Novartis made slight changes to their leadership competency set and this has been reflected in minor changes in the module content. A tightening of the budget available has meant that the participants do not gather for a night together before the start of each module but otherwise the format remains much the same.

As described earlier, the programme had a 'formal' element in terms of the module content but there was an equally important 'informal' element that took place outside the modules. There was pre-work to do before each module, there were action plans from each

module, there was personal reflection time and there was interaction with other programme participants. All of these things worked well on Leadership 2000. However one thing that did not work so well was coaching between the modules. Although a system of coaches and coaching meetings were set up, in practice the arrangement did not work as well as it could. The main problem was the work pressures on both coach and coachee, meaning that meetings were frequently postponed or cancelled. In addition it is probably true that the coaches received insufficient briefing and training for their role. Learning from this experience, the graduates of Leadership 2000 will be the mentors for the Leadership 2001 group. The graduates of 2000 appreciate the value of the coaching relationship, have been trained in coaching and will now be very effective coaches to the participants of Leadership 2001.

One of the significant aims of the programme was to increase the awareness of the participants of their responsibility to develop their people and to increase their ability to do it. Has this worked? Ian Ritchie says, 'I'm really confident that the 16 graduates of the programme will be good at developing the people in their teams, informally when they go out with them on customer visits and formally through helping them put together personal development plans, involving training. The graduates of 2000 are all committed to the principle of developing their people, not least because they see this as a means to their own successful promotion.'

Another aim of the programme was to encourage cross-functionality within Novartis UK. Previously there was a traditional silo structure, where if you were working on a particular drug family you would be disconnected from others working on other drug families. For example, as a GP representative selling one drug family to doctors, you would not be mixing with hospital representatives selling other drug families to secondary care users. Novartis recognized that this meant that potential learning was not being spread efficiently throughout the organization. On Leadership 2000 there was incredible bonding between the participants and they all remarked upon it. As a group they worked their way through some difficulties. Initially there were one or two who were problematic, generally trying to succeed individually at the expense of the other group members. However, over a short period of time they all came together and recognized the power of the group. Through the five modules they were mixing all the time, formally and informally. The composition of small sub-groups was constantly changing, promoting a lot of exchanges of views. It is not fanciful to call this real learning – and it grew organically formally and informally throughout the programme.

Ian Ritchie comments, 'That's why I'm disappointed about losing the night before each module as a time for everyone to get together. When asked, people often say that they learnt a lot in the bar on any training programme they attended. That was certainly true in Leadership 2000! We gave them things to do in the evenings but they were fun things that got them working together in groups and in teams. There was lots of evidence of people from different silos, once they'd broken the barriers down, calling each other about work-related issues. A programme contact list was given to them but sub-groups set themselves up independently. The programme put those 16 people under a lot of pressure and they spent a lot of time together in quite intensive situations. This helped to break those barriers down and has strengthened inter-departmental links. The formal structures may have been in place, but the programme has certainly boosted their effectiveness.'

The Oxford Group holds a strong view that reflection is a key element of learning and it is a key element of the Oxford Learning Model. When Claire and Ian were designing the two modules that the Oxford Group were solely responsible for and talking with Fiona and Tony from Ashridge about the whole shape of the programme, they found that both sets of tutors

had built in a significant element of reflection into the programme. For instance, at different parts of the programme, participants chose course partners, with whom they would go off and talk about their learning. They would be given specific time to reflect upon sessions and make notes about the learning they had gained in their learning logs.

One of the most powerful examples of reflection as a learning technique was the final presentation by the Leadership 2000 participants at the end of the programme. They invited Adrian Adams and all his executive (30 of the most senior managers in Novartis) to the second day of the fifth module. They set up the room as the interior of an aircraft, gave everyone boarding cards to enter, and used the airline analogy as a vehicle to bring out the learning points from the whole programme. Various 'employees' from the airline (the 16 participants) gave their messages in an entertaining way, illustrating the most important learning points from the entire programme. Ian comments, 'It was an imaginative way of pulling the learning together and presenting it. They presented it to the executive but also to each other. They all worked on it. We gave them some time on the fourth module and some time on the afternoon of the fifth module to get ready for this, but most of the preparation was done in their own time. You could genuinely call this reflection, because they were going back through all their notes, all their slides, all the material, the exercises they'd done, their own learning logs, pulling all of that together – this is what we've got out of Leadership 2000. It was a way of reinforcing the value of the programme and celebrating their collective success.'

The learning from the programme can be characterized as improvement in performance (single loop) and improvement for transformation (double loop). In terms of single-loop learning, the participants became better at doing many things. Some of the classic theory around leadership and communication was conventionally improving their knowledge and understanding. Most of the exercises and role plays resulted in significant skills development. All through the programme the participants received behavioural feedback from the tutors which, combined with the outputs of the diagnostics, gave the participants deeper self-awareness and an understanding of the effect of their behaviour on others. Over the months of the programme it was possible to observe real positive behaviour change in most of the participants as a result.

On the transformational side there was significant reflection and appraisal, challenging some of the things the participants had traditionally thought they had to do. When a person is first appointed to a leadership role, they have much personal past experience of being led to influence them. Participants on Leadership 2000 were invited to consider the question 'Do I have to do things the way others have done them before?' They discovered that there are different ways and better ways to lead and be led, better ways to work in teams and to communicate with others, more effective ways to get results and to introduce new ideas and ways of working. They gave each other the strength and confidence to experiment and to share their experiences with the rest of the group.

As mentioned earlier, there were some specific measures of success for the programme, in terms of retention levels and promotion rates. Before the intervention, Novartis were suffering huge levels of attrition at this level, because young graduates in the pharmaceutical industry are a scarce commodity and can easily find new jobs with more money and a bigger car. There was an urgency to address these issues.

Against these two hard measures of success, the programme has delivered brilliantly. Over the 12 months of the programme, not one of the participants left the company. In addition, and perhaps more importantly, 15 out of the 16 participants has been promoted to a higher-level role in Novartis.

In addition to these two hard success measures, Novartis was looking at a broader picture of organizational transformation. They are a profitable and successful pharmaceutical company and they are innovating faster than most of their competitors. They are growing faster than the industry norm. To the world they are an admirable organization. But in his closing address at the end of the programme, Adrian Adams said, 'If we don't continue to change, we'll fall behind in the race. Change is a continuous process that must be part of the Novartis culture. It seems to me that you have taken this message on board as you have gone through this programme, and I now exhort you to keep doing so as your career in Novartis opens up for you. Good luck!'

Some personal reflections

Looking back on Leadership 2000, Ian Ritchie believes it was a very successful programme: 'I'm very proud of what we achieved and the client is very pleased with the results. I know we have made a real difference to the lives of the individuals who went through the programme, and as a consequence, we have made a real difference to Novartis.

There was some good learning in the project for Claire, myself, and the Oxford Group. Winning half a project was unusual for us and we had to learn how best to collaborate with Fiona, Tony and Ashridge to develop the best solution for the client and the participants. We would have felt quite competent at covering the whole range of the programme ourselves and no doubt Ashridge felt the same. However, I genuinely believe that by collaborating we brought an extra dimension to the learning for the participants.

Splitting the programme between two providers cost Novartis more. Using two providers meant that we needed to talk to each other and this cost was borne by the client. I know, however, that Novartis believed that the extra cost was worth it, and the proof of the pudding is that they asked us to work together again on Leadership 2001.

We shared information about the material in our modules freely between the two faculties and this helped us to develop the programme holistically. I think some consultancies are too precious about the confidentiality of their material – once material has been passed out to participants on a programme it's in the public domain so this has never been a problem for me. I'm sure that Claire and I picked up anecdotes from Fiona and Tony that we will use in the future, and vice versa, but this should help enhance the learning experience for future participants. It was a good relationship that worked well. If there had been difficulties at a personal level between the four tutors then I am sure that would have manifested itself in some way to the participants. Comments from the participants suggest that they valued the two-faculty approach, perhaps identifying an emphasis on practicalities from Oxford and a more rigorous approach to the underlying theory from Ashridge.

I think there's lots of other things I've learnt from this programme that take me more steps forward on my personal learning journey. The idea of using imaginative venues linked to the themes of the modules worked well and is something I would do again if budget constraints allowed. The mix of activities we built into programme would encourage me to go further down that direction in the future. I think the way that Claire and I worked together was classic Oxford Group style in that we worked democratically and collaboratively.

If there is a danger in the two-faculty approach, it is in assuming that the other faculty is going to cover their subjects comprehensively and that they will stick to the script! In real life this never happens and therefore it was difficult to know what went on in the off-line discus-

sions around the topic. How could this be done? I suppose by spending more time together as a tutor group. Two things militate against this: time and cost. We tended to be there at the end of each other's modules, briefing participants with the pre-work for the next one. However if someone has just spent two days on their feet delivering a module, they don't want to spend two hours at six or seven o'clock at night on the second day, doing a de-brief to the other tutors. They want to go home.

There's a graph that shows that if you want to improve something that is already good, it costs a lot of money to obtain a further marginal improvement. I think that this would be the case here – no doubt spending more time (and therefore money) would have improved the programme but frankly the return on the investment would not be worth it for Novartis.

The only worry I'm left with is for the client. The successful first programme has given them a pressure in that it's a hard act to follow for the next cohort. Novartis spent more on the first run of the programme than they intend doing on the second. The venues were a notch higher the first time round. For example, we're using the Twickenham Rugby Union ground rather than the Williams Formula One Centre. They're not giving the participants the night before each module in a hotel or at Ashridge so there's less time for networking and doing things together. This is bound to affect the learning environment, as are late arrivals when participants are not in residence. Having said all this, Leadership 2001 will be another great programme and I am looking forward to my involvement in it.'

10 Pearl Assurance – Better by Miles

Tom Heywood

This is a tale of two companies. One is a well-known organization faced with a demotivated workforce, a blame culture, an out-of-date management style and a rapidly diminishing market share.

The other is a 46 per cent increase in sales over the previous year – a 'can-do' culture with managers who trust and empower their people. With a 70 per cent drop in staff turnover, it is officially one of 'Britain's Best Employers'.

In fact, they are the same organization some three years apart. This is the story of Pearl Assurance (now a business owned by the AMP Group, a global financial services provider) and how its commitment to a new training and development strategy was a major reason for a radical business turn-around.

There were four key stages in the development of the learning solution at Pearl: defining the need, designing the solution, delivering the programmes, and deducing the results. This chapter looks at those four areas in detail, as a way of sharing good practice in helping others learn.

Defining the need

In the mid-1990s, Pearl Assurance, a company with over 130 years of insurance and pensions sales experience, was under serious and lengthy investigation by the regulator over compliance issues. Added to this, Pearl had huge commercial problems: 16 months of consecutive falling sales, an outdated hierarchical structure and an over-reliance on a traditional approach to management and customer service. Front-line staff were continually frustrated by the way the system worked in their efforts to provide excellent service to their customers.

It is important to see the learning intervention as part of something bigger. A new Managing Director put in place a series of key projects aimed at building a new culture and transforming business performance. Training was seen as one of those key projects. In order for the training to work, it needed to be inextricably linked to commercial reality for the business. An off-the-shelf training approach would have had little impact here. The traditional training approach for an individual at Pearl is familiar to most of us: perhaps a little on-the-job training from their neighbour, and a bit of advice from their manager. There was little that was consistent, planned or cross-functional. The result was that at best staff got to know their own tasks well enough. And in today's business world that is not enough. So the training intervention was designed by the Oxford Group to give staff the opportunity to understand more about their customers, each other, and themselves.

First, we conducted a major training-needs analysis across the business. This determined what key competencies people needed to take the business forward. But it did more than that. By actively involving over 500 of the 1800 staff in interviews, job shadowing and focus groups, major buy-in was achieved for the programmes. People could see that the intervention was being designed for and with them, rather than done to them. All layers of the business were consulted and involved in the process. All of this meant that the *spirit* of the learning process was established very early on, and almost subconsciously through the manner of the training-needs analysis: involvement, partnership, working together were key implied fundamentals and these values were transferred. In a way this was a kind of virtuous Hawthorne effect:[1] people seemed to become more motivated to do a good job because there was so much investment of time (and money) in their development needs. Even just the observations and focus groups appear to have energized employees. This energy, though, may partly have been due to the fact they knew a 'formal' development programme was coming up.

Design

As a result of the analysis above, the 'Better by Miles' programme was created. Three core programmes were at the centre of the intervention, for operational managers, team leaders, and customer service employees. The three tailored programmes were called Miles Better Management, Miles Better Team Leadership, and Miles Better Customer Service. This branding of the overall programme was significant for more than just the name: it gave a consistency to the learning initiative, and it helped staff to see the company pulling together as one. The name helped to engender a positive approach at a time of difficulty in the company. It suggested that the company was aiming to be 'miles better' than its competitors. Perhaps more significantly, it implied that the learning programme would make Pearl 'miles better' than it always had been. In this way the branding helped subtly to both recognize the company's situation, and to focus people on making significant improvement. We'll return to the branding later.

Each of the Better by Miles programmes consisted of six or seven modules, lasting one or two days each. The modules were a blend of skills, behaviours and a deeper understanding of the company and its business. For managers and team leaders, the modules looked at Pearl's vision and values, performance management, communications, creativity and customer service. A particular emphasis was put on helping managers to use a coaching style with staff. For the 1200 front-line staff, verbal and written skills were paramount, as well as understanding how to work better as a team, and how to share skills with each other. Typical content included:

- company values, vision, the manager's role, self-awareness
- performance management
- customer service skills for internal and external customers
- firm and fair management of our people
- listening and communicating
- creativity and problem solving
- celebrating success.

The key to the programme's success, however, is more in the approach than the content. A

number of design decisions were taken to enhance the learning opportunity, and these were taken with the Oxford Group Learning Principles© in mind (see Box 10.1).

The Oxford Group Learning Principles©

Transparent: we ensured all the objectives and aims of the programme were available and open to everyone.

Transferable: we made sure the learning in the training room was relevant to the business, by using real examples and tailoring the programme.

Measurable: we designed measures to ensure people knew how successful were they – and the programme as a whole.

Memorable: we designed the programmes to be interactive, fun and memorable, because only then will key learning stay in participants' minds.

Reflective dialogue: we built in as many opportunities as we could (before, during and after the training events) for people to share their thoughts with others in a constructive way. This embeds and personalizes the learning.

We helped people learn through their **Hand, Head and Heart**, that is, doing, thinking and feeling, more of which later.

And we helped people learn holistically, using all their **five senses**, by providing a stimulating and interesting environment.

Specifically, our design team produced the following solutions. First, there were overt sessions about how Pearl worked and made its money. The training needs analysis had demonstrated that employees had little understanding of the way the business worked, and a resulting lack of knowledge about what other functions actually contributed: they knew about their own piece of work, but not how it linked in with the bigger picture. This gave them that bigger picture, but was also a key way to establish the commercial credentials of the programme.

Second, and perhaps more significantly for sharing learning, all delegate groups were to be comprised of mixed functions in the organizations, providing a ready-made opportunity to share experiences and gain a better understanding of where things 'fitted'.

The impact on the learning effectiveness of the above two points should not be underestimated: staff learnt, often *for the very first time*, how their company actually functioned, and they did so through some input, but largely by meeting in their delegate groups with staff from other functions with their own stories to tell. In this way, a whole host of informal stories about the company were told and learners reflected on where the business had come from and where it was going (akin to the power of corporate stories in Johnson and Scholes, 1993). Critically, perhaps, this 'cross-swapping' of functions demonstrated that it is people who can make a difference in a company like Pearl. Any mystique is stripped away as delegates could see that the company is made up of people, striving to do their best in difficult situations. Traditionally at Pearl, people sat and worked in their own functions. Now as part of this learning process they were brought together with others from across the business in small intensive groups. Here was a very real demonstration of the power of the company pulling together.

Third, learning was enhanced by the modular approach taken. The programme was split into modules spread over a year, which meant the business had fewer interruptions to its core work (it was still fighting to consolidate a weak position). More than that, it meant delegates had a chance both to reflect between modules and to put learning into practice in a real situation. This latter opportunity was enhanced by the design of work-based assignments (WBAs) (see Box 10.2)). The WBA was established to reinforce the learning from that particular module. However, there were some critical elements to it without which it would have failed as a learning technique.

First, the assignments had to be 'real'. In other words, we made sure they were activities that were *genuinely useful* for the business. This was important not only for the learner's motivation, but for the whole credibility and aim of the programme (in terms of its bottom-line impact). We designed the WBAs fairly loosely, and invited every delegate to reflect on them and do their own customizing so that the assignment fitted their role. So rather than be faced with delegates saying that the task was 'irrelevant' to their job, our challenge to them was to make it relevant using the framework we provided. The underlying message here was: do not just do a task because you are told to (the traditional way in companies like the old Pearl), take responsibility to ensure what you are doing is the right thing for the business.

BOX 10.2

A sample work-based assignment (WBA):

Departments at Pearl had traditionally worked in 'silos', and carried out their duties with little understanding of and some preconceptions of (internal) customer needs. After the first module for managers and team leaders, we asked them to conduct a Stakeholder Analysis with their internal customers. We had run this in the training room, and they had brainstormed their stakeholders and the needs of those stakeholders. Now we were asking them to do it for real. It was quite a daunting prospect for some of them, but the results brought to the start of the next module were enlightening. Some delegates had spoken to their key stakeholders about their needs for the first time, and been surprised at the findings. And we asked them to reflect on what that told them about how the company had traditionally functioned, where activity had been praised over effectiveness.

The above example shows the WBAs were a good demonstration of the head, hand, heart approach we took all along:

- *Head:* give people some input and mental stimulation on the subject, in this case, an introduction and a worked example of the stakeholder analysis.
- *Hand:* let people experience and have a play with the concepts introduced. In this case, the delegate 'practises' the stakeholder analysis in the safety of the training room, and then embarks on it for real in the WBA.
- *Heart:* with a chance to reflect and share feelings about the experience, people genuinely understand the concepts at a deeper level, they mean something personally to them. In this case, delegates came back with great stories about their stakeholders, and we provided them time to reflect on what this was telling them about the company, the future, and themselves.

Delivery

The training was staggered. All members of staff received training, but not at the same time. The programme started with managers and cascaded on to team leaders and front-line staff. This means that all line managers are both in a position to support their people through development, while at the same time receiving that support from their own boss.

Training took place in a building purposely fitted for it, and away from the building where people worked. This meant the learning environment was conducive.

The delivery style of the programme mirrored the desired change to management behaviour for the business: trainers were coaches and facilitators, not instructors or presenters. Core skills like coaching were transferred to managers, and embedded through exhaustive practice and review.

Furthermore, learners came prepared, thanks to a fun, branded communication programme. There were a series of large briefings before the whole initiative took off, which prepared staff for the key messages to come. Briefings were hosted by Human Relations (HR) and senior managers. The environment was informal. Lunch was provided in the briefing room, as well as a 'Time Out' chocolate bar which linked to the day's message of 'Take Time Out For Training'. The briefings covered the – by now well known – key projects designed to get Pearl fit for the future. Employees heard about the aims of the programme, the approach to be taken, and an overview of the content for every strata. The presenters took an interactive approach and questions were taken during and after the session. Questions and answers meant people could have their queries and concerns answered in full. And the answers were added to a 'Frequently Asked Questions' list which everyone had access to through the intranet. The whole briefing process meant people came to the learning programmes enthused and set up for success, rather than apprehensive or cynical. This way of involving people built on the earlier training needs analysis, which as we have seen helped to get staff on board with the programme. The briefings also helped us in finalizing the design of the programmes, because we could see at first hand what the remaining concerns of the staff were, and attempt to deal with those concerns.

Another reason for the success of the initiative was the deployment of 50 Pearl managers as co-trainers on the programme. The Oxford Group trained board and senior managers in facilitation skills to help them co-deliver the sessions. The fact that senior managers were using their time to deliver on the programme sent a very clear message to delegates: we are serious about this programme. It also meant the sessions could be assured that real live issues could be discussed. The managers gained too, not only in new skills, but in hearing first hand the concerns and suggestions of the workforce. As with the stakeholder analysis example earlier, some of them had never spent any real time genuinely listening to their people.

Learning logs and a learning contract were designed to help individuals capture and track their key learning as well as tools for reflection. The logs were also a symbol of giving power to the delegates to take responsibility for their learning. This in itself was indicative of Pearl's new desire to empower rather than 'tell' people as a management style. The contract helped the learner and their manager get together before and during the programme to make sure the individual and corporate learning needs were met. This last point was a constant source of concern for us. The balance was to ensure that individuals were learning useful skills for work and life, while at the same time we were rightly charged with enhancing business performance.

The key from a delivery point of view was for our training designers and deliverers to

have a real understanding of the business. In fact, we kept our core team as tight as possible, and made sure that wherever possible, trainers had been involved in the design stage, so that by the time they came to deliver their knowledge of Pearl was quite comprehensive. We also extensively briefed our trainers, and produced an in-house newsletter specifically about the Pearl project. Co-delivering with senior managers also really helped to ensure we married the personal with corporate learning goals, as they were well in touch with business needs, at least at the strategic level.

There was also an emphasis on ongoing development using self-study packages, computer-based training, and job rotation. Mentoring schemes were set up, as well as a buddying system for delegates. A new learning centre was set up to assist with ongoing personal development. In this way the 'formal' training part of the programme was surrounded by a range of learning methods from which each delegate could choose according to need and preference.

Outside of the training-room environment, development opportunities continued. One particularly relevant example was an on-the-job coaching day provided for every participant. Coach and delegate would agree in advance what they would be discussing (a key, practical business issue relevant to the person being coached), and would get together in the most appropriate way. For some participants this meant they requested to be observed in a key situation (running a critical meeting, perhaps) and then given feedback. For others, a preview session to help them plan for a difficult one-to-one encounter, and then a session to review it and understanding the learning points. Again, the emphasis was on the learner to identify the approach to be taken, with guided support. These on-the-job coaching sessions really helped people get into a double-loop learning mode, enabling learners to recognize the taken-for-granteds (tfgs) in their behaviour. Real breakthroughs were made when people could see how the skills discussed on the programme could be put into practice in their own way. They began to believe in the power of the development solution because they started to see how they could *practically* apply it in a whole range of situations.

Delegate groups were kept the same throughout the year of the programme. This provided opportunities for delegates to network and to genuinely understand how other parts of the business worked. To ensure this worked, a robust administration and logistics exercise was needed.

Employees also benefited from the chance to gain new qualifications through 'Better by Miles'. It was always the stated aim of the programme to recognize people's learning achievements by offering them some external qualification. But what Pearl did not want was to make people have to sit exams or go to night school. Instead, Middlesex University was approached to accredit the work-based assignments. These credits count towards a Certificate in Management, a Diploma in Management, or even an MBA. Customer service staff were given the chance to take an NVQ. At its height it was the country's largest work-based accredited training scheme.

Results

The 'Better by Miles' programme was one key project of nine. Because it was seen as one of the key Change projects it had business credibility and its status was thereby elevated above the norm. This was partly a result of the creation of a steering committee made up of executives and key managers, who met monthly to review the progress of the training pro-

gramme. This closeness to the business meant the programme was used as a vehicle to convey the organization's values, goals and service proposition. These are then clearly linked to delegates' own initiative. This supports learning because people can see how their own needs are complementary to the needs of the company. The importance of Better By Miles to the success or failure of Pearl as a whole meant that the results of the programme were critical.

Measures of success were established for the programme at the beginning. In this way the value it provided could be uncovered and translated quickly. Delegates could see they were part of something that was working, and this helped to make them feel more accessible to the learning opportunity presented.

The programme was based around a competency framework, offering people the chance to develop the competencies they personally wanted, and at their own pace. The modules were book-ended by a 'before and after' 360-degree feedback analysis for all managers and team leaders. This provided some key success measures: people could see how much their colleagues perceived they had developed in the organization's core competencies. And for many this progress was marked. These were built on by developing behavioural objectives for employees as part of the training programme. The underlying message here was that Pearl was now not just concerned with what you do, but *how* you do it as well, the behaviour we show to our customers and to each other is of paramount importance.

At the start of the programme, few employees had – or admitted to having – Pearl products themselves. After the 18-month run of the programme many did so, encouraged also by increasing employee ownership through AMP, the parent company of Pearl.

Surveys showed the workforce at Pearl to be more motivated than before the programme. A 46 per cent increase in sales over the previous year was recorded. A 70 per cent drop in staff turnover was seen. Pearl officially became one of 'Britain's Best Employers'. Better by Miles was spoken of with enthusiasm amongst the employees, and the 'language' of the programme was used everywhere. When asked, nearly every staff member felt the programme had better equipped them to do their job, but more than that had provided them with the tools and skills to help them to keep developing and improving in work and life.

Note

1. 'Hawthorne effect' refers to research carried out by Elton Mayo and his team at Western Electric's Hawthorne factory in Chicago, Illinois, in the 1930s. Results showed that *any* intervention which alters the working environment leads to increased production.

11 *IMPACT at Thus plc*

Peter McInnes, Anne Shiels and Stephen Davis

Background

Thus plc is a publicly listed telecommunications company based in Glasgow. The company was forged from the amalgamation of a number of businesses acquired during the mid-1990s by the privatized public utility Scottish Power and unified under the banner of ScottishTelecom. Although these businesses had a common theme of telecommunications, their development reflected very different cultural backgrounds, ranging from the entrepreneurial spirit of Demon, an Internet service provider, through to staff drawn from the regulated environment of a public utility company.

The disparate nature of the company cultures within the constituent companies of ScottishTelecom presented a sizeable challenge to the management group on a number of fronts. In addition to the geographical spread of the business and the variety of policies and procedures in use across the organization, the management skills and style varied enormously; ranging from the relatively well-trained, but bureaucratically driven, utility employees, to the technically competent entrepreneurial individuals who had been promoted to management positions in some of the acquired businesses. Combining these business entities brought together a number of highly integrated cultures (Martin 1992). Without intervention, there was a real potential for people within these cultures to begin stereotyping the behaviour of others, leading to the build-up of conflict within the organization, ambiguity of practice and unfavourable comparison of treatment of staff in the various subsidiaries. From a commercial perspective, integration was seen as essential in delivering the synergistic benefits of the merger. However, integration could not be an assimilation of the acquired company's employees and imposition of ScottishTelecom's practices – such an approach would mean an unacceptable dip in performance. Rather, it needed to be a process of mutual learning that would lead to a degree of organizational transformation.

In response to this environment the management group of ScottishTelecom, and in particular the Chief Executive, initiated the IMPACT (Improved Managerial Performance As a result of Continuous Training) management development programme. Specifically targeted at the more senior managers in the organization, this programme had numerous aims, the main ones being the building a unitary culture reflecting the slogan of 'One company, one voice, one team', while providing a baseline for management skills, promoting lateral communication and as a result lessening conflict and rumours. In addition, in order to promote improved organizational performance, IMPACT concentrated heavily upon the external environment, the requirements of the customer and the company's strategic response to the market.

Course design

The course design consisted of modules as follows:

- Developing Business Performance (three days), where groups of around five people put together a business case to solve a perceived problem
- Understanding Your Markets (two days), identifying the markets in which the company operates
- Financial Management (two days), concentrating on value creation and evaluating strategic choices
- Leadership (two days), designed to communicate what it means to lead in Thus
- Concepts and Practice of Strategy Implementation (two days), considering the way strategy can be implemented by thinking about how groups and individuals tackle problems and solve problems.

The modules were distributed over a period of about one year. The daily schedule consisted of classes in the morning and afternoon punctuated by plenary sessions where the implications of the topic, for the individual and the company, were discussed. Some modules utilized group-based project work, related to the module itself, being taken back to the workplace for completion, with presentation and feedback. Each module was sponsored by a director who was scheduled to attend during the module in order to lead a frank discussion on the topic area and its consequences for the company. This was done to clarify direction and impress the participants of the commitment to the ongoing development initiated by the programme.

In order to reinforce group coherence and encourage people to work together on a significant customer-focused task using the theories they had gained from the course, each cohort undertook an action-learning project over the course of the programme. A rigorous introduction promoted cross-functional/cross-business project working using Ford as an example of best practice. The projects were selected by the groups themselves but had to address a customer service issue that would be relevant to the company in the medium term (three to five years). Over the year, projects were allowed to progress in a mainly self-managed way. This placed responsibility for arranging meetings, managing attendance and ensuring completion of actions squarely on the team. During each module a number of questions, derived from the module's material, would be posed to the group. The group would reflect and take actions based upon these questions in the evening during the module and between the modules. These reflective sessions were facilitated and at the end of the evening, groups spent time in a plenary where they discussed each others' analysis of their project and action steps. (It should be noted that this process was, in a sense, a cross between project teamwork and action learning, and it would not conform to the more strict definitions of action learning used in other cases.)

Three specific deliverables were expected from the teams:

1. a report to the board outlining the project
2. a statement of three measurable improvements that their project would achieve
3. a skills audit of the company in relation to the plan's implementation.

The final module of the course involved two presentations. The first was a presentation to the

remainder of the cohort on the process of project work and the learning gained from it. The second presentation was of the project proposal itself and was made to one, or a number, of the company's directors who presented a certificate of completion after the presentation. Not only did this ensure completion of the work, it also provided closure for the participants as well as providing an audience in which their ideas were listened to. In a number of cases this led to implementation being authorized. Each cohort consisted of around 16 members, with 8 cohorts giving a total of around 130 participants in the IMPACT programme. Although measures were taken to ensure that cohorts represented a cross-section of the organization, selection for the course was relatively unscientific. The human resource department simply chose those whom they thought were senior members of their respective organizations, had strong influence or were recommended as having potential. Although it wasn't specifically planned to achieve this, this approach gave exposure to a number of people with good ability who would otherwise have remained hidden in subsidiary companies.

In order to mould the course materials towards practical application in the organization, Strathclyde University and Thus jointly developed course material. The teaching, or rather facilitation, was guided by the discussions and concerns generated by the participants. This centred the delivery very much upon the cohort's reflections upon the subject rather than being a fixed corpus of material. The design of the course focused heavily upon encouraging reflection upon practice through the lens of theory. To achieve this the programme employed multiple time-frames and vehicles for the application of theory, for example, class-room with plenary discussion, modules with project work running through, and between them and finally the action-learning project running across the whole time-frame. These action-learning projects also encouraged the implementation of the theoretical material in the workplace, reinforcing double-loop learning for the participant and spreading the lessons from IMPACT through the organization. The course sought to further embed these new skills through feedback from the individual to the cohort and from workplace colleagues to the individual.

Material for the following discussion has been derived from feedback after completion of the programme, through direct experience of the course and from interviews conducted during 2001 with key members of the human resources team. First we consider a key event which occurred during the course that impacted upon the standing of the course in the eyes of the organization, before turning towards some specific features of the course that proved effective.

The best-laid plans

The initial launch of IMPACT was well received and support from the executive group, in particular the commitment of the Chief Executive, was clearly indicated. This impressive start was, however, interrupted by a sweeping change in the boardroom involving the replacement of the Chief Executive and a number of his management team. The programme continued, but the replacement of the Chief Executive precipitated a number of strategic organizational changes as the company moved towards the flotation and renaming of ScottishTelecom as Thus plc.

For the IMPACT programme, the changes had some serious implications. The programme was seen in part as 'belonging' to the outgoing Chief Executive, therefore the participants brought into question the importance that they should attribute to the course.

Managers from the early cohorts reported their superiors being ambivalent, if not directly oppositional, to their attendance. This ambivalence was exacerbated when members of the executive team failed to attend the 'open and frank' discussions. Cohort members were left with a feeling that the executives considered the programme less important than what was happening in the business. The depth of the unease and confusion that the groups were dealing with was reflected in some executive seminars not going ahead. Even when these did go ahead, the groups questioned the authenticity of some contributions and the motivation behind them (particularly where it emerged that the individuals concerned were about to leave the company). All of these factors contributed to the disbanding of the first cohort.

Despite these challenges the programme continued, indeed it increasingly proved a useful arena in which the participants could reflect upon the changes in the organization. The change of Chief Executive signalled a change of strategy that included flotation of the business. This heightened the awareness that, as leaders of the business, the participants needed to focus upon delivering shareholder value through concentrating upon what the customer wants. This increased the salience of many of the modules, particularly marketing and strategy, and feedback on these reflected the depth of discussion that had taken place within them.

Making the IMPACT – what worked well

The environment within Thus became, understandably, turbulent during this transitional phase. Many of the original design intentions seemed to lose their importance as more immediate issues superseded them. This is not to suggest that the programme failed to deliver on any of its intended outcomes; as will be clear from what follows, these were attained but not necessarily by the intended route.

PROVIDING A SAFE HAVEN

Instead of being a learning environment where old preconceptions were questioned, the cohorts provided a safe environment for participants to reflect upon the strategic direction the company was taking in its targeted markets. As well as reconceptualizing the direction of the organization, the cohorts also served as an arena where rumours and stories could be discussed (and in a number of cases quashed), through triangulating responses from different parts of the company. Facilitators were able to listen to organizational stories and discuss them in relation to theory, often surfacing the underlying rationale. Facilitators were also able to feedback concerns and issues to the human resource managers, enabling them to address organizational problems.

As the organization moved towards flotation, a number of people left the company, including some participants in the course. Again, these were significant events for the other cohort members. At least one participant reported apprehension regarding his position in the organization when one of his colleagues disappeared. However, being part of the IMPACT programme gave members an opportunity to talk candidly about these events and the exit of colleagues from the workplace, an opportunity that was not readily available in their work environments.

LEADERSHIP AND MANAGEMENT SKILLS

The session that attracted the most positive feedback was undoubtedly the management training and the 360-degree appraisal. The latter was conducted, with teams, peers and managers, across the time-frame of the programme which allowed participants to gauge their behavioural change over an extended period. For some this was the first such feedback they had ever had and the results were, in the main, taken positively as opportunities for development rather than criticism. In particular, the longitudinal nature of the review provided an opportunity to see improvement reflected in the comments of their workmates.

The effect of this training, coming at a time of dramatic change, was extremely valuable to course participants. The combination of improved managerial practice along with increased understanding of what was happening across the organization and, more importantly, why these moves were a necessary part of the company's strategy, gave cohort members a good footing on which to operate. Additionally, bringing together people from disparate parts of the business allowed them to compare their own abilities with those of their peer group. In this way people could find their level and be sure that their behaviour and decisions were not out of step with those of any of their peers in a similar situation. As a result many members of the course reported greater self-awareness, and were observed to exhibit increased confidence. In effect, a reflective dialogue was enabled amongst a group of peers who would have met rarely if at all were it not for the IMPACT programme.

ACTION LEARNING

This aspect of the course received a mixed response from participants and yet achieved many of its objectives. The task of selecting an appropriate project proved particularly troublesome as it revealed the lack of knowledge people had of what different parts of the business were involved in. A positive consequence of this was that through working together the process surfaced and challenged many of the myths and stereotypes held by participants. On the negative side, this often meant that project work started in one area only to find that another project team, or indeed another IMPACT cohort, was working on the same task.

Numerous examples exist of successful action-learning projects. In particular, one cohort took the opportunity to investigate the practicality of introducing a new product. Indeed this product idea was one that had been considered by the company over an extended period, but time constraints had prevented its full investigation or implementation. The group in question completed a feasibility study and business case for their new product and were authorized to implement their proposal when they presented their idea to the directors during their last module. The group undertook this, and the product was launched successfully as a result of their action-learning project. Other groups undertook projects ranging from a pilot scheme for an improved billing procedure through to a package that coupled the Internet, mobile phone and call-centre technology to provide reception services to customers who operated small- to medium-sized enterprises. This proposal extended what would at first appear to be a phone-forwarding service by employing Internet technology to provide company-specific data to the call-centre operative enabling that person to complete simple information provision and consequently appear to all intents and purposes to be an employee of the client firm. What these projects had in common was a focus not necessarily on internal efficiency but upon adding value through meeting the needs of customers or even the customer's customers. The improvements to business represent single-loop learning, but the

project groups also engaged in reflective analysis and action with the cohort, and this, along with the new cross-functional working, produced double-loop learning.

NETWORKING

Although not directly targeted at establishing a network, one of the biggest gains for the participants and the organization from IMPACT was the network that the cohorts built. This has, and continues to have, an effect on the way that the organization operates. Informal networks enable people to shape their actions by gaining a broad perspective on what is happening in the company by eliciting information from people in other parts of the organization. The informal network can also be used to complete tasks more quickly than through the formal structure of the company and indeed gain approval for projects by rallying support from elsewhere in the organization. That this was useful to the participants can be seen in the feedback which indicated that people were anxious to broaden the network by integrating with other cohorts and meeting with more of their peers and senior managers.

For the organization, this activity has clear advantages in terms of getting things done. Additionally, the programme's success in this respect indicates that the programme met one of its initial design criteria. The integration and networking of people across the business broke down the barriers that may otherwise have developed between different companies, different locations and different levels in the organization. Good managerial practice was encouraged because managers not only became more aware of contextual factors and comparative practice but thought in terms of 'one company', with a focus on meeting the customer's requirements.

Continuing IMPACT

CONTINUING DEVELOPMENT

The IMPACT programme was a powerful initiative whose effects are still being felt in the company. Many of the participants have flourished in the company, some as a direct result of the exposure gained during the development programme. Thus plc have continued to implement new projects and initiatives that encourage reflective learning. For example, in an effort to reinforce the management learning gained from IMPACT, the company have progressively introduced a mentoring/coaching scheme. Here senior managers are assigned managers and conduct periodic meetings to review their handling of difficult situations. The initiative specifically sets aside time and space to encourage thoughtful reflection upon practice. This has a learning effect for both mentor and mentored as the space is created to reflect first upon the situation as presented by the mentee, second by the mentor exploring what their reaction to that situation might be and then jointly exploring different solutions and discussing the implications of that action. This process serves to utilize the management skills material that was taught on the course and integrate this through reflection with the everyday practice of managers.

Learning loops

Numerous learning loops are in evidence occurring at an individual, group and organizational level, and the outcomes may be regarded as examples of reflective dialogue:

- On an individual basis, managers reflected upon, and modified, their managerial practice over the programme through feedback gained from their 360-degree appraisals. In order to ensure that good practice continues to be followed, the mentoring programme aims to cement reflective managerial practice as a norm.
- Perhaps one of the most dramatic consequences of the programme was that participants realized how little they knew about the whole organization. Course members learnt about other parts of the organization and the activities they undertook. Not only did this serve to challenge a number of the stereotypes and preconceptions that they had, it led to double-loop reflection upon the aims and direction of the organization.
- Reflection upon peer performance was significant. An improved self-image was achieved for individual managers, through being identified for the course in the first place, and through comparison of their own behaviour and knowledge levels with those of their peer group. This served to build confidence in their abilities.
- Managerial turnover during the transitionary period had an effect on the workplace and the cohort. Although this served to reinforce the feeling of dramatic change, these events had an emotional impact on course participants. The programme provided a safe environment for participants to rationalize these events in relation to what the company was trying to achieve.
- Managers reflected upon the strategic changes in the work environment that directly effected their operating environment. Counter (or in addition) to the initial intention of provoking double-loop learning by challenging core underlying assumptions amongst the staff, the programme became an arena in which the participants were able to reflect on the plethora of changes that they were seeing in their workplace and through sense-making realign their own thinking and actions in response to this environment.
- Reflective learning also occurred within the teaching staff and human resource department. The programme evolved through feedback of what worked and what didn't as well as making changes to reflect the work background. For example, early cohorts criticized the academic nature of some of the material being presented. In response to this a new approach was developed where staff from Strathclyde University would co-facilitate some sessions with members of the functional area under discussion. This served to make the material more directly relevant to the situation within the organization rather than being general theoretical statements on the subject.
- It is necessary for reflective practice needs to be committed to over an extended period of time. Even after completion of the programme, subsequent initiatives reflect the values and ethos established through the IMPACT programme. Ongoing reflective practice is enabled through the mentoring programme. This encourages reflection upon workplace experience and enables practice to become informed by theory.

Lessons learned

The IMPACT programme has proved a useful basis for learning for both Thus and Strathclyde University. There are, of course, a number of lessons that will be carried forward to the design

of future programmes. During research for this chapter, some very practical suggestions were made as to how the programme might be improved if it were to be run again.

In the action-learning phase of the programme, it is suggested that a steering committee for these projects might be useful. Whilst primarily there to look for overlaps between similar projects underway in the company and to provide communication on other action-learning projects, members of this committee might sponsor a project to add weight to the group's efforts and reinforce the importance of these projects in the participant's minds.

It was suggested that for future programmes cohorts should be selected to ensure an appropriate blend of people. For example, consideration of relative abilities, group working and learning styles of individuals could facilitate a better learning experience for the whole cohort. The critical success factors in the action-learning groups appear to have been the constitution of the group and the nature of the task selected. The group who developed and introduced the new product, for example, consisted of a mixture of individuals with creative flare and a number of managers who could exert influence in the right arenas within the organization.

Finally, two things became evident that proved crucial to the successful design and implementation of a management development programme. The first is that top management support is crucial and the effectiveness of the programme is in part reliant on continuing support of the management group. The second point is that many of the positive outcomes from the programme have appeared to be unintentional. Therefore the key message for this case is that even when 'best practice' doesn't produce the intended outcomes, a little persistence is often worthwhile.

12 *e-Learning at Kodak*

Nigel Purse and Anne Brockbank

The modern firm known as Kodak evolved from the Eastman Kodak Company, which was established in 1892 and made photography available to everyone using film in rolls for the first time. George Eastman pioneered the creation of profit-sharing systems for employees, as well as retirement, disability and insurance benefits. Eastman held four basic principles:

- mass production at low cost
- international distribution
- extensive advertising
- a focus on the customer.

In addition Eastman advocated that his company should adopt the following policies:

- growth and development through continuous research
- treating employees in a fair and self-respecting way
- reinvesting profits to build and extend the business.

In today's firm, these principles and policies influence Kodak's values and style of management.

The Oxford Group is one of the UK's leading providers of training and consulting services to many of the world's top companies. With 200 consultants based in the UK, Australia, Belgium, France, Germany, Hungary, India, The Netherlands, Singapore, Spain, Switzerland and the US, we have been custom designing learning solutions for managers since 1987 in the areas of:

- organizational change
- management development
- personal development
- leadership
- people assessment
- customer relationship management.

The Oxford Group has always embraced the latest technology to support its learning solutions, but has sought to apply it intelligently and creatively, driven primarily by learning objectives, never by technology itself. Its approach to the potential of e-learning is based on the following assumptions:

- Tailoring the learning experience to each person's unique learning style is the biggest single e-learning challenge.
- To be effective, e-learning should exploit technology that is widely available rather than technology which is clever.
- The real e-learning opportunity is to use emerging technology to integrate the full range of learning channels – face to face, self-study, internet, coaching, e-mail, etc. – into a package that is appropriate for the subject and meets each person's unique needs and learning preferences.
- The Internet and remote communication technologies can be exploited to meet the growing needs of people for just-in-time, personal support and learning that also delivers measurably improved business results.

Rather than starting with a piece of technology, and seek a training need for it, the approach is to start the principles of effective learning design which already guide their work – the seven principles of the Oxford Group Learning Model (see Box 10.1, p. 80).

The challenge is always to deliver:

- the highest quality learning experience (that is, that which will lead to real change in behaviour, and therefore more sustained impact on business performance)
- at the lowest total cost to the client
- whilst minimizing time away from work.

Based on these principles the approach has been to provide customized in-house e-learning programmes comprising a blend of:

- on-line self-assessment of individual learning needs
- a tailored package of Web-based learning materials (including mastery tests and course assignments)
- personal coaching support on-line and by telephone
- short face-to-face skills workshops
- lifetime access to a personal Learning Log.

This means that learners can undertake a programme of self-managed, but supported, learning over a period that suits each individual. It also means the programme will integrate on-line learning, practice of skills in real-life situations, and unlimited coaching support for the duration of a given programme.

Kodak came to the Oxford Group with a request from their EAMER region: Europe, Middle East and the African Region, for support for two thousand managers operating in 28 different countries. Could help be provided with a specific challenge they will face in 2001? The challenge was this. During 2000 Kodak announced (from the US) that there would be global changes to their performance management process which would affect these two thousand managers and their employees in two ways:

- On performance appraisal forms there would be a new five-point rating scale where the employee would be rated specifically on the results they achieved against their objectives. Previously different countries used different scales, and people had not been clear that they were being assessed on their results. The new scale clarified this.

- In addition to this rating, all employees would be rated against the Kodak values, that is to say, an assessment of the degree to which somebody's behaviour is living and demonstrating the Kodak values. Previously the values existed but were not part of the assessment process. Clearly the purpose of this step is to further embed the Kodak values by ensuring they are considered and reflected upon during day-to-day management of performance, as well as at appraisal time.

When these changes were announced within the EMEAR region, there was a variety of responses. In the large and more established EMEAR countries like France, Germany and the UK, where there is already a well-established Kodak operation, most managers said 'No problem to move to a different rating scale because we're already using a scale and we know what you mean.' However they were much less clear about what was meant by assessing people against the behavioural dimensions represented by the Kodak values, and said they needed much more help with this.

In the smaller Kodak countries in the Middle East, Europe and Africa there was a much more fundamental need, as there was no track record of understanding and implementing performance management in a consistent way. Clearly the concept of performance management (PM) is not universally understood and we clarify here some of the issues.

What is performance management? Performance management (PM) has been defined as 'a systematic approach to improving individual and team performance in order to achieve organizational goals' (Hendry et al. 1997).

At its simplest, PM generates learning for improvement (single loop) by setting performance objectives, reviewing past performance, and relating results to reward. For more complex development or double loop learning the system should include a reflective process, and time and space for reflective dialogue. Such a system needs to be constructed within a framework of goals and values, and a successful PM system aligns objectives and incentives with corporate goals and values. The potential of PM to stimulate development or even innovation depends on the prevailing culture. Where control and blame are strong cultural variables, managers will struggle to develop a transformative learning approach. Where company values nurture growth and development, there is likely to be learning support for reflection, and the Oxford Group e-learning model addresses this through personal coaching and lifetime access to a learning log, both of which are potential vehicles for reflective dialogue.

Kodak's challenge was to support two thousand managers spread across Europe, Middle East and Africa. How to communicate with them effectively given the usual business pressures of tight budgets and no spare resource to allocate to an expensive training programme? Through an existing relationship with the Oxford Group's French office, Kodak approached the provider and a blended learning solution was designed and delivered.

The programme

For each participant, the access to the programme is via a Website at <www.oxfordelearning.com> which the manager enters using a Kodak ID and password that identifies the manager as coming from a specific Kodak region, but does not identify them as an individual.

The entry point of the Website is a Home Page that explains in detail how the following learning options and resources work, with links to the full spectrum of resources described below.

Managers are directed first to a self-assessment instrument which enables them to assess their knowledge, skills and confidence in applying PM in general, and the specific changes required by Kodak in their new approach.

Depending on the results of this self-assessment managers are offered three alternative learning options:

- Four hours of self-study delivered through this Website, consisting of a mixture of reading, case studies, self-tests, graphics, etc. This option is for people who felt confident in their skills in implementing PM but just needed to update themselves on the technical changes which Kodak required.
- The above, plus two half-day live virtual classroom sessions delivered over the Internet. This option is for people who had completed the four hours of self-study but needed more help with the practicalities of operating the new scheme and making a values assessment.
- One day live face-to-face training to follow self-study and virtual classroom sessions for behavioural and interpersonal skills development.

THE SELF-ASSESSMENT INSTRUMENT

The purpose of this self-assessment is to help learners to decide what level of support they need to successfully implement Kodak's new, global, standardized Performance Assessment (PA) process, and Performance Management (PM) in general.

The self-assessment covers three critical elements:

1. understanding of the rationale, principles and processes of the new, global PA approach
2. understanding of the practicalities of implementing the PA process with team members
3. competence and skills in handling the interpersonal and behavioural elements of giving positive and negative feedback.

The Kodak self-assessment process is shown in Box 12.1.

BOX 12.1

The Kodak self-assessment process

Read the questions below and follow the guideline.

1. Understanding of principles, process, paperwork and timing of new PA process and existing PM process.

If you are not confident in answering any of the following questions you should complete Section 1 of the self-study materials.

- What are the four main reasons Kodak has introduced a new, standardized, global Performance Assessment process?
- Does the new PA process have any impact on the existing Performance Management cycle?
- When does the new PA process takes effect, and to whom does it apply?
- How do you incorporate Kodak's Values when setting Performance Objectives?
- What does it mean if an employee is rated very high, or very low, against the Kodak Values?
- How does the new PA process affect pay decisions?

- How should the new PA process be implemented in the Matrix and Virtual organizations?

If you answer 'No' to the following question you should also complete the appropriate Sections from 2 to 8 of the self-study materials.

- Do you understand Kodak's full PM cycle and how to implement the various stages apart from the new PA process?

2. Understanding of the practicalities of conducting PAs and PM, especially anticipating problems and handling difficult situations.

If you are not confident in handling the sorts of situations listed below, book on to the Virtual Classroom sessions where they will be fully discussed through a number of Case Study examples. These sessions will also review your understanding of the principles of the new PA process.

- Making practical performance assessments using the new rating scales, and communicating these to people in a positive, constructive manner
- Dealing with setting objectives in high-change environments
- Handling a Performance Assessment situation where significant changes in the business have made an individual's objectives irrelevant
- Handling Performance Assessment when you have recently taken over managing an individual or team, and lack personal knowledge of their performance

- Handling a situation where someone disagrees with the PA rating you have given them
- Putting together a practical development plan to improve poor performance
- Managing the performance and development of a high-potential employee.

3. Competence and confidence to handle the face-to-face, interpersonal and behavioural elements of giving positive and negative feedback, coaching for improved performance and agreeing good objectives.

If you are not confident you have the skills and behaviours described below, book on to a Skills Workshop session where you will have numerous opportunities to practise your skills in a safe environment.

- Do you have the practical skills to prepare for and conduct an effective, face-to-face appraisal interview?
- When discussing an example of poor performance with an individual face to face, do you have the skills and confidence to achieve a successful outcome?
- When discussing a poor Performance Appraisal rating with an employee, do you feel confident that you have the skills and behaviours to achieve a positive outcome?
- When giving positive feedback to an individual, do you have the questioning and listening skills to understand the reasons for their high performance, and to create with them a development plan that plays to their strengths?
- Do you have the interpersonal and behavioural skills to deal with an employee who disagrees with your assessment of their performance?

The self-study material is presented in eight sections:

- Section 1 contains most of what managers need to know about changes to Kodak's Performance Assessment process. If the learner is only interested in changes, then the other section to look at is Section 3 on setting objectives, which has more information on preparing people for a Values assessment at the end of 2001.
- Section 2 contains an overview of Performance Management which will be helpful for those who have not systematically applied this process before.
- Section 3 describes the process and principles of setting performance objectives, with some ideas about unfreezing people's thinking so they can add value in new ways.
- Section 4 has information about the important skill of coaching, to help set people up for success in the future.
- Section 5 contains information about the process of making assessments of employees' performance, a key management responsibility.
- Section 6 is about the skill of giving effective feedback, and describes a simple agenda for doing this on both formal and informal occasions.
- Section 7 is about developing planning and contains information on a range of different personal development strategies.
- Section 8 covers preparation for, and an agenda for conducting, the appraisal interview.

THE VIRTUAL CLASSROOM SESSIONS

People would book on to the sessions by e-mail and then up to twelve Kodak managers would log in from wherever they were, either from a PC at their desk top, or from home. Simultaneously they all joined a live audio conference call.

We grouped people by language and ran the sessions in English, French and German (to be extended to cover Italian, Spanish, Polish and Russian). The twelve managers are guided by one of our trainers through the four-hour study materials.

Sessions were designed to be highly participative. The trainer guides participants through a series of interactive presentations which appeared on their PC screens, with the trainer controlling what appears on their screen at any particular time. Virtual flipcharts and white boards also allowed participants to collaborate in designing good questions and gathering learning points.

The most important part of the design was the creation of a case study about two fictional Kodak employees, John and Maria. Learners met John and Maria in their Web-based self-study material, where there were in-depth descriptions of John and Maria, a rich account of their biographies, objectives, behaviours, dreams and dreads, as well as their actual performances.

The case studies were used to bring to life the changes required by Kodak in their new PM process. On the first of the two half-day sessions we looked at past performance, and on the second we followed the case studies through and talked about agreeing objectives for future performance. This mirrors the Oxford Group's coaching model which has two modes: preview coaching and review coaching. For the poor performer a performance improvement plan was needed, and for the high performer a career plan was appropriate.

Before the case-study work, we gave participants a coffee break, asked them to disconnect from the conference call, and put them into pairs for a one-to-one discussion before reconnecting with the conference call, in effect simulating the break-out groups that would often be used in more conventional classroom-based training.

THE FACE-TO-FACE TRAINING-SKILLS WORKSHOP

In addition to self-assessment, self-study and virtual classroom sessions, learners were offered a one-day live face-to-face workshop. The Skills Workshop is a day of skills practice sessions, with video feedback delivered by an Oxford Group tutor, for up to twelve Kodak managers. Each workshop lasts a day and contains a varied mixture of discussion, case studies and skills practice sessions. To participate, learners need to travel to a training venue. Information on-line about the skills workshops is shown in Box 12.2.

BOX 12.2

The Skills Workshop

- *What will I get out of attending the Skills Workshop?*
 Attending the Skills Workshop will enable you to check your understanding of the new PA process, in discussion with a tutor and other Kodak managers (although you will be expected to have completed at least Module 1 of the self-study materials). You will discuss the practical issues of implementing the new PA process, and other aspects of performance manage-ment, especially how to handle difficult performance issues. You will participate in a number of role play and skills practice sessions where you will receive feedback and coaching on your behaviours and interpersonal skills.

- *Who are the sessions designed for?*
 The sessions are designed for managers who want more support in implementing

 the new PA process, and performance management in general, than can be provided by just completing the self-study option and Virtual Classroom. They are specifically designed to help you increase your confidence and skills in the interpersonal and behavioural elements of giving feedback and coaching.

- *What preparation will I need to do before the sessions?*
 You will need to have completed Modules 1 and 3 of the self-study about the new PA process and objective setting, and taken self-tests 1 and 3. You must have read the case study material about two fictional Kodak employees, John and Maria – see the links on the Virtual Classroom page – and have sent an e-mail to the tutor with a brief summary of what you wish to achieve from attending the sessions.

Between March and May 2001, there were 1500 hits on the Kodak PM Web-based support materials, and five of the virtual classroom programmes were run, with 60 Kodak managers attending from as far away as Saudi Arabia and Kenya (feedback is shown in Table 12.1). In this period no participants opted for the full programme, choosing to take the self-study and virtual classroom options only, citing time and logistics as the barrier to attending face-to-face events.

Table 12.1 Evaluation of e-learning programme at Kodak

Course Content	D1	D2	D3	D4	D5	D6	D7	D8	D9	D10	D11	D12	D13	D14	D15	D16	D17	D18	D19	D20	D21	D22	D23	D24	D25	D26	D27	D28	D29	D30	D31	D32	Totals	Average
Quality of the content of the self-study web site containing information about changes to Kodak's PA system?	5	4	4	3	4	4	4	5	4	3	4	0	0	0	0	0	0	0	0	0	0	0	0	0	0	0	0	0	0	0	0	0	44	4.00
Ease of access and navigation around self-study web site?	3	4	4	4	3	3	4	4	4	4	4	0	0	0	0	0	0	0	0	0	0	0	0	0	0	0	0	0	0	0	0	0	41	3.73
Joining instructions for Virtual Classroom?	4	4	4	5	3	3	3	3	3	2	2	0	0	0	0	0	0	0	0	0	0	0	0	0	0	0	0	0	0	0	0	0	36	3.27
Quality of trainer's input in the Virtual Classroom?	4	4	5	4	4	4	4	3	4	5	4	0	0	0	0	0	0	0	0	0	0	0	0	0	0	0	0	0	0	0	0	0	45	4.09
Value of the case study in the Virtual Classroom?	5	4	4	5	4	3	4	4	4	3	4	0	0	0	0	0	0	0	0	0	0	0	0	0	0	0	0	0	0	0	0	0	44	4.00
Value of the discussion in the Virtual Classroom?	5	4	4	5	3	3	4	4	4	4	4	0	0	0	0	0	0	0	0	0	0	0	0	0	0	0	0	0	0	0	0	0	44	4.00
Overall, amount learnt from self-study and Virtual Classroom?	4	4	4	4	4	4	4	4	4	4	4	0	0	0	0	0	0	0	0	0	0	0	0	0	0	0	0	0	0	0	0	0	44	4.00
Value of self-study and Virtual Classroom in terms of lessons you have been able to apply at work?	4	4	4	4	4	4	4	3	4	3	4	0	0	0	0	0	0	0	0	0	0	0	0	0	0	0	0	0	0	0	0	0	42	3.82
How does this format rate by comparison with travelling to, and participating in, a conventional course?	5	4	4	5	4	3	3	3	3	4	4	0	0	0	0	0	0	0	0	0	0	0	0	0	0	0	0	0	0	0	0	0	42	3.82

Key:
1 = poor 2 = less than satisfactory 3 = fully satisfactory 4 = very good 5 = excellent

100

Table 12.1 concluded

What would your estimate be of the time/cost saving for you of this format of training by comparison with a conventional course?
Time: ½ a day; Cost: Flight and hotel saved but extra on phone communication.
You waste less time, you are less tired. The difficulty could be that as you are alone in a room, the concentration is not easy, so it has to be lively, and in this case it was.
No hesitation, the time and cost saving is very appreciable.
Lost time of travel to/from (20 hrs). Cost US$1.5K excluding cost of the programme.
From the point of time saving it's yes as this saved the time of travelling. Each participant only has to give time for the training then he'll switch again from the same room to his daily work, but this will never compensate the face-to-face interaction between the trainer and the group and among the group itself. From the point of view of cost savings, again it's yes. This virtual training saved the travel and accommodation cost, but at the same time it's still high as international phone cost comparing to a local training course.

As the e-learning course does not include role plays, the same time is spent on other subjects when compared to a conventional course. Cost saving: Yes
I think nothing if the conventional course is in my building.
Difficult to estimate – depends on location of course, whether overnight accommodation is needed etc.
Time saving: 5 days cost saving US$2K

What was the most memorable learning point for you from the programme?
This kind of training is very effective and that a good user interface makes it a success
The case study, which really helps you to learn through a concrete example.
Multiple choice approach.
Two things: 1) setting SMART objectives and how this will help a lot both the manager and the employee during the performance appraisal 2) How we assess the value by gathering facts from all the surrounding people and I see that assessing values is fair enough to the employees who are role modelling the values or demonstrating the values comparing to the others.
How to set objective, how to measure them.
The case study.
Good demonstration of how technology enables learning in a different format.
The Kodak Values
Group discussions and trainer input.

Do you have any other comments or feedback about the web site or Virtual Classroom?
The most important part of success is linked to the discipline of the participants. This means giving priority to the course and not being absorbed by general job issues and doing other stuff at the same time e.g. some participants disappeared during the work group sessions on cases. The preparation of the cases is key, so invest some time in it. I also think that a logical order must be set up at start so that every participant knows his number in a row for reacting on the questions that are asked by the chairperson. Otherwise people start to speak together or are waiting one for another.

The main weakness of this type of learning was that it was, most of the time, very difficult to hear well the teacher and the other participants! You had to really concentrate to hear well and considering that the course was quite long, it is very tiring. Two half-day courses might be too long for some employees because of their heavy work schedule. The other thing is that it would be much nicer to receive this type of questionnaire the week following the course to give more accurate answers. My personal conclusion is that I would not hesitate to participate again in an e-learning course!
Thank you
I don't have any feedback regarding the web site, but I would propose if we can organise other PA training sessions for other managers and supervisors in the company as this will help them a lot during next year's performance evaluation process.
E-learning material on the web site should be in local language.
It's necessary to book a room, to follow this learning.
Main disadvantage of Virtual Classroom is that it is not always as participative as traditional training courses, and miss opportunity to network/talk 'off-line' during breaks etc. You can also get distracted when sitting at your own desk - important to be disciplined/focused.
No
A great experience, the virtual tool gave me ideas for other parts of our working life outside of training.

Feedback on the programme

FROM PARTICIPANTS

It was the first time any of the participants had taken part in a live virtual classroom and many said they had serious doubts about it, having grim experience of isolated text-learning at a terminal. Their expectations were therefore quite low. They thought it would be boring, sounded like a long time, and they were not sure whether it would be worthwhile (fairly typical course participant expectations). On completion their view had completely switched and they rated the programme as extremely valuable. In particular, the case studies and the amount of discussion were cited as the most important parts of the learning process.

FROM KODAK

Kodak felt that they had a duty to support their managers, following their announcement of changes to the PM system, and the programme fulfilled this duty. Kodak was happy with the learning levels achieved and found the programme to be practical and good value for money.

During June and July an evaluation was conducted which showed that those who had attended the virtual classroom sessions and used the Website rated their experience between 'fully satisfactory' and 'very good'. A copy of the evaluation is attached as an appendix to Table 12.1 (pages 100–101).

Conclusion

Clearly the e-learning solution is attractive where staff are likely to be numerous and geographically disparate. On the assumption that the e-learning blended solution represents a saving in costs, the main question is 'How effective is it for reflective learning?' The provision of opportunities for reflective dialogue was included in the programme (the pairs work) and this could be developed to include intentional dialogue focused on the learner's performance or perceived difficulties. The self-assessment process in itself generates self-reflection, as does skilful use of the case studies where learners may distance themselves from poor performance but can identify characteristics of it for themselves. Moving toward action for improvement is likely to be achieved through the personal coaching option, and electronic learning logs are vehicles for reflective records. The design of the programme can develop to include scheduled and intentional dialogue between learners (the course partner method) and there is no obstacle to such development. The face-to-face training offers a valuable opportunity to model dialogue with learners if they take up that option and future programmes are including the face-to-face element as compulsory. The Kodak work was experimental and the Oxford Group will build on the good results from this programme to offer similar blended solutions to their clients, incorporating the potential for reflective learning on-line.

13 Organizational Change and Learning at Allied Distillers

Nic Beech, George Cairns and Tom Robertson

Allied Distillers Limited (ADL) is based in Scotland and is part of the international Allied Domecq group. Its main business is the production of whisky (particularly Ballantine's) and other spirits-based drinks. ADL was formed through the merger and acquisition of a number of independent whisky companies, and it operates in a market which has seen little or no growth in demand for many years. Competition with other spirits producers is intense and there is a need for ADL to maximize its productive capabilities. This need has led to a change process which has its roots in 1993, but which became firmly established in 1996 and is still ongoing. This case traces some of the major changes from the perspective of learning and development. In particular, there was a perceived need to achieve an effective mix of formal and informal training, with an emphasis on learning through doing, and an integration of people development policies with other human resource management (HRM) and operations policies. ADL provides us with a lesson in perseverance – the radical changes they have achieved do not occur overnight, and there has been a longitudinal commitment to change.

ADL had been organized in the pattern that was normal for the industry, in other words it was a mechanistic and hierarchical structure, and it was highly unionized, with adversarial 'us and them' relations between management and the workers. In that atmosphere, training was often limited to the functional, that is, the basics needed by shop-floor workers in order to do the job. Development, where it occurred, was for managers. In addition, development was often thought of discretely. For example, managers were sent on MBAs and other external courses, but there was not a strong focus on the *processes* of learning transfer and development within the workplace. The changes have challenged this traditional way of thinking and acting, and there has been a movement towards a more integrated and developmental culture. The driving force behind this was not simply based on valuing development, rather there was a conviction that development and organizational performance are inextricably linked.

The information presented in this case is derived from numerous interviews and focus groups conducted in ADL between 1996 and 2001, and from personal experience in the company.

Key achievements through the change process

The 'Change Agenda' was established in 1996. It placed emphasis on flexibility, a partnership with unions and employees, an increased customer focus and a move to a structure based on team working. This change programme was accompanied by reviews of various areas of operation, and subsequently a project 'Building on Success' which culminated in the relocation of physically dispersed parts of the business in a central site. Integration was a theme underlying the changes and as Richard Turner, President, Customer Service and Planning for Allied Domecq, put it 'During this period we have seen significant change and continuous improvement. This has been a total team effort from all parts of ADL and I think that is the most gratifying part.' So improvement was not achieved simply in a top-down process of change, rather it drew out and built on skills and knowledge within the workforce. According to Commercial Director John Corrigan:

> Our employees provided a wealth of knowledge and experience which was tapped and their help was used to manage the change ... this not only saved hundreds of thousands of pounds on consultancy fees, but also provided a large number of employees with a new stimulus and challenge that many enjoyed, working and participating on the various project teams within BoS [the Building on Success project].

The changes led to significant outcomes. Productivity has increased greatly. Over the period of change the staff numbers have reduced from 1600 to 970, but the same output of 12 million cases of spirits per annum has been maintained. Output per employee has risen by 65 per cent. Cost savings have been made throughout the business and the BoS project alone is estimated to save £6 million per year. Notwithstanding the need to make savings, the investment in training has been maintained at the level of £500,000 per annum. These changes would be comparable with some of those organizations that are held up as examples of international best practice in HRM (for example Becker and Huselid 1999; Pfeffer and Veiga 1999). The productivity gains and cost savings were achieved whilst simultaneously operating a policy of no compulsory redundancy. There has been what is seen as a culture change which enables increased cross-functional working, communication and involvement. For example, project teams from the workforce were involved in designing the new facilities – something that would be unimaginable in the old culture. Ian Gourlay, Managing Director, commented, 'I have been really impressed by the way that our entire workforce has handled BoS, whether it be in designing the new bottling hall, how the offices should look or even what kind of food should be served in the restaurant. This is a great success and I am extremely proud of our people.'

Internal recognition of the contribution and development of the workforce was supported by external recognition through accreditation by Investors in People.

Processes of learning and change

The key achievements derived through the change process are impressive. Following the 'what did they achieve?' question, the next is 'how did they do it?' The following section seeks to explore some of the processes of developmental change. The starting-point was change in the management population. There was an assessment centre through which man-

agers were chosen for various positions. For some, the outcome was redundancy. Having selected the people for the job, training included a major event called 'Transfusion'. As the name implies, the aim of this was to radically shift the attitudes and approaches of the new managers. This was followed by a greater concentration on training and development for the whole workforce. Development was fostered through the use of project teams, a move to having shop-floor facilitators (rather than supervisors) and a longitudinal training programme for 'change leaders' in the business.

Change and development of the management population

ASSESSMENT CENTRES

Top management, influenced by input from Allied Domecq level, had identified a need to shift the culture of ADL. Their change model entailed getting union support through the Change Agenda, but also reselecting the management population. This was done in line with criteria which entailed different managerial competencies to those prevalent in the old culture. Whilst the old managerial style had been control-centred, the new approach was to more facilitating. Workers were to be enabled to operate in teams in a high-quality mode, and this would require a different approach from managers. The assessment centres for managers were run over three days and included a range of selection techniques. Participants were asked to role-play handling an aggrieved employee, with the employee being played by a professional actor. There were group exercises in which people sat round a table and were allocated roles as directors of different electronics companies in the same group. One company had to be shut down, and the exercise involved arguing the business case to defend the company you had been allocated. Other exercises included analysing information about the Allied Domecq group and writing a 2000-word essay on the business strategy.

The outcome of the assessment centre was a reduction of 30 per cent in the management population, with a number of non-voluntary redundancies having to be made. There was also a significant reduction in the layers of hierarchy, so that a new structure with only four layers was produced. This was negative for some. Obviously those who lost their jobs would be unlikely to feel the process was effective, but in addition, the workforce did not unanimously think that all the best managers had been retained. It is unlikely that any such process could be perfect, and for ADL it was necessary to make a radical shift, and the assessment centre served a purpose in achieving this.

Once the management population was selected, it was important to establish a new way of behaving and to reinforce attitudes that would foster the desired new approach to work. One means towards that end was a training event called 'Transfusion'.

TRANSFUSION

Transfusion was a three-day event for all of the newly appointed/reappointed managers. Participants were grouped into cohorts of 50. The purpose of the event was to enable people to break with the traditional norms which had been pervasive in the company culture. The event was held at a hotel, and the dress code was casual. As participants entered the room, which was spacious, the chairs were arranged in a horseshoe and loud Celtic music was playing. The event leader started by pouring water from a jug into a cup, but he did not stop as

the water overflowed. As a senior manager explained, 'As the water cascaded onto the floor he was totally unconcerned. It was intended to demonstrate the brain full of data with lots of knowledge passing by.' And a middle manager commented, 'The water incidents did make me sit up as I was disappointed that someone could be so callous as to pour water over the room. But then I entered a mode which I felt removed much of my inhibitions and I felt more of a risk taker.'

Exercises were planned to disturb the 'old ways of thinking' and to stimulate double-loop learning, that is, learning for transformation. These included: Tai Chi, relaxation techniques, guided fantasy sessions and role playing/dramatized group interaction. There was a focus on 'the whole person', well-being and group membership. Coffee was discouraged and water and fresh fruit were provided. The hours with the group were long, lasting from 7.30 a.m. to late at night, and through this time people were encouraged to open up to each other in personal and revealing ways: '[it was] an astonishing session as many extremely private disclosures were made, as well as some tragic events' (Senior Manager), and 'items discussed were of redundancy, divorce, deaths, serious illness and so on. To this day I remember an issue of a child death ... I see the people and I see their predicament. This alters my behaviour' (Middle Manager).

The outcome of such sessions was an increased bonding within the groups and members reported seeing others quite differently, and more sympathetically, than they had previously. This broke the established norm in ADL in which communication could be characterized as rational engagement between post-holders, and instead emphasized a person–person form of interaction.

Clearly there can be advantages to such an approach – greater tolerance and team working between managers from different functions is encouraged. However, it should be noted that the process can also be highly invasive. The levels of revelation were unnatural for the organizational culture at the time, and once one has made a revelation it cannot be taken back. Hence, if someone has said more than they meant to, the knowledge about them has become publicly owned and will impact on the perceptions and behaviours of others (even if only those present at the session).

Transfusion was not only about getting to know the person behind the role and achieving integration, it was also concerned with performance. The use of 'Power Time' was an example of this: 'The programme was to ramp up using the phrase "power time", which was to maximize each minute of your time to be of value. Tasks would be set which you would immediately dismiss as unachievable, only to find that by eliminating idle chat, toilet visits and coffee breaks, a large task can be completed in a small time' (Middle Manager).

Power time was subsequently transferred back into the workplace. When facing a blockage, groups would focus for a particular time period (sometimes as little as ten minutes) to derive observable outcomes. For some groups this was very effective. For others, it was a fairly short-lived initiative.

As with the rest of the programme there are both pros and cons with this approach. Whilst it can be effective in mobilizing activity and avoiding passivity, it is not necessarily conducive to reflective thought and decision making. In combination with more contemplative phases of team behaviour, however, it can be effective.

Transfusion was a high impact event. Although it can be criticized as being invasive of participants, and its focus on dramatic events may have short-term effects, none the less it was important in turning a corner in the change process. It was a strong symbol that behaviour and attitudinal approaches had to change, and it engaged the three domains of think-

ing, doing and feeling which must be involved if learning is to be significant for transformation. However, Transfusion was directed only at managers. Development of the workforce is considered below.

Development of the workforce

PROJECT TEAMS

'I would say most of the learning in this company is through doing. We are encouraged to do that. I can't think of one instance where someone has been told "you can't do that" ... this place is awash with project teams!' (Middle Manager)

There is a focus on recognizing ideas and suggestions from throughout the organization, and prizes are given for successful ideas. In the old culture, there would have been considerable scepticism about such an approach, but now things have changed to the extent that people from the shop floor are involved in the editorial team of the company newspaper which was previously regarded as a 'propaganda machine' (Middle Manager). Teams have been involved in a range of functions including the design of the new facilities. The project team included people from many levels in the organization, and they visited other notable developments in the UK. They could not command the same capital expenditure as some of the 'best practice', but they developed their 'own take' on a number of prominent themes and have transformed the production and office facilities into ones which encourage team work, which are highly functional and cost effective, but are also very attractive. This is a radical move for an organization which for many years had separate dining facilities for directors, and workers would not be expected to walk through the directors' corridor, even if it were the most direct route to where they were going. Displaying this level of trust in the workforce has been important in establishing a new form of relationship which achieves greater integration between managers and workers. And this is crucial when it comes to learning. It is only in an atmosphere of trust that project teams can really develop and try out their ideas, because learning through doing may entail mistakes. Whereas in the old culture the reaction to a mistake was to find someone whose name could be attached to the problem, now mistakes are seen as routes to effective learning. However, the ever-present 'bottom line' ensures that mistakes, once identified, are not repeated.

Other projects have been in response to challenges from management. For example, the directors set a target of making a £750,000 saving through the reduction of waste. A project team was formed and was given the brief of coming up with the strategy and process to make the saving. They produced a range of cost-saving ideas including using a different quality of cardboard in packaging, altering the way that cardboard is packaged and stored on pallets and managing the way that pallets were returned to the suppliers. They also developed a plan for more efficient deliveries so that now there is one instead of the four that were previously made. This involved approach contrasts with that experienced by a middle manager who joined the company in the 1980s at a more junior level:

Back in 82 when I joined the company I was amazed at this big building 50 yards across the road, and I remember saying to my boss 'what happens in there?' and he said to me 'if I catch you in there I'll fire you, you stay here.' For three years I never

knew it was the drain and fill, I didn't know that was where the whisky came from. All I knew was I press this button and it comes out.

More recently, when John Lloyd of the AEEU visited the plant there was a radically different atmosphere. 'I was introduced to people by those on the line – not by an HR person, or worse, a PR person . . . everyone was very relaxed about being stopped and asked about their work . . . everyone was trained on how to explain what they were doing, what the processes were and where it led to'. There is evidence of single-loop learning, aimed at improvement, and double-loop learning, aimed at transformation. People developed new skills and processes, and also were 'different in themselves' in the workplace.

SHOP-FLOOR FACILITATORS

Part of the developmental philosophy was to make the most of the potential contributions of shop-floor workers. With the increased use of project teams and greater autonomy for teams it was necessary to identify people who would take responsibility for decisions and keep things going. 'Grade 4s' were in a sense deputy team managers who were to fulfil this need. One middle manager described the developmental process as follows:

> I took them away to a venue and went through self-awareness type training, and training of what the job was about. We worked on how they could best work with each other, and did some role-play to emphasize the points. I didn't seek the authority to do it, so I took a bit of a risk. These people were under a lot of peer pressure from their colleagues, being accused of being managers on the cheap – because it was breaking a tradition. We took a bit of a risk, but it worked . . . They changed because they had been made to feel special.

Subsequently, there was far more openness in volunteering for project teams and for getting involved. Over time, and through positively reinforced experience, the spread of involvement has increased greatly. An individual example was of a person who joined the company as a temporary worker. He took on responsibilities for forklift truck driving, and later joined a small project team:

> That guy has just rocketed from being a temporary fork-lift truck driver, shoving things about a yard, to moving possibly onto the managerial ladder. It's through taking these people and building them up. Before these people were seen as a threat to the management. Now it's actually a feather in the manager's cap to develop somebody through . . . previously he would have been kept at bay . . . that's a sign of the culture change. [Middle Manager]

A change in direction towards facilitation rather than supervision, and using such roles as ways of developing individuals has been important in making the culture change real. It is people's everyday experience of work that has most impact on them, and that everyday experience is strongly associated with the way they are managed face-to-face, and probably only weakly associated with more remote statements of strategy and policy.

In addition to personal development and style changes, formal programmes have been used to support the change. One such is the 'change leaders programme'.

Change leaders programme

The change leaders programme was instigated to support the change in role from supervisor to facilitator. It entails formal training supported by less formal peer support. On the programme, team leaders go through a series of modules covering a set of competencies that were regarded as largely missing. These include: influencing and leadership skills, decision making, time management, presentation and motivation skills and fundamentals of manufacturing. The programme is phased over 12 months, with two-day sessions every four to six weeks. Participants are expected to undertake some course work between the modules. One of the dangers of formal learning away from the workplace is ineffective transfer of learning back onto the job. In the design of the change leaders programme, relevance and transfer are put centre stage through an individual business improvement plan (BIP). Before participants start the programme, they meet with their managers and agree something that will make a difference to their area of the business, and this is formulated into the individual's BIP. The BIP is worked on throughout the year, with the help and support of others on the programme. The intention behind adopting this approach was, in the words of the organization Development Manager, 'to make it different from just a training event ... this would be a valuable tool for people to have completed in that when internal positions arose they would be at an advantage.' The link between development and an expressed commitment from the organization to the participants was thought to be important in heightening motivation. In addition optional events on specific topics such as finance, the operation of customs and excise, and procurement were run. Wherever possible, these were facilitated by internal staff. The impact of using internal staff was to acknowledge their expertise, and to make it better known and understood in the organization, in addition to saving the cost of bringing in external consultants (which had been the previous norm). The facilitation met many of the requirements to be seen as reflective learning as it involved the three domains of thinking, doing and feeling, and it involved people in being different as well as applying new skills. This further fostered the spirit of integration which was central to the culture change. Cohorts were of 16 people on average, and by 2002, 60 people will have been through the programme.

Conclusions

In ADL there were strong business imperatives for change – demand for the main products was tight and competition was strong. ADL had the advantage of some strong brands, but it needed to recreate itself as a highly efficient producer of quality product. It has done this through the way it has managed and developed its people. It has combined cost reduction with people development. At the beginning of the change process, there were about 1600 employees, by 2001 there were 970, but the volume of production had been maintained at 12 million cases of spirits per year, and quality and customer feedback have improved over the same period. External recognition of the achievements has come through the Investors in People award.

The key to the increases in productivity has been to enable people to work differently and more flexibly. This has entailed a focus on learning through doing. Project teams involve people from all levels of the organization, and people have developed skills through working on real problems and issues. The organization has exhibited double-loop learning through its

adoption of recommendations and solutions which have emerged from the project work, and there has been upward learning. For example, the design of the new facilities was developed by a project group, which involved all levels of employee, and this has contributed to the success of the move.

There have been formal elements to the training – such as transfusion for managers and the change leaders programme for team leaders, but these have been placed in the context of changing behaviour. This is reinforced through the performance management system, and managers' pay is contingent on their performance against behavioural objectives. There have also been links to other human resource management policies – such as the use of assessment centres for the selection of staff, and to new ways of working based on teams and the use of new technology.

In a sense, the change will never stop. It is necessary for ADL to maintain its flexibility and to be responsive internally to the abilities of employees and externally to changing markets and competition. This is likely to mean that their longitudinal commitment to change and performance through people will have to continue. Perseverance is the name of the game. In the words of the organization's Development Manager: 'I think the one thing you have to get clear in your mind, and it's difficult, is that it takes time . . . and the frustrations . . . you start to question your own competence and approach to things when you don't get early returns . . . but when it starts to come through . . . it's almost like dragging a boulder up a hill, when you get to the top you'd better run because it's coming after you!' While it takes time to build trust and involvement with the workforce, once it starts working the initiatives and development will move at a pace which even those who started the ball rolling will find unpredictable.

On the Journey – Enabling Effective Learning

14 Learning from the Evidence of Co-Inquiry Based Practice and Research: Explorations in Primary Care

Susan Weil, Jyoti Bhandari and Sonal Shah

Starting points

This chapter explores a research project that began with a 'respectable passion': to reduce coronary heart disease (CHD) amongst men in the UK originating from Indian subcontinent countries of India, Pakistan, Sri Lanka, and Bangladesh ('South Asians'). A core team of health care professionals, concerned with improving the quality of primary-care health strategies with respect to this challenge, comprised four General Practitioners, including Jyoti Bhandari (JB), Sonal Shah (SS) (both co-authors here) and a Community Trust Link Manager – all South Asian women. Susan Weil (SW) an Anglo-American, worked with us throughout. She brought expertise, including within the health service, of the approach we adopted: critically reflexive action research (Weil 1998).[1,2]

Here, we open to view our sense-making about different ways of being and knowing in research and why these matter in practice contexts where complexity and 'mess' reign. We outline our approach, why this was suited to such conditions, and share learning trajectories of significance for all involved. We focus here on reflective learning processes, since other outcomes will be published elsewhere. We explore how and why our taken-for-granted practices have been challenged and changed in ways that have made a difference for ourselves, high-risk patients, and partnerships with others. We never envisaged such outcomes at the start of our project. We tell the story that follows in a first-person plural voice, and also as interweaving and separate voices.

Setting the scene

Traditional medical research has demonstrated that first and second generations of South Asians in Britain have a significantly higher death rate from CHD than the indigenous white population (Balarajan et al. 1984; McKeigue et al. 1991; McKeigue and Marmot 1988). In the

Brent and Harrow Health Authorities of Northwest London, where the core team members practise, South Asians make up just under one-fifth of the total population (Brent and Harrow HA 1991).

Our starting question was 'How could health care professionals reduce disproportionately high and premature rates of death from CHD amongst South Asian men, hit hardest by this disease?' Our focus was on CHD risk factors amenable to a primary-care approach. These included adverse dietary practices, certain biochemical factors and a lack of aerobic exercise.

For many primary-care professionals, traditional research can fail the 'so what' test. For example, the double-blind randomized controlled trial remains seen as highest-quality research. However our research question – and primary care – are not reducible to pre-specifiable variables or cause-and-effect linear relationships. However, much primary-care research generates standardized taxonomies and population-based data sets. These do little to improve the health of people in specific cultural subgroups within communities (Seng 1998). We wanted to tackle this gap, and this contradiction.

We approached 'knowledge' not as a fixed commodity or its production as a decontextualized activity, but as a collaborative and relational process that is embedded in dynamic social, cultural and political discourses and practices. We were guided by the principle of 'doing research not on people', or 'for people', but 'with people' (Heron and Reason 1997; Weil 1998): that is, in our case, with people who (potentially) suffer from CHD, or who can influence South Asians' risk of this disease. Our concern has been the co-generation of knowledge that can make a difference in people's lives, and the practices and systems which influence them.

This alternative research stance has opened up pathways through the many tensions and uncertainties that beset primary care. In the medical world, evidence-based practice is highly valorized. This project raises challenging questions about the risks of limiting what we mean by evidence. What has challenged and changed us in this project has been evidence generated through rigorously pursuing powerful questions about our practice intentions and choices relating to CHD, and systematically inquiring over time about whether and how we are realizing these as effectively as we might in primary care.

We hope that by sharing our story, we shall encourage others who, like the core team at the beginning of this project, do not see themselves as 'researchers' in any traditional or alternative sense. We also go further than this. Through this project, we have begun to come to grips with what it may mean to be not merely reflective practitioners (Schon 1983) but actively co-inquiring professionals in our everyday practice. This entails being continually self-challenging and in dialogue with others about the intended and unintended impacts of our practice choices on health outcomes in communities.

Research approach

Critically reflexive action research (CRAR) (Weil 1998) provided the starting-point for our enactment of alternative epistemological commitments than those that dominate in medical and primary care research. CRAR (and related theories of practice now emerging at the SOLAR Centre)[3] comes from a fertile mix of influences. These include critical systems thinking, complexity theory, field theory generally (as developed within Gestalt theory and the field of sociodrama) and participatory action research traditions (Midgley 2000), Flood and Romm 1996; Reason and Bradbury 2000; Stacey 1995; Reason and Goodwin 1999).

Principles and practices emanating from this work guided us in meeting our own concerns for rigour, quality and ethics, in ways that remained flexibly determined by us in the project throughout. These enabled us to explore what it may mean to enact science differently, so as to create socially robust knowledge with others (Nowotny et al. 2001), rather than merely 'reliable knowledge' as understood within a more traditional research frame. CRAR has recently been characterized by Midgley (2000) as a 'third wave' systemic inquiry and action research approach: that is, multi-methodological in its practice, and multi-layered in its processes and focus, all the while actively engaging with the lived dynamics of power and choice in complex systems and professional practice.

After introducing some key principles and inquiry practices that have influenced this project, we go on to contextualize these, as lived in the journeys of this research.

The first principle is that of *collaborative and relational inquiry*. This derives from an action-research tradition that seeks to be both participative and democratic (Reason and Bradbury 2000). It 'honours an holistic perspective on what constitutes valid knowledge' (Bray et al. 2000). Effective collaborative inquiry 'demystifies research and treats it as a form of learning that should be accessible by everyone interested in gaining a better understanding of his or her world' (Bray et al. 2000).

In traditional research, we are taught to objectify 'the field' and to discount anything that dislodges the design or hypothesis/question, except in ways that have been predetermined. In this approach, the 'field' for data collection is not out there, but we are in and of that field, embedded in the realities we create. CRAR challenges us to experiment with the potential of everyday practice for testing out and learning more about:

- what we do
- why
- with whom
- with what other meanings when viewed from diverse perspectives
- and with what intended and unintended consequences.

In this approach, everyday situations become opportunities for creating relationships and dialogue that open up possibilities for co-inquiry based practice. This principle enabled our research design to adapt and change in response to what emerged from different cycles of knowing from, for and within action. We worked with others to generate alternative framings of the problem with which we began, based on deeper insights into the limitations of our own mindsets, assumptions, metaphors and ways of being in learning and change with others. This collaborative and relational knowing within the core team took us into further cycles of co-inquiry, at the boundaries of our 'not knowing'. Rather than allowing solutions to drive action, we explored how powerful questions can galvanize participation in action-based co-inquiry that, in turn, can generate possibilities for change with which people identify.

The second principle is that of '*grounded systemic inquiry*'. We approached knowledge co-generation as a process that is situated within dynamic fields of practice, of which we are a part. For example, the field of inquiry at one point may be our own individual practices and assumptions within complex systems; or it may be at the dynamic interfaces of interacting subsystems, focusing perhaps on the taken-for-granted constructions of quality amongst a group of practitioners delivering a service; or alternatively, within the field created by two interacting systems, such as an interprofessional grouping working together reflexively and

through dialogue with others, such as users, on powerful questions that might enable a service to be understood and delivered quite differently, through new forms of partnership.

Whatever the starting-point for systemic inquiry may be, we remained alert throughout to the patterns that emerge from the particular, the local, and the contingent and that need tackling at other levels of the systems in which we practise.

CRAR is concerned with how we can learn in the spaces in between 'story and ground' and intentions for policy and practice (Weil et al. 2001; Weil 1999). Some aspects of the principle of grounded systemic inquiry, as applied to our own work here, will be illustrated below, and expanded upon in future publications (Weil 2002, forthcoming).

A third key principle is that of remaining *critically creative and reflexive in relation to our taken for granted 'topographies of attention and action'*. CRAR challenges us to engage at once a collaborative process, a creative one, and a critically reflexive one (Weil 1998). It focuses explicitly on becoming more self-challenging, individually and with others: about our taken-for-granted meaning and intentions for practice, as well as the assumptions and mindsets that influence actual decisions we make in action. Such choices are seen as situated within 'fields of possibility', the depth and potential of which often remain vastly unexplored. For example, bringing this principle together with the previous ones, CRAR challenges us to bring into awareness social discourses and boundary-setting practices, to explore within the real time of projects how these can act like invisible fences, and structure how we see possibilities for choice and action. We attend to what is insufficiently understood and possibly silenced, at the margins of our fields of practice and to how context and meaning shape each other. This can include searching out what remains unspoken in the formal system but spoken in informal systems, such as within corridors but not at formal meetings! Throughout, we are challenged to reflect critically on how these insights sit with the values and intentions we claim matter, such as for a profession, a field of practice, or a social policy. For example, what are the different meanings and modes of power being manifested, and how are these enabling and disabling for diverse but significant others? We can also become more creative in how we bring what is invisible and unspoken into view and into new forms of hearing within a system. The active engagement of different forms of knowing, such as experiential, metaphorical, narrative-based and embodied forms of knowing, help to go beyond the limitations of overly rationalistic and analytic/reductionist modes of thought. These can so easily keep our hearts, minds and eyes closed (Heron 1996; Belenky et al. 1986; Weil 1994).

At the same time, as we become more alert to the forces that influence our field of vision, and our concepts for practice, we explore these as questions with others, considering how we might transform our practices and the fields of which we are a part.

The final principle is that of *'tracking trajectories'*, the pathways of which cannot be known beforehand. This kind of research engages us to begin research by reflecting critically and creatively on our taken-for-granted frames of reference, practice assumptions, and the biographical, practice and social learning that has helped to generate these. We then open these up to scrutiny with others, which in turn surfaces more 'baseline starting points.' We problematize with others how we understand 'the starting problem'. Cycles of critically and creatively reflexive action and learning are supported by the continuing data analysis and 'play back' of emerging questions, themes and patterns, using creative *and* propositional forms of representation. Fields of possibility emerge through new forms of dialogue and reflexive action. Returning to rigorously kept research journals enables us to see patterns across these interweaving cycles of reflection, action and learning. Narratives about trajectories begin to emerge over time, but not as linear, neat accounts. These are multi-voiced,

messy and full of potential that often cannot be understood in the moment. In such work, the ultimate challenge is to communicate learning trajectories from co-inquiry-based practice and research in ways that may stir others into alternative forms of seeing, thinking and acting differently. Rather than using 'tracking' to prove or generalize, this instead becomes the material through which multi-voiced narratives invite others into a co-inquiring relationship with what is being represented.

For example, in our account below, we document how the core team's attention to boundaries, and processes of inclusion and exclusion in the context of intentions to reduce CHD, shifted over time. We had to rethink the most appropriate use of professional expertise and 'reliable evidence-based knowledge' in context, and in interaction with patients and the community. This brought into view taken-for-granted assumptions about the effects of our practices that we opened up to deeper scrutiny in dialogue with others, as we moved out of the safety of our offices and into the community, including into mosques and temples, in order to set up patient co-inquiry groups. To our surprise, we encountered highly sophisticated knowledge about CHD amongst South Asians. But our initial research questions had only focused on how we, as experts, could increase awareness, using the evidence of traditional research. Instead, we found we had to change our questions, and challenge ourselves about why we had framed it as such in the first place. We tracked self-challenges about what we excluded from our awareness in giving meaning to our primary-care intentions, and with what intended and *unintended* consequences – and how we learned and changed from this! Rather than 'cleaning this all up', this learning is all part of the story, and helps to establish the trustworthiness and social robustness of this knowledge co-generation process.

These processes are anything but linear, and will often not manifest, unless we systematically involve critical friends, challenging co-inquirers, and revisit documented material over time, with others. The recording and tracking processes become essential, 'since the emancipatory possibilities in such [work] are enormous, but they are also fragile and easily lost' (May 1998). Failing to attend to events as they unfold in such research can be at great cost, since genuinely seeing and acting differently is no easy matter.

Through this project, in summary, we brought reflective learning, action for change and research into new forms of relationship in our everyday lives as professionals and local policy makers. We became more appreciative of what was entailed in re-storying our practice and our worlds and activating the knowledges that were available to us within a 'knowing field' and at the edges of our 'not knowing'.[4] We learned that confusion and clarity interweave in a complex mix, in such work.

But now we wish to give life and meaning to these inquiry principles. In the section that follows, our different voices seek to bring the reader into our metaphorical navigation of this project's gullies, mountains and varied terrains – and the 'ah-has' generated along the way.

Living cycles of knowledge cogeneration and critically reflexive action research

The CRAR cycle set out in Figure 14.1 below provided a structure for our project and the account, which follows. This is used recursively, and is adapted as projects develop, as will be illustrated below.

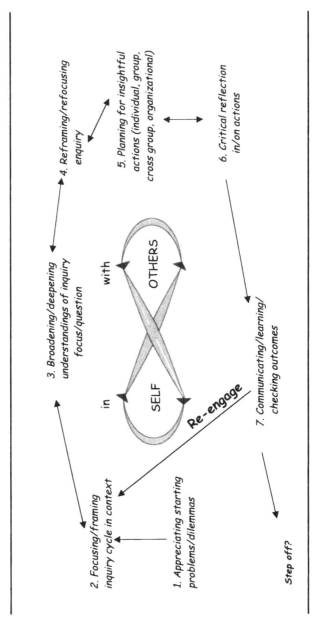

CRAR
Critically Reflexive Action Research
key cyclical processes

4. Reframing/refocusing enquiry

5. Planning for insightful actions (individual, group, cross group, organizational)

6. Critical reflection in/on actions

3. Broadening/deepening understandings of inquiry focus/question

with

OTHERS

in

SELF

Re-engage

7. Communicating/learning/ checking outcomes

2. Focusing/framing inquiry cycle in context

1. Appreciating starting problems/dilemmas

Step off?

Figure 14.1 CRAR: Critically Reflective Action Research

STAGE 1: APPRECIATING THE PROBLEM

Funding enabled five workshops to underpin this research project.

JB/SS: 'Before the first workshop, we rang Susan to say we would do our literature review before we met, as we knew was customary in research. She said no, which surprised us. She explained that traditional academic research defines problems in terms of prior research: the "building blocks" upon which knowledge is added.

'She suggested that further in-depth searching of the medical literature, beyond that which we had done to secure research funding, could lead to us unwittingly devaluing the depth of our own practice-based knowledge, and experiential understandings as rooted in our identities as South Asian women and health care professionals. Susan spoke of the "standing on the shoulders of giants" double bind, whereby we start squeezing down the rough edges of our own "respectable passions" and research questions, feeling as if we must now fit these into others' frames of meaning. This can lead to our reproducing the status quo, albeit unwittingly. Later, we realized that, had we then done a more in-depth search, this research might have had a less significant impact on our own and others' practices.

'Instead, Susan encouraged us to capture as much as possible about why this project mattered to us, and what we hoped to get out of it as the core team, and to record initial thoughts and assumptions in our "research journals" in ways that suited each of us. She mentioned drawing, images, scribbles, anecdotes, stories, and talking alone and with each other into tape recorders and writing in journals. We continued this process, begun individually, as a group when we met on the first Saturday morning workshop, in one of our surgeries. A range of black-and-white photos (Weil 1994, Midgley 2000) helped us go further in this. For example, through our *photo* choices, we were helped to voice tacit knowledge and assumptions, about, for example, why this project mattered, what might be difficult, and what we hoped we and others might get out of it. As insights surfaced through dialogue, we began to see patterns and connections across our stories. All of this was taped and later transcribed. We were to recognize later how invaluable this baseline documentation would prove.

'This introduced a novel way of approaching a research problem in a fun and interactive way. It gave us confidence later to use different ways of opening up knowing and dialogue with project co-inquirers.'

IMPACT AND OUTCOMES FROM STAGE 1: APPRECIATING THE PROBLEM

Through such stage 1 processes, we discovered that the our dominant baseline assumptions and taken-for-granted patterns of thinking in action could be depicted as follows:

- Taken-for-granted assumption: South Asians would have low awareness of risk factors for CHD.
- Ensuing taken-for-granted choice of action: That if health care professionals improved their awareness of risk factors, such as through giving them information during our consultations, they could change their behaviour and therefore reduce their risk of CHD (an assumption we later found to be dominant in primary-care research literature).
- Taken-for-granted assumption underpinning that choice: Reduction in the prevalence of CHD would also result from more effective dissemination of information to other primary-health care professionals who could utilize this in their dealing with high-risk South Asian men.

SS/JB: 'Little did we know how subsequent stages of CRAR would challenge and change this highly rationalist position!'

SW: 'In this kind of research, such emerging insights and questions stirred by processes of critically reflexive dialogue are taken back into the messy world of practice. There, we start noticing our normal ways of thinking, seeing and acting, and whether, how and with whom we reflect on these. We start exploring emerging insights with others, in ways that invite challenge.

'We begin to see what it may mean not to "extract data" from people as if it were separate from relationships and the context in which understanding is located. Instead, we co-inquire, using dialogue that seeks to minimize power differences, while paradoxically enabling critical reflection on these. And we write, draw, talk into recorders, capturing things that we think may be of importance in all this, or perhaps not, but dating entries and depictions of our 'coming-to-know' processes as we go on. At the beginning, this discipline is challenging, and it is difficult to know whether and why such jottings matter. But later, this data becomes as important as any other, such as interview material, in terms of substantiating claims for challenging and changing our practice – a key quality concern in such work. As the saying goes, "the fish does not know water until it is out of it."'

JB/SS: 'This research approach also encourages you to think about these things from diverse perspectives: for us, this meant as South Asian women, as members of extended and diverse communities, and as primary-care professionals working within health care delivery systems.'

SW: 'Part of my role was to offer examples of how the core team could become critically reflexive co-inquirers in their everyday practice, in ways that stayed manageable yet fruitful, in terms of everyday pressures. In other words, this approach offers a way of being and thinking, that does not create an artificial distortion between research and practice.'

STAGES 2 AND 3: FOCUSING/FRAMING INQUIRY IN CONTEXT AND BROADENING/DEEPENING UNDERSTANDINGS OF THE INQUIRY QUESTION

We condense and merge these two stages, to focus explicitly on issues of relevance to this book.

JB/SS: 'Using principles of boundary critique (Midgley et al. 1998), we tried to ensure that participants reflected the diversity that characterizes the South Asian communities in Brent and Harrow (for example, social class, age, gender, religion). We met with South Asian patients (16), relatives and friends (22), members of South Asian Community Organizations (4) and primary-care team members (6). We used semi-structured interviews, informal conversation and collaborative inquiry groups. When the latter met, we expressed our hope to keep meeting over the course of the project, bringing in others as things emerged.'

SW: 'This "networked inquiry" approach, with permeable group boundaries, distinguishes CRAR from cooperative inquiry approaches where processes of trust and continuity membership are given more weight (Bray et al. 2000; Reason and Hawkins 1988; Heron 1996). In complex systems and communities of practice in today's world, coming and going is the norm. The challenge is how to sustain and deepen possibilities for reflective learning and change across diverse communities of practice over time, space and boundary.'

The first workshop resulted in the following three questions to underpin the next stage of the project:

• What do you understand about coronary heart disease and its risk factors?

- Do you believe that these risk factors *can* be changed or influenced and if so how?
- What experience do you or your friends, family, colleagues have of doing so?

JB/SS: 'Throughout, we stayed alert to how South Asian men might feel about opening up to us as women, but also as health care professionals and in a number of instances, as their own GPs. We shared the same ethnicity with many of our co-inquirers and we did not know how this would influence the quality of dialogue. When we began Stage 3, we tended to ask our questions opportunistically as part of our ordinary surgery consultations, but we were anxious that patients were only telling us what we wanted to hear. However, in the collabora-tive inquiry meetings, co-participants seemed more relaxed about sharing their true thoughts and beliefs. They told many powerful stories about personally encountering CHD, and why they had or had not changed. On the whole, we felt that our common ethnicity was an asset in this research, improving its quality as well as the depth of insights surfaced by the process.'

STAGE 4: REFRAMING/REFOCUSING INQUIRY

In our next workshop, we worked with the many outcomes generated from Stages 2 and 3.

SW: 'My role at this stage was mainly to help draw out the core team's learning, including critical incidents and narratives, relating to what had happened since our last workshop. Throughout, I would raise questions about how their inquiry thus far seemed to relate, or not, to the core team's baseline assumptions, and intentions for primary-care practice. Transcripts of interviews and the co-inquiry groups provided reference points for dialogue around particular themes, such as awareness, as explored further below. These workshop dialogues were also themselves transcribed.'

This workshop marked the first of more structured processes of data reflection, analysis and preparation for 'playback' of data, with which different groups of co-inquirers could now engage.

JB/SS: 'This process helped us to recognize key themes, and patterns, and to explore these across the experiences of each of the core team members. We explored their possible mean-ings in a wider social and cultural context, and for professional primary-care practice, as will be illustrated below. We kept connecting what was surfacing to our various practice fields. For example, what did emerging insights mean for how we enacted our roles, individually and with others? We could challenge and support each other in thinking about contradic-tions and paradoxes related to what it might mean to make a difference to CHD under the conditions within which we were each working.'

SW: 'Team members' explorations of their interpretations of their findings from different role perspectives opened new lines of inquiry. Stories from everyday practice and living as members of different South Asian communities emerged. These help us problematize things that had been outside of their previous topographies of attention and action – and were at risk of slipping back out of view. Throughout, we documented perceived commonalities, differences and tensions in what was being presented. In keeping with a "grounded systemic approach", I suggested that they consider the tensions that they were surfacing as not merely negative, or positive, but rather, when and how such tensions were disabling or enabling in specific contexts for action. And how they might influence or release flows of energy and participation that were more congruent with their practice and research intentions? For example, it is not "wrong" to provide evidence to patients from traditional CHD research, such as about dietary influences. But if this is *all* that is done what possibilities for stimulat-

ing and supporting behavioural change may be missed? If we only focus on *disseminating* evidence, what evidence do we also deny ourselves? What other questions and issues might usefully be explored during, say, a ten-minute surgery consultation: for example, to learn more about how and why risk-prone lifestyle practices are sustained in that patient's context? This requires a shift from conceptualizing our roles as "knowing professionals" to being professionals who are able to "not know" and co-inquire with others, in ways that are experienced as authentic.'

Tensions and dilemmas around giving, gathering and co-generating information will always be at play in consultation situations. But how do we stay reflexive about dominant patterns across our choices over time that then begin to restrict the field of possibility? We continue to explore and ground the implications of this particular dynamic below.

IMPACT AND OUTCOMES FROM STAGES 2–4

The CHD learning trajectory

JB/SS: 'By this stage, it was more and more evident to us as health care professionals that the "low awareness problem", as we had initially framed it, was of our own making. We were struck by the sophisticated in-depth understanding of South Asians and health professionals, of CHD risk factors with respect to stress, diet, exercise, smoking, alcohol, and obesity!'

For example, South Asians associated stress with:

- racism
- pressures to succeed academically and financially
- over-working, often in family-owned businesses
- intergenerational conflict
- absence of stress-relieving strategies, such as seeing the value of leisure time and exercise for reducing stress.

But whereas patients had elaborate understandings of stress and gave it a high priority, health care professionals did not. We wondered whether we too were downplaying patients' accounts about stress in their lives. As GPs, we began to listen differently to such accounts, and be more attentive to possibilities for action that lay within patients' own stories.

The complexity of South Asians' 'lay knowledge' was also very apparent around diet and exercise. In contrast, the health care professionals emphasized the impact of risk factors – rather than the reasons for the behaviour. We began to ask 'How *do you* think these risk factors could be changed?', 'What experience do you have of doing so?' and 'How could we help?' These questions opened up worlds that had been invisible to us previously, in terms of our practice choices. For example, critical coronary events involving family members or friends were often cited as having changed South Asians' lifestyles. One patient reported how shocked she was to find so many South Asian patients in the coronary care unit with her father. We too had encountered a cardiologist during the course of this research who said that any Asian man over the age of 30 presenting to Casualty with chest pain was at risk of CHD.

We began to experiment more with our ten-minute consultation with South Asian high-risk patients. We became more proactive about using family consultation positively to encourage change, based on emerging evidence here of the impact of peer and family pressure/support on changing behaviour.

The trajectory related to living and learning new forms of inquiry

SW: 'Any such project raises issues relating to power dynamics and difference, especially in the context of forming new potentially long-term relationships. For example, how could I stay inquiring about whether and when I was riding roughshod over their meanings and social learning? Was the quality of our own dialogue and inquiry such that we could trust that we would test each other's assumptions, and risk challenge of each other? Were we staying sufficiently alert to absences, silences, "unspoken knowns", and patterns and processes in the "spaces between ourselves", not just with others? How did we stay reflexive not only about our own membership in this system, but about the wider system dynamics that would be impacting upon this field of inquiry? We all struggle with how best to open up exploration of such things. Although to do so is congruent with the approach, it can also feel potentially intrusive, and impositional, in the living of it. What does it mean to stay respectful of how participatory practice does not guarantee freedom from oppressive or stuckness? (Cooke 2001; Weil et al. 1996). To illustrate, one member of the core team voiced at this stage the possibility of doing a questionnaire about awareness of CHD risk factors. This suggestion came, after spending a morning sharing insights from Cycles 2–4, and moving into rich territories for deeper knowing and knowing differently. I had to take a deep breath. What to say, how, whether to say it? Fortunately, the tape recorder had been on. I suggested we all listen to a replay of the previous ten minutes.'

JB/SS: 'This helped us to become more acutely aware of how quickly we can lose sight of opportunities to re-story our practices, and undermine the fragility and power of what was opening at this point. We too were also hesitant about what to do at this point. Susan opened up the space we needed to voice our own concerns about such a retreat from the exciting (yet challenging) cusp that was only just coming into view.'

SW: 'As we built confidence in the robustness of these processes and the culture we were jointly evolving, the depth and quality of our work could also develop, as well as our capacity to navigate differences at times of tension. As is likely to be clear by now, CRAR does not operate as a neatly sequential or uni-directional cycle. It works recursively in stages and cycles. It enables co-inquirers to reframe and refocus, and both broaden and deepen understandings, while learning in the midst of action in ways that take account of emerging insights.'

JB/SS: 'To illustrate, referring back to Figure 14.1, we were now "officially progressing" to Stage 5. We had revised our research questions and were now planning for more insightful research and practice actions. We were more explicitly focusing on the implications of our learning and action at different levels (individual, group, organizational) in keeping with what is seen to distinguish "third wave action-research approaches". We were considering intended and unintended impacts of our own choices, as well as those in different parts of the primary-care system. At the same time, we were still developing our appreciation of the starting problem, and problematizing it, using multiple dialogues and perspectives for doing so (Stage 2). We were also more alert to subtle but powerful nuances of difference arising from appreciating this problem in different contexts (Stage 2) and the possibilities being revealed for more insightful practice with high-risk patients and the community – and ourselves as a core team.'

SW: 'In a "quick fix" oriented world, learning is more and more seen as something that can be predicted, packaged and delivered. Sustaining reflective-learning processes at any level of depth can become more and more counter-cultural. However, prolonged engagement in such inquiry practices help us to trust that living and learning our way through the mixed feelings that change can engender is often worthwhile, and in the ways that we often claim matter.

'Unlike in traditional research, this approach also enables us to take account of complexity and the impact of engaging with diverse perspectives flexibly throughout. To have stayed entrapped in a pre-determined design would have de-railed the possibility of reflective learning.'

JB/SS: 'Susan was still formally in the position of "inside outsider" and critical friend to the core team. But the sense was increasingly of being "alongsiders" to each other. She too was learning about what it may mean to use a CRAR approach in relation to an actual medical risk, within a diverse yet specific cultural context. She was working with GPs for the first time on a problem that impacted directly on South Asians' lives. We were all beginning to appreciate better how in primary care, disseminating evidence is not enough. How do we also seek out "evidence" from within our own fields of practice, in ways that enable us to know differently and better in the fields we navigate daily? Different choices for action can flow from different ways of seeing the world, and relating to others. But the simple power of such insights can be hard to catch sight of without having support in standing back, in relation to what is emerging from co-inquiry-based research and practice.

'Both prospectively and retrospectively we were appreciating at this stage the principle of having "critical friends" and multiple-reference groups who had challenged us along the way, as well as our research journals and the growing pile of flips, transcripts and notes.'

STAGE 5: PLANNING FOR INSIGHTFUL ACTIONS (AND REVISITING OF STAGES 1, 2 AND 3)

As a result of interweaving learning trajectories, related to CHD and to the processes of learning and change such research can support, we now changed our questions:

- How many people co-inquirers knew within their immediate or extended family who had suffered or died from CHD?
- Why did they think that they had developed CHD?
- What impact did this have on co-inquirers' own lifestyle or other choices?
- Had they changed?
- What barriers to change did they perceive?
- What had helped and what would help them to change?
- Were they happy to continue as a co-inquirer in this study?
- Did they perceive any gender issues relating to how they sought health care?

JB/SS: 'We took our new questions out into the community and now included women. We better understood that we neglect the social and cultural context in reducing CHD at our peril! We met with 12 male patients in our surgery, 8 people participating in a local community-centre exercise class for South Asians, 30 people in a local community prayer group, 16 men and women from a Hindu temple religious group and 12 worshippers from a local mosque.'

In our ongoing patients group, to which new men were also added, we asked people to use a family tree to trace and tell stories of how CHD had impacted on their own families. In the community settings, we explored peoples' expectations of GPs' roles (actual and potential) in community-based interventions – a most unsettling but illuminating process! South Asians appreciated our coming out of our surgeries and our normal working roles, and shared far more with us than we expect they might have, if we had talked to them in our offices.

We also began to involve our practice partners and other work colleagues in this inquiry, sharing what had happened and questions that were now emerging for us. This process created opportunities for reflective dialogue and active co-inquiry over time, as the team began to talk to patients differently.

In our groups, we also encouraged participants to think explicitly about co-inquiry processes, and how they might relate these to their own lives. These sessions were all taped. In addition, we provided each group with summaries (either written or verbal) of what had emerged from other groups to support and stimulate their own reflections, dialogue and actions, with each other and others.

IMPACT AND OUTCOMES FROM STAGE 5

The following story from Stage 5 captured something quite powerful about how taken-for-granted topographies of attention and action can change through the evidence of co-inquiry-based research and practice. One team member, a GP, went into the local community centre for one of her group meetings and encountered a high-risk patient. She had only recently arranged a third appointment for him with the surgery's dietician. Once again, he had failed to show up. But here, in the centre, she found him hard at work on the exercise bike in the gym. She expressed her amazement, asking him whatever was he doing. He replied that he was exercising. She challenged him about not keeping his appointments. He expressed his amazement in return: 'My wife does all the cooking, so why should I go to the dietician?'

SW: 'We all felt excited about this story. I could also help in focusing the team's attention on stories like this – critical incidents – that offer evidence of alternative futures for primary care in the here and now. The dominant culture often dismisses story as something peripheral to what is learned from research: "just an anecdote". However, the process of systematic inquiry and documentation over time enabled this story to come into the foreground. Critical incidents if honoured, can speak volumes, if we only stop to listen to them. The quality and extent of his knowing in action was invisible to the surgery: but not when looked upon from another angle. The field of possibility for action, choice and co-inquiry with others was continuing to expand.'

JB/SS: 'We had also encountered by this stage the cumulative impact that participation in this study was having on patients and community members participating as project co-inquirers. Throughout, we had summarized insights, questions and outcomes from across our various groups. But now we began to see what we were doing being "mirrored" by them. For example, some of them spoke about noticing patterns relating to changing or failing to do so, in themselves and others with respect to unhealthy lifestyle factors. They shared stories of trying to influence their family, friends and work colleagues. They told about asking others to reflect on what they did and why, if they knew people who had died? We began to appreciate how involving them in the inquiry groups, and being genuine about wanting to be challenged by them, had itself generated reflective learning and practice in everyday contexts. They too were understanding better how awareness does not necessarily change behaviour or help them learn from within the lived situations and circumstances of their families and communities. This was a very exciting moment in the research!

'These experiences encouraged us to engage the community more actively in the stories of this research through Sunrise Radio and Channel East breakfast television show. We have also found ways of involving other local policy makers and practitioners, such as through

participation in different local efforts to reduce CHD. We have worked with others to increase the sensitivity of services to diversity, for example by introducing an "exercise on prescription" scheme at the local leisure centre. In doing so, we were able to address some culturally sensitive issues, such as offering "women-only" exercise classics. We have liaised with physiotherapists in the cardiac rehabilitation programme, in hopes that they will also work differently with families and friends who visit people in that unit.

STAGES 6 AND 7: CRITICAL REFLECTION IN/ON ACTIONS AND COMMUNICATING LEARNING AND CHECKING OUTCOMES

JB/SS: 'A final group workshop enabled us all to work with the full range of insights and outcomes from Stage 5. For example, Susan supported us in "working our data" to ensure we were taking full account of what South Asians thought hindered or supported change in lifestyles. We scoured transcripts and our research journals to actively honour the different impacts of the study on us as individual GPs, as health care professionals working within members of the South Asian community, and as local policy makers. We could now better appreciate our own learning trajectories, as professionals who had set out to reduce CHD in South Asian men and the South Asian communities; and for others, such as our local Primary Care Groups who have a role in implementing coronary heart disease policy as outlined by the National Service Framework.

'We began to raise questions about dominant assumptions and status quo practices, and how these are reproduced by systems, despite illusions of "radical new practice". For example, having a blanket policy on health promotion can be taken as a "big bang solution" to community-based health. However, this is likely to only continue to serve the needs of the "worried well". Primary-care strategies that are focused on working with patients in their family, cultural and community contexts require very different uses of resources and alternative concepts of organization and "outreach". Investing in new buildings or new centres may distract our attention from what may matter much more in making a difference.'

Two of us (JB and SS) then followed up this workshop to work in depth with all material, now covering numerous flipcharts and pages. We systematically reviewed interview transcripts, research logs and documentation from previous workshops.

SW: 'This was when the documentation of original assumptions proved so powerful. Examples of insights such as those arising from the story of the man on the exercise bicycle can all too easily shift to the background within our usual "topographies of attention and action": dismissed as serendipity or "just a story". In traditional research, only interview data would be given weight. These other forms of knowing are seldom neat. They can threaten our sense of order, so we dismiss them, or push them back into the shadows, saying in traditional research, for example, that this does not "fit" the design. But the wealth of material dated over time helped the core team to grant a different currency to stories. They also came to value the extent to which they had re-storied their own practice, and the patterns of their relationships, attention and action in relation to patients, the community and primary care itself.'

JB/SS. 'We were now ready for our "literature review", and to adopt a very different stance towards published work than we might have earlier. The full importance of our review is beyond the scope of what we can report here: however, suffice it to say, it enabled us to value how differently we were now seeing, knowing and acting within the primary-care field. Not surprisingly, like the core team at the beginning, we found a dominant preoccupation in

primary-care research literature with how best to communicate to patients the evidence from traditional research about the causes of CHD. We found *no* documented research that sought to understand from the perspective of South Asians themselves, their awareness and perceptions of CHD and its risk factors, or what kinds of change strategies supported by primary care interventions and resources they thought might make a difference.'

This project has not only helped to redress such gaps. It has also generated knowledge and evidence that has made a difference to our own practice, and the behaviours of patients.

Closings and openings

Health care professionals often turn to evidence-based medicine to guide decision making and everyday practice. Such research increasingly informs policy decisions and assessments of quality practice. However, evidence-based approaches do not in themselves address the complex uncertainties and dilemmas that we may face in most fields of practice. But that they can do so is an idea gaining increasing sway in many different fields. Is this a case yet again of what Schon (1971) called the defensive retreat to certainty in the face of growing uncertainty?

In medicine and primary-care practice, there are few documented examples of what it may mean to generate socially robust evidence, based on alternative understandings of research quality and rigour. We hope that we have reduced this imbalance, in our presentation of this study carried out on the basis of epistemological commitments that are not the norm in this field.

However, we made claims at the outset of this piece to have gone further than this. We have been exploring research principles that may help us to revise and to re-vision professional practice and choice in community contexts – as an ongoing process of action-based co-inquiry. In doing so, we are raising questions about the limited and potentially damaging effects of restricting current notions of evidence to that which is associated merely with traditional forms of 'high-quality research', such as randomized blind control trials.

The sharing of stories with others throughout this project has galvanized the energy and attention of many others. Our narratives have inspired conversations that we could never have envisaged. We have learned how story begets story, strengthened by our sustained inquiry over time. We see over and over again how analytic reports anaesthetize us to our own knowing and meaning-making, and how neatly sanitized bullet points distort our own lived sense of being in a complex world.

We note that we cannot put a neat boundary around what we have done as merely a piece of research. Instead, our experience of this project has generated a way of 'living life as inquiry' in our everyday practices and relationships with others (Marshall 1998; Weil 1999). This has been true for all members of the team. We only hope this will continue to have a ripple effect on those who participated in the inquiry process, and on the quality of our own practices and partnerships with others.

We might have called this chapter 'Coming to know collaborative inquiry-based practice as a way of life'. We have certainly come to know better that uncertainties cannot be easily resolved, and that nothing stays the same. We have learned that unsettling our taken-for-granted topographies of attention and action is anything but easy. We also know that new forms of dialogue, co-inquiry and attention can reveal alternative choices for learning and action in primary care. We keep learning how tentative and partial our knowing always

is, and always will be. And we will never be free of contradiction in our practice or our systems. However, we can create new forms of capacity to learn from these in ways that reduce the wastage of precious resources, and that might make a difference in peoples' lives.

To assert such things is itself challenging. But as anyone who fishes knows, the same place on the river is never the same place. That is what keeps us going back there each time, always in hope of creating the possibility of a different story. And hopefully, not another one, about the chance that, yet again, got away.

Many thanks to the following for their guidance and assistance in the development of this chapter: Laurie Bidwell, Carlis Douglas, Jo Ellis, Emrys Jenkins, Judi Marshall, Michael Powell, Martin Rhodes, Dianne Walsh – and Ian and Anne for their encouragement, expert support and patience.

Notes

1. The other two General Practitioners (GPs) were Tayyaba Sherif and Goodi Irani (GI) and the link manager was Bharti Sapra. We wish to acknowledge here previous presentations of this Project at the Royal College of General Practitioners' Inner Cities Conference, May 1999 by GI and SW; the WeLReN June, 1999 and 2000 conferences by the full team; the Annual University Department of General Practice Conference, February 2000 by JB, SS and GI, and at the Annual Primary Care Ethnicity Project Conference, 1999, 2000 by JB, SS and GI.
2. Susan's involvement and this project overall were made possible by WeLReN, the West London Primary Research and Development network, which provided funding under the Ethnicity Project and also introduced us to a range of research strategies, including action research.
3. The SOLAR Centre, founded in 1996 by SW at UCN, in the UK, is concerned with social and organizational learning as action research. It is developing alternative theories of research practice to support knowledge co-generation and action-based co-inquiry to support learning, innovation and change in complex systems.
4. Ways of doing this that are less demanding of those involved are also being evolved at SOLAR, such as through the use of learning histories at MIT (Kleiner and Roth 1998). The use of storyboards is also being developed to create new insights at the interface between users' and practitioners' stories and those at other levels of systems, and to focus action-based co-inquiry around 'logjams' emerging from these connections. Such work is currently being undertaken in relation to realizing social policy intentions in complex social and organizational systems (Weil and Samson-Barry 2000).

15 *Action Learning at the London Borough of Ealing*

Stella Binns and Ian McGill

In this chapter we show how action learning is utilized for staff and organizational development in the London Borough of Ealing. In particular, we convey specific examples of how staff have applied their learning from the experience of action learning to their work and how this has benefited the organization. This entails taking very specific and concrete examples in their action learning process and asking the question: what was it in the action learning process that enabled them to transfer that learning into their working practice? How did the organization benefit?

We have asked participants who have had a high level of involvement with action learning to elicit their learning and applications to the workplace. These participants experienced the process, initially, as part of an in-house management development programme (MDP) and then became members of a set designed to develop facilitators so that the authority was not dependent upon external facilitators.

Stella Binns was the coordinator of an action learning programme for the London Borough of Ealing from 1999 to 2001. Ian McGill was one of the original external facilitators later invited to develop interested staff in becoming in-house facilitators as well as sharing in the creation of the accreditation programme at City University.

Introducing action learning into the London Borough of Ealing in 1995 was a way of bringing reflective learning into the organization as part of a new management development programme. The aim of the programme, promoted and supported by the Chief Executive, was to support managers in the face of extensive organizational and cultural changes affecting the Council, like other local authorities in the 1990s. Action learning could provide managers with the opportunity to take time out, reflect on their practice and explore new ways of managing: to 'see the wood for the trees'. It would help them get the most from the management development programme by supporting, reinforcing and developing their learning. And because it was much more than problem solving, it would give them transferable skills, and make them better managers.

How did it work?

Ealing adopted the model of action learning originated by Revans (1980) and developed by McGill and Beaty (1995), and Gaunt and Kendall (1985) amongst others. Action learning is a highly structured form of group working. It provides a 'safe' environment for learning and development to occur in the context of the person's work. For Ealing the action learning 'set' consists of six to eight participants, with a facilitator, who meet regularly (approximately

monthly) for four to six hours over a period of around six months. Thereafter the sets may, and often do, decide to continue meeting on a self-facilitated basis.

Individual set members take it in turn to have personal time in the set where they can 'present' an issue, task or problem relating to their work. The role of the other set members is to help the presenter explore the issue deeply and identify appropriate action. They do this by questioning, clarifying, challenging and giving feedback in order that the presenter can find their own answers. It is not about giving advice or brainstorming; it is based on the assumption that the presenter has the personal resources and knowledge they need to find their own appropriate answers.

This is the 'content', or problem-solving part. Equally important is the reflection on 'process', which follows the presentation, for example: What happened during the presentation? What questions were useful or not useful? Was there rapport and empathy and how did this relate to the presenter accessing and exploring the issue? By identifying the process by which successful outcomes happen, members learn about what works and are able to use these skills again themselves and 'model' or teach them to others. Equally important, they learn about what doesn't work and a prime example of this in the set is advice giving which is something people naturally want to do to be helpful. In the early days of the set, this is a common occurrence and people must learn that rather than closing off the exploration with a piece of advice, open questioning enables the presenter to discover her own answers, appropriate to her own situation. The skilled facilitator needs to deal with this sensitively.

Learning for all within the set is linked to action and reflection on the action and learning for the presenter is linked to action in the workplace, which they will feed back to a future meeting, when it is possible to further reflect on the process.

What happened? – facts and figures

In the five years since it started, some 200 people have participated in action learning. Interim results from a recent evaluation show that:

- 52 per cent of respondents have continued to participate in a set after the initial six-month facilitated period.
- 95 per cent of respondents consider that action learning has partly or fully contributed to their effectiveness as a manager.

The following skills were identified as having been developed as a result of action learning:

Active listening and attending	95%
Reflecting back	76%
Rapport	66%
Assertion	38%
Empathy	57%
Questioning	66%
Managing conflict, challenge and confrontation	43%
Giving and receiving feedback	81%
Awareness of group process	76%

The following learning was identified:

Awareness of relationships at work	62%
Communication	62%
Awareness of self and others	71%
Awareness of process	52%
Awareness of transferable skills	67%

Other benefits gained by participants were, above all, networking and information exchange. The sets also became safe places to be vulnerable and to gain support from the group.

When asked what might hinder continued participation in action learning the most commonly suggested factors were lack of time and lack of support from the manager.

Facilitation

Initially the facilitators were two external consultants and one internal facilitator. As more people went through the management programme some became interested and involved in developing skills as a facilitator. This interest, and the identified cost savings that would be obtained by having a team of in-house facilitators, led eventually to a planned facilitator development programme. The facilitators were themselves facilitated in a set by an external facilitator (one of the authors of this chapter). At the same time, each facilitator started to facilitate a set, initially with an experienced facilitator and then on their own.

This facilitator set met in two ways, first with their external facilitator for their continuing development and supervision, and subsequently as a self-facilitating group becoming a force for developing and promoting action learning practice. Thus not only were they active and consciously developing as facilitators but they also met regularly for business meetings in order to discuss and develop good practice and organization. Some examples of this practice included:

- *Steps to becoming a facilitator – code of practice:* This document identified five steps for the would-be facilitator: (1) to have been a member of a set for at least six months; (2) to co-facilitate with an experienced facilitator; (3) when ready, to facilitate alone; (4) to take on a new co-facilitator and be their mentor; (5) to engage in appropriate study to develop a wider appreciation of theories and practice in facilitation through an accreditation programme developed with City University (London).
- *Outline programme for two-day start-up event:* Derived from pooling best practice we wrote a programme, which can be used by facilitators. This includes a short introduction with slides for a large group and a programme for the set process.
- *Person specification for new facilitators:* To give guidance to would-be facilitators and assist in the selection process.

THE FACILITATORS' STORIES

In addition to the in-house development some of the facilitators began a programme designed to give further recognition of their role by accreditation. In 1999/2000 a group of eight facilitators completed the Independent Learning Module from the City University's

MSc in Continuing Education and Training. This was the first qualification programme specifically for action learning facilitation. In compiling this chapter we approached facilitators who had undertaken the City University programme. Each was asked to describe, in personal accounts given below, what they did in facilitated action learning sets that they gained personally and what the organization gained. The emphasis is upon personal improvement and/or transformation for themselves and colleagues in the organization.

Ann – really working with process

My starting-point was to recognize the crucial role of the start-up event in preparation for action learning sets. The start-up event supports my role as facilitator in building trust within the set and establishing the group identity. In addition, this particular start-up event emphasizes the important distinction and relationship between task/content and process. When designing the programme I was looking at exercises which would build trust and teamwork; and I chose the exercise 'Moving the Piano', an energizer involving a shared activity (see Box 15.1).

BOX 15.1

Exercise: Moving the Piano

Summary	Energizer involving a shared activity
	Attention Switcher
	Cooperative energizer
Materials	None
Timing	Up to 20 minutes
Procedure	1 Have participants form into groups of four or five.
	2 Ask each subgroup to imagine that they have to move a grand piano from one side of the room to the other.
	3 Give them five minutes to plan how they would achieve the task, taking into account the different group members.
	4 Ask the groups in turn to act out their task.
Commentary	It is possible to ask people to actually move an object, but it is important to be aware of the health and safety implications in doing so.
Variations	The object to be moved can be varied (for example, you might choose an elephant, a tree or a motor bike).

Source: Exercise taken from 'Icebreakers', Kirby (1993), contributed by Di Kamp

First of all I tried out the exercise on my peer facilitators set to see how it would work. The outcome was that it was felt to be a very useful exercise and we agreed that those of us who were about to run start-up events would all use the same exercise in order to have a comparison.

Those facilitators who used the exercise found that each set carried out the task in a completely different way. For example, one set started out discussing a variety of physical methods of lifting such as pulleys and trolleys; another role-played it and enthusiastically acted the part. Another set, whilst entering into the fantasy of it, elaborated the fantasy and imagined a super-light elephant and one set member suggested delegating the task to the caretaker.

Although all did the task differently, the outcome appeared to be the same. The task brought people together to work cooperatively and with great fun (energizer and mood shifter) but more importantly when unpacking what had happened it was a very useful way of demonstrating the use of process in a non-threatening and experiential way. People were able to reflect on what they had done and why they had acted in the way they did. For example, one participant recollected that taking charge and directing was her role both within her family and at work and added that perhaps she needed to be more self-aware around this aspect. She wondered how that might conflict with the need to enable her staff to grow and 'stand on their own two feet'. Another person said that although she had cooperated with the task because I was the 'teacher', inside she was 'cursing' me for getting her to do 'bloody silly things' which made her look foolish and went on to reflect that she often was at odds in how she presented and how she was feeling. In subsequent presentations she talked about her lack of confidence.

This activity, in demonstrating process over content, was a revelation for me as I have struggled long and hard to grasp its meaning or purpose over the years. For me, it demonstrates experiential learning very graphically. Also I realize the method of completing the task is determined by the nature of the individuals making up the team. People's models of the world are based on their values and experiences and their individual ways of learning make each person's contribution unique. When I bring together combinations of unique individuals I always get a unique team and this perhaps explains how each set is unique. This start-up event is also classic team-building material and applies to any work situation where people can understand what contributes to the way they interact with others. This awareness has added to my managerial skills.

Meera – how action learning has transformed my practice

My project was based on understanding the role of action learning within the context of learning and development in the organization.

With this in mind I read up on the theory of learning organizations because this was of particular interest to me. I used examples from two main pieces of research (Newman 1996 and Clutterbuck 1994). Then I considered where Ealing was in terms of being a learning organization and looked at the role of action learning within that and finally looked at how the facilitator programme could be developed in terms of delivering action learning more widely. I also based my project on experience from the one-to-one work that I do (advising potentially redundant staff on job opportunities), plus some issues that came out of facilitating action learning sets.

What I discovered was that there are many strands within Ealing that work towards encouraging us to think about our continuing learning. I looked at Investors in People (IIP) status and how that fits in with the corporate strategy; I looked at the appraisal system in terms of encouraging personal development plans, and so on. There may have been gaps

where employees don't have appraisals or even supervision and are effectively blocked from training. I then looked at making a case for other developmental activities that would enable employees to consider their own development – important if we were to consider Ealing a learning organization.

From a personal point of view, I found that I gained tremendously from action learning because its format focuses on questioning which opens up issues for the presenter. Above all, it has enabled me to think critically and to think about how I phrase questions. In my job role particularly, it is very easy to fall into a help mode – people are distressed and it is really hard not to try and rescue them. Action learning addresses this particular issue in the role of the facilitator who is there to keep the set on track and not prop it up. Compared with five years ago, I am much less prescriptive and this is very much linked into all the things we are encouraged to do in the set process: I don't lead someone along a particular path; I create an environment where individuals take responsibility for their own actions, their own paths, their own lives.

Years ago I used to physically thrash out a skills profile form. (This is a template that guides people through a range of skill areas.) I used to spoonfeed them and suggest what individuals could write about their skills under each heading – very much a one-way process. I don't do that any more. I take people through that form with some guidance and I will give them another appointment a week on and ask them to come and see me with a first draft. That way they are already buying into part of the process, taking control and thinking about where they want to go and where the gaps are. That is much more beneficial first because it gives them the opportunity to think in their own time, and second, it enables them to focus on whether they want to work here, what they want to do and if they don't, what their options are. I make it clear that they must take ownership and responsibility for this process and really positively think what the outcomes are in the short, mid and longer term. This is a learning process with individuals taking responsibility for their own future development, through planning a career move and/or more training and development. Most people seem to be able to be enthusiastic about this.

I wouldn't have done this without being exposed to the action learning set process because it has taught me the skills of open questioning, reflecting back, the value of reflection and critical thinking and individuals taking responsibility for their own actions.

I thought that one way of expanding the possibilities for personal learning and development in an organization such as this would be to extend the opportunities to be involved in action learning to non-managers. I would love to see Ealing as a place where each employee really wants to buy into his or her own development. I am really enthusiastic about that – because primarily my role is about developing people and getting them to realize their own potential. We need structures and processes in place to realize that – we have tremendous qualities in individuals out there which if shared could then almost mirror the practice in other parts of the organization. Knowledge and experience could be shared and employees would not feel they had to go through hoops in order to get a basic bit of development opportunity.

Clover – learning through action learning

In early 1998, I joined the Facilitators Development Programme. The aim of the programme was to develop action learning skills within the organization. This would provide a pool of in-house facilitators who could be called on to facilitate action learning sets and other corporate events and activities.

My motives for joining the programme were twofold: first, my only other experience of

action learning was part of the corporate Management Development programme, which left me feeling 'I can do this better!' and second, action learning would consolidate and hone my skills.

However, very early on in the programme it became apparent that the skills I hoped to acquire were *not* going to be available through the traditional teaching methods, that is, teacher/student relationship – there were no lectures, hardly any notes and no grades. I was to learn through experiencing action learning.

I found this method of teaching very frustrating. There were no rights or wrongs, and although there was a need for a structured process, there was some flexibility within it. All that was happening, as far as I could see, was that at the end of each day, I was exhausted from having to grapple with the rudimentary skills of actively listening and phrasing probing questions – which were usually redundant when the presenter took a different track! – and at the same time having to be process conscious. And on top of all that, I was expected to be empathic!

And then one day, I presented an issue. Experiencing the role of a presenter put me in a different place. I was allowed to feel angry, frustrated and emotional, because they were my emotions. I experienced being challenged in a supportive, non-judgemental, empathic environment. At the end of my presentation I felt liberated. Through shedding my own perceptions and interpretations of the situation, I was able to focus on the issue and plan constructively about how to resolve the situation. This is the outcome of effective action learning.

McGill and Beaty (2001) suggest 'the most important aspect of action learning is the relationship between action and learning. We can learn about the world and about ourselves through reflection on past action. We can construct our future actions from our reflections on our learning.'

There are different types of facilitation required by the organization: first, the more 'formal' which is task oriented and time limited, and second, the more 'informal', which taps into a deeper level within the organization and which enables and empowers staff and which supports them in their learning and development. There is a place for action learning in an organization that wants to develop. In particular for my organization, the Government's Modernizing Agenda requires authorities to become more accountable to their stakeholders and engage in new and better ways of working, which will involve consultation, negotiation and agreement. The skills developed in action learning are all compatible with these challenges.

And how has my 'learning through action learning' benefited the organization? First, my presentation work on policy and strategy: I 'sell' policies in a different way. As opposed to telling people I now invite their reaction, the result being that they own the policy. Second, in terms of training I now share the learning experience instead of imposing a teacher–student relationship. I don't always know best! This mirrors the action learning process of trust, risk, open questioning, feedback and shared learning. Learning is about personal development, it is not about control.

My assignment for the accreditation programme was about the role of a facilitator. I drew upon my experiences of facilitating in different environments – action learning sets and formal organization events. I reviewed what went well and what didn't go so well and as a result have my 'black book' of best practice, based on experience. Top of the list is: maintaining integrity, being open and genuine, empowering set members to take responsibility for defining their own issues and learning, and defining and modelling action learning process and the relevant interpersonal skills, for example, rapport, empathy, active listening and so on.

I embarked on action learning with a very simple idea: 'I could do it better.' I wanted to acquire something without quite knowing what success looked like. Action learning is a very different animal to anything I had previously known. It is not about project management – you cannot develop a project plan, there are not always tangible outcomes, it is not a one-man band and it's not about control. It is primarily about risk, trust and enabling individuals to create their own personal development 'black books'.

John – thinking 'outside the box'

For me, getting involved in action learning meant thinking about what the word 'learning' might mean: what happens during a learning experience? Where and when does it happen? What interferes with it? Why do different people draw such different conclusions from the same event? I decided to use the critical reflection model of action learning (after Mezirow et al. 1990) to explore the argument that we construct experience to a greater or lesser extent, and to reach some conclusions about how useful the model was for personal development in a work context.

This led directly to a close encounter with philosophy. I learned that we filter events that happen out there until they fit the world, as we already understand it. In the process of making events fit our understanding we may, and often do, distort them. if I listen but for a few moments to rival politicians debating the implications of this or that event, I become aware of the lengths to which both individuals and groups will go to achieve a reassuring distortion.

It was necessary to undertake some critical self-reflection to try to understand how I manifested this behaviour. I made a series of presentations to fellow set members to try to expose my belief system and its impact on my learning and working practices. A little auto-biography was required.

From childhood, through adolescence and into adulthood, my feelings towards 'grown-ups' centred on contempt, mistrust, anger and disappointment. These feelings were balanced by a simultaneous desire to be acceptable to the grown-ups, on their terms if necessary. In general I filtered my experience of the grown-up world through a repressed rage. There were personal reasons for this, but I did not feel particularly exceptional. Most of my peers seemed to exhibit similar feelings. I revelled in the culture of youth protest, which grew through the 1960s, and identified strongly with popular icons of rebellion.

In middle age, a residual mistrust of authority persists, along with dissatisfaction with prevailing cultural values. The need for acceptance remains to some extent. These are the dominant perceptual filters through which I experience the world, and which inform many of my assumptions.

So, with this capacity for self-reflection how have I benefited from action learning, and how does this relate to my work practice?

Action learning has provided me with a space in an otherwise hectic working life to examine these filters, to understand how they might impact upon my experience, my capacity to learn and my behaviour. I also, regularly, ask myself what, if anything, I am going to do about it, and to consider what the answers to that terrifying question may be.

I no longer feel that there is any such thing as a stupid question. I ask them all the time and find that they are the most revealing questions of all. I have learned how to think 'outside the box', to walk around a problem and see it from different viewpoints. I have realized that I do not have to be especially clever to do this. I merely have to listen to others. I have learned how much fun, and how vitally important, continuous learning is.

Specifically, I have adapted my style in one-to-one supervision meetings with my staff. I have consciously tried to adopt a more developmental approach, by questioning colleagues more thoughtfully, and encouraging them to develop their own solutions rather than wait for me to supply one for them. From a professional viewpoint I feel able to lead (and be led by) fellow learners on occasional journeys out of their boxes and into the unknown. I am part of the struggle to create a genuine learning culture in the place where I work.

Sally – applying facilitation skills to successful team building

I got involved in action learning initially because it was a compulsory part of a management programme I was attending. I discovered how useful it was being with other people from different departments in such an open and disclosing atmosphere, learning about what was going on in other parts of the authority. Importantly I learnt that others had issues, which were similar to mine, and I built a lot of confidence from this because I could see that I wasn't different from anybody else. I became more aware of some valuable skills, which promote good communications and help get the best out of others.

However, although I was extending my awareness and insights, I knew that I wasn't making the best use of what I was learning. I was not taking it back as well as I could do to the workplace. My project for the MSc course module set out to address this by examining what could be done to apply the ethos and skills involved in action learning more consciously in my work practice.

A particular case study for the module was the merger of two teams, and looking at how I could effect that merger more successfully using skills and practices derived from action learning. In particular I considered the planning process – how we would join up and then how we would work together.

I described a specific example of how I used action learning methods in a planning day around the merger. I introduced an icebreaker exercise with the aim of building mutual understanding, trust and respect. We did exercises around unpicking what people were doing in their jobs and ended up with a much better shared understanding of people's roles. This also gave each individual an opportunity to contribute – an important principle of action learning.

I introduced exercises such as a value shield of work-related and personal issues – this provided an opportunity for people to reveal something of themselves – another trust-building and sharing exercise.

For parts of the day I got people to work in pairs – they picked names out of a hat so they weren't just working with someone they knew well; this broke down barriers and gave people a better understanding of each other.

Most importantly, I introduced a 'check-in' and 'check-out' – to create boundaries around the meeting and also to encourage each individual to say how they were feeling or just to contribute.

Finally I paid special attention to the environment and 'hygiene factors' by making it comfortable and making sure drinks, 'breakfast' and lunch were provided.

Having approached it with more conscious attention to the action learning framework and ethos, I think that the session was far more successful in terms of business outcomes – we achieved a lot in one day which could easily have been diverted into side issues; we kept on track, remaining focused and refreshed, and to some extent we addressed people's different styles. The work that people did in pairs achieved team building and a greater mutual understanding of each other's roles and issues.

Business outcomes were also positively developed in a project group I was managing for the department. We formed the group, melded together quickly and were very active and successful in our first major task. We also achieved a great deal of groundwork for communications policy – this was in part due to my improved management skills and conscious effort to bring in some of the action learning skills, for example, a modified check in/out and giving people the opportunity to contribute, instead of allowing individuals to dominate. I used a metaphor exercise to establish a common meaning for the 'communicating department' – the feedback from people was that this was really useful to achieve a shared understanding.

Having more awareness of the significance of the basic skills, for example, of listening, giving space, questioning, I found that my management has improved as a whole and meetings, appraisals, supervision and most communications with staff and colleagues have been more productive. This was probably derived from my experience of action learning as a set member and facilitator. In addition the MSc module prompted active application with the objective to improve.

Stella – tapping individual knowledge for the benefit of the organization

The more I became involved in facilitating action learning the more I realized that successful personal outcomes depend on someone exploring deeply their own assumptions and patterns of behaviour and through this to identify which, if any, of these need to be amended, changed or done differently. This is a major 'learning' part of action learning. Following the 'action' identified and carried out there will be more reflection and more learning. Embodied in this learning is also the learning about how the person accessed this knowledge in the group process. Both the content of the person's exploration and the process of developing the action plan are examples of 'tacit knowledge'.

I became interested in the idea of accessing tacit knowledge in terms of the benefit to the individual but also in terms of the benefit to the organization. Organizations, in theory, can gain some of the vast wealth of knowledge and skills locked up in the individual and revealed by action learning. And when I thought about how so much of this is revealed I realized that a major role is played by storytelling and metaphor.

At the start-up event that precedes joining an action learning set, we aim to establish rapport and trust, and start to develop action learning skills. The method used is to ask people to address two questions: 'Where have I been?' and 'Where am I now?' They go away with a sheet of paper and do a drawing, or text or diagram and return to tell their story. The outcome is invariably a fluent, compelling story peppered with metaphors. Then in the set meetings the presenter, when exploring their problem or issue, tells a story; they become enveloped in their story and they connect with it emotionally. They will sometimes seem to be in a semi-trance with a glazed look, unfocused, with deep breathing and long silences. The others listen, empathize and engage emotionally with the presenter.

What I gained from this is real clarity about the way that stories and metaphors are a powerful way of accessing tacit knowledge – this is the first step in transferring this knowledge back into the organization. I am very aware of this when running groups or meetings where it is important to elicit individual knowledge and experience and transform this into group meaning and understanding (for example, brainstorming). One example was in a planning meeting about launching a new service where we were able to create visionary language to describe what the service is and what opportunities it can provide for our customers.

In considering gains to the organization I make a distinction between actual and potential gains. An actual gain by one manager was how she demonstrates better interpersonal skills at work, another told me how she has run more effective team planning meetings by the use of action learning methods to build up the team role and establish trust, and another described how he was able to model and teach useful ways of dealing with customers such as establishing rapport, matching and mismatching, and appropriate language. Our evaluation (see p. 130 above) identified potential gains to the organization by having more managers with better confidence, self-awareness and understanding of people.

Conclusion

Action learning was seen in 1995 as a support to the then new management development programme. By the end of 2000 a group of experienced and skilled facilitators had emerged – we were the engine driving action learning forward – and it now has a life of its own outside of the management programme. Inside the space provided for facilitator development we discovered a wealth of creativity, which has benefited us individually and can have an impact on the organization.

Ann's description of the value of process over content and John's understanding of the use of critical reflection can help managers to extend their boundaries and challenge their constraints. Thinking 'outside the box' is both a metaphor for the individual and the organization. Clover found her personal development impacted on her managemeent style and both Sally and Meera demonstrated practical methods to empower staff – an active learning model rather than a passive instructing one. And Stella explored the capturing of tacit knowledge and keeping it within the organization to enrich it rather than lose it.

We have tried to show that organizations as well as individual managers can benefit from reflective learning practices such as action learning, if they want to. Our evaluation has shown that there have been benefits to individuals involved in action learning and the account above suggests benefits to the organization. The drawbacks have been partly cultural and partly practical. Culturally we are still a long way from acknowledging the value of ongoing development in the 'soft' management skills, or 'emotional intelligence' and practically we need to allow all managers time out from, what is for many, a highly pressurized work role. Ealing has supported action learning and provided funding for it; the reality for many middle managers is justifying to themselves as well as their managers, staff and colleagues that they are not on a 'skive'. The key for us is that action learning has motivated and inspired people – and Ealing like all organizations needs to be motivated and inspired in order to enable others.

Acknowledgements

A big thank you to Suzanne Binns, John Burgess, Sally Davies, Thelma McKay, Clover Rodriguez, Arvind Sandhu and Ann Wake, not only for their contributions to the material for this chapter but for their invaluable help and support during our joint discovery and experience of action learning at Ealing. They have been an inspiration.

16 *The Salford Cathedral Centre*

Joy Wanless

'Love thy neighbour as thyself' Matthew 22:39

The Cathedral Centre

The second of Jesus' greatest commandments is lived out daily in the Cathedral Centre where eighty clients per day are served by five paid management staff and a workforce of approximately sixty volunteers. Each volunteer works on average one shift per week of four hours. A management team of seven volunteers, drawn from the diocese and statutory and voluntary sector agencies, take responsibility for the strategic planning of this service.

The clientele they serve are the marginalized of society, the homeless and disadvantaged. The Centre staff aim to provide basic human requirements of food, clothing, hygiene and shelter, and above all the most needed commodity – *unconditional love*.

The Salford Diocese generously donates the Centre's premises. These comprise the basement of the Cathedral, with limited daylight entering through small high windows looking out onto a wall. A steep flight of concrete steps gives access to the Centre's facilities for cooking, dining, laundry, showering, recreation and medical care.

The facilitator

My first contact with the Centre was working as a volunteer counsellor with clients of the Centre. Relationships are as vital for the homeless as for all groups in society. My vocation is relationship counselling and the organization I work for as a volunteer, Marriage Care, was approached to provide this service for Cathedral Centre clients. I also work as a management trainer and supervisor. Having been awarded a MSc in management, which was achieved by action learning and research, I am committed to experiential learning.

It is a great tribute to the dedication of the already overburdened paid staff that they worked with me for two years to sow the seeds of a learning organization. They were motivated by their desire to offer best service to their clients and by the increasing necessity to be better equipped to meet the changing needs of their clients in an ever changing political, economic and social climate. We could not envisage at the start of our journey together the power which would be generated by these five core team members to exert influence in political and religious arenas.

Motivation for change

I perceived two factors contributing to the start of the Cathedral Centre's journey to becoming a learning organization. The greatest by far was the tremendous frustration experienced by the five paid staff in feeling increasingly inadequate in their work to promote their clients' efforts to live with dignity and have control of their life situations. This frustration fuelled their later work in exploring the political and economic arenas when becoming more involved in outreach. Outreach work, that is following work through with clients outside the Centre, acquired greater importance when a client with severe medical problems got 'lost in the system' when left unsupported. In one case, staff outreach support enabled her to receive necessary medical treatment and probably kept her alive.

The second factor which motivated staff to embrace change, which was much harder for the staff to concede, was their own frustration with their work roles: too much work, too little time to do it in and, only occasionally verbalized, a sense of isolation from other staff members. Might this be seen as a lack of control of their own life situation, the very thing they aspire to encourage in their clients? This incongruence between their expectations of themselves and their aspirations for their clients, once owned, fuelled their later work in exploring their own cultural and social arenas.

The Catalyst

In 1998, a MSc student (herein known as the 'Catalyst') who wanted to hear the voice of the marginalized explored the work of the Centre. The frustrations of the staff might still be unvoiced were it not for her intervention. She was given access to staff and clients to encourage each of them to tell their story.

An assumed expectation of the paid staff is that they also work voluntary hours in the Cathedral Centre, thus keeping in tune with the ethos of service and the spirit of the Centre. The Catalyst found herself volunteering to work in the Centre and thus validating her sincerity in the eyes of the workers. She earned their respect. This helped engage the staff in the process of change, which she and I later worked through with them.

No one conceived that her research would, in unlocking each contributor's story, enable much pain to be heard. This demonstrated strongly the power of unconditional listening, and supports change equation theory where momentum for change is fuelled when pain experienced is greater than resistance to change.

She perceived a need for the staff to be enabled to voice their feelings about their work and initially they approached me for supervision. For the staff this service mirrored that which they made available for their clients.

Establishing a learning environment

WORKING AS A GROUP

I provided individual supervision for the paid workers as this respected their culture of working as individuals. In order to make progress I suggested the best way forward was to meet as a group. This immediately raised a problem area that would recur frequently – time manage-

ment. More importantly, meeting as a group challenged their management and working styles, which were respectively reactive rather than proactive and autonomous rather than cohesive. The initial group meeting of four paid workers, Worker 'F', Worker 'C', Worker 'K', Worker 'A', was interesting both in terms of content and organization.

CONTENT OF INITIAL GROUP MEETING

In order for their needs to be expressed I wanted to establish an environment of trust, where each manager felt equal to and valued by others. I invited the workers to use imagery by drawing a picture to portray their immediate feelings. An image of an animal, drawn by Worker 'C', gave rise to lively, animated discussion. The range of interpretations, from a cuddly cat to a frightened rabbit, gave opportunity to discuss different perceptions of the same situation. The skill of active listening was encouraged and the facilitator modelled listening and reflection. The fact that the original image was of a frightened rabbit opened emotive dialogue that enabled the workers to begin to listen to each other. The content of this meeting was important as a starting-point for them to learn more about each other.

ORGANIZATION OF THE MEETING

For all workers to meet at the same time the Centre needed to be closed to clients. The staff volunteered their time without pay, and the meeting was held in the Centre's office. The phone was not switched off on the principle that clients come first. Interruptions did distract from the meeting. Anxious clients knocked repeatedly at the external door and staff answered them, if only to explain opening hours and the fact that the Centre was closed. These details are offered to give a taste of the culture where clients come first and availability is perceived as reacting to their demands and needs. Also, as it was rare for the workers to meet all together, time was taken for business issues, for example timetables and client problems. The workers deemed this meeting successful – it was 'good enough' in that they met together, the clients did not suffer from their absence and timetable issues were discussed. The input from the worker who portrayed the frightened rabbit was not fully valued and her needs were not resolved. Self-disclosure was an unfamiliar skill.

I shaped future meetings to begin with reflection on the previous meeting and end with an agreed agenda for the next meeting. This involved a worker taking responsibility for preparing items for the agenda and usually taking some action in consultation with others. The idea of consultation subgroups meeting together was fostered and reporting back was encouraged. This group of workers functioned by consensus management in theory, but in practice always looked to the same worker, Worker 'F', when decisions were needed. This worker, the founder member, was instrumental in initiating and opening the Centre and therefore held its history and the respect of the other workers.

Building for the future

In order to establish all workers as equal members in building a team from a group, I organized an away-day to revisit the vision of the Centre and root it in today's world. The group had grown to include two new workers and the Catalyst, eight of us in total. We invited the Catalyst to provide input on poverty in Salford today, part of her MSc research. We dreamt of

what we would like to be able to offer the clients. We constructed an image of the Centre today and devised goals for the future. This generated much enthusiasm and renewed us in our values and beliefs. We were encouraged by the scale of work being undertaken daily and began to recognize the volume of business. A SWOT analysis, exploring the strengths, weaknesses, opportunities and threats of the Centre, helped us conceptualize the work of the Centre in the wider environment. Opportunities were highlighted.

Either the Catalyst or myself offered management input at each stage to provide a theoretical base for the learning. Experiences from the Centre were offered by different workers as material to use to process the theory. One of these experiences was an example that is now referred to as 'The mushrooms', and never fails to bring a hysterical reaction when mentioned.

Mushrooms as a learning experience

A donation of mushrooms was offered to a Centre worker at the end of the day. It was unquestioningly and gratefully accepted. The vast volume of mushrooms had not been anticipated. The collection needed a van and a worker as driver. Packing and unpacking took time and energy. The short lifespan of fresh provisions required immediate preparation of the mushrooms. The limited storage space was oversubscribed. Mushrooms were served in a wide variety of recipes for as long as they stayed fresh. Everyone felt like they lived and dreamt about mushrooms for days. Importantly the staff resource used to manage the mushroom 'crisis' left the Centre understaffed.

The Catalyst was working as a volunteer on this shift and a violent incident between clients caused her distress. She felt unable to cope and felt unsupported by experienced staff. A client physically intervening in the violence in fact bailed her out. She found it difficult to voice her distress to the workers and her suppressed feelings inhibited her contribution to the group. I facilitated an open and honest discussion where her disclosure helped the workers to explore another perspective on the mushroom story.

This example helped the workers to explore their response to donations. They created a proactive policy where they produce a wish list of donations to circulate to parishes. This also helps address the donations at harvest time when they are often inundated with fresh produce that might exceed the storage space available. However in order to do this they first had to acknowledge their cultural belief that all donations should be gratefully received, in order to move towards a responsible policy to make the best use of donations. This example is offered to illustrate how a facilitator can encourage reflective dialogue, which may result in transformation of working methods and ideas. The need for a policy to address violent incidents in the Centre was also reinforced and noted for a future meeting.

Processing the learning

The learning takes place in a neutral environment. As a facilitator I always model disclosure. I offer a trigger input, usually management theory, on a topic relevant to the meeting, which has been agreed in advance. This stimulus encourages sharing in a non-threatening manner. The workers are generous in their disclosures and are committed to output because they contribute input and their emotive feelings complement factual details. The time structure

allows for reflective dialogue, an activity that is often sacrificed when time is short and pressures high.

Further away-days were structured to preserve the fundamental values whilst providing information and support to explore alternative strategies. A team-building exercise helped staff to appreciate their individual special talents and to begin to separate out roles and responsibilities. The relief of each person at not being responsible for everything was tremendous.

Culture

Interestingly, given time and space to share ideas, some of the workers returned repeatedly to frustrations with their own job performance. I encouraged them to explore social and cultural aspects of their work, which helped them to identify constraints to their work input. Once these were identified and partly resolved, energy was released to explore the wider environment and make progress politically and economically.

In trying to define the culture at a later away-day, it was agreed that the founder member of the Centre, Worker 'F', was regarded as the overall manager. She was involved in initiating, building and maintaining the Centre. Worker 'F' believed in consensus management and preferred shared responsibility for management of the Centre. She saw the kitchen as the heart of the Centre, the provision of food being a basic requirement.

When our learning process began, all staff were expected to work a number of shifts in the kitchen regardless of their other talents. The culture of service was rooted in the kitchen, reactive to the basic needs of the clients. Our reflective process of the illustration of a frightened rabbit at our first group meeting challenged this taken-for-granted assumption. Self-disclosure from Worker 'C' encouraged staff to explore other approaches to service and this opened the way to best use of talents, where experience and expertise could be valued and new perspectives could be explored. In turn this enabled the work of the Centre to develop.

CULTURAL ISSUES INFLUENCED BY STAFFING

Originally nuns staffed the Centre and the culture as described above was one of service. The mission was to live the Gospel by following Christ's commandment, 'love thy neighbour as thyself.' All donations, as demonstrated by the Mushroom Story were gratefully received – premises, food, clothes, and so on – and working hours were as long as the staff was physically able to provide the service.

As the mission grew, paid staff were employed to enable more hours to be offered. This was not viewed as a job but as a vocation similar to the nun's calling. As more specialized services were required by clients, staff were sought from different sectors. Worker 'C' had a nursing background. She shared the vision of the Centre, that is, service to those in need. However her own professional needs were rooted in the health service culture where ongoing professional development was a requirement for her professional validation. She did not feel as though her needs were understood. The frightened rabbit image was the first effective way of voicing her unease with the culture in what seemed to her a cohesive and otherwise satisfied group.

Worker 'B' was employed with a background of managing a care organization. Her management expertise had been highlighted as highly relevant to the team's needs. Her first

culture clash came when she realized contracts were based on trust rather than explicit documentation. The calibre of staff was high. Each manager was willing to learn from the others' values and beliefs. However the learning could be painful, self-disclosure being the pertinent skill to effect any change.

Socially I realized that the 'comfort blanket' of the team members most affected by the changes was the kitchen. Once the away-days became established and clients realized that the Centre was closed on these days and staff would not be available, we moved the venue to the kitchen and started the day with a shared brunch, shared in preparation and consumption, and a prayer service. This environment was much more conducive to work and change. The agendas for the days moved towards embracing a more responsible management style. This was partly necessitated by the requirements of funders and other stakeholders. As the work expanded, the Centre became more accountable to a wider range of stakeholders. These individuals and organizations contribute to the ongoing development of the Centre, through funding or other measures of support, for example providing premises or volunteers.

The communications worker

The part-time paid post of communications worker, fulfilled by Worker 'A', held the key to interfacing with the wider environment. Worker 'A' had a long history with the Centre, mostly as a volunteer. Having taken time out to work in other projects she developed rich experience of acquiring funds, an experience of much value to the Centre. Again the team meetings offered an environment conducive to her development as a team member. When her talents were valued and necessary structures put in place her work became proactive. Her skills and knowledge were harnessed once her contract was formalized and her hours increased, giving her the required 'permission' to expand her role.

Her frustrations led her to request that I facilitate a formal review of her post, for which I used the Appraisal Model. The affirmation she received from positive feedback was very motivating. She raised the team awareness of the requirements for funding applications and amazed the team with the amount of money that was available for bids. Her frustrations at not having the necessary documentation to respond effectively to bids were taken on board by the team and provided the agendas and time-frame for future away-days.

However, this aspect of the Centre's work, competing for money in a commercial environment, is most alien to the Centre's culture. It is a constant battle to keep other team members on board with funding requirements. This area of voluntary work has probably changed most in recent years. There is currently an expectation that voluntary organizations should contribute to their funding costs or meet the contract specification of the external funding source.

The voluntary sector

The Cathedral Centre is a medium-sized voluntary organization. The significant difference between voluntary and commercial organizations is that the economic aim of voluntary organizations is not for profit. Finance is still of prime importance to fund the operations and provide opportunity for increased operations but all surplus money is ploughed back into the organization. Fundraising requires detailed accountability, which in turn requires policies

and procedures to be in place. Thus the three Es of management are still pertinent: economy, efficiency and effectiveness.

Salaries to paid workers are usually offered at a level that is fair, just, and not excessive. Motivation to work in the voluntary sector is usually from shared beliefs in outcomes to be achieved, rather than in financial gain. Government funding is usually contract based, thus bids must be clear and focused.

My reflections

HOW MY ROLE AS FACILITATOR ENABLED LEARNING

The Catalyst recognized the potential for the workers to better serve themselves, the volunteers and their clients. She appealed to their missionary zeal to encourage them to embrace change. My role as facilitator was to help them to unlock the potential and harness their energies into an ongoing programme of change to meet the changing needs of staff, both paid and voluntary, and clients.

I genuinely admire the work of the Centre and I communicated this to the staff. I also shared with them details of my own vocation with Marriage Care to help them understand my value base. I familiarized myself with their culture and actively respected it. The staff themselves generated the agenda for change. I established an environment of trust and equality where each member's contributions were valued. Active listening and reflection encouraged self-disclosure.

Task issues dominated early meetings. I gradually modelled process issues and encouraged workers to offer their perspectives on process. The different preferred learning styles of the workers emerged. It is sometimes assumed that in community service the preferred learning style will be of a pragmatist or activist. We worked with these styles and also the styles of reflector and theorist. We valued the differences and learnt from each other's preferred styles. A maze game provided the trigger input for this work. This was instrumental as a levelling exercise, raising the self-esteem of individual workers as their individual strengths emerged, and valuing the different working styles. The workers generated the agenda issues. Content of later away-days contained management input from the Catalyst or myself; we also generated the framework. Timing was agreed by all in advance of work rotas being prepared.

ORGANIZATIONAL LEARNING FOR IMPROVEMENT

Organizational learning occurred at these away-days: workers learnt more about each other as they began to function as a team. They clarified their vision for the Centre and identified their tasks, and in the process learnt more about themselves. They identified their own training needs, some of which could be addressed at away-days, while for others, courses were booked with specific agencies. This learning resulted in improved performance, freeing workers more from 'housekeeping tasks' and leaving time for more creative work to be undertaken.

Structures were created, giving more flexibility to workers' interpretations of their tasks. Job descriptions liberated rather than restricted creativity by describing core tasks and identifying responsibilities. Policies for dealing with violent clients, health and safety, and volunteer induction regulated processes instead of each individual reinventing the wheel. Client

files became more accessible due to the introduction of new technology. Regular procedures were documented, enabling a more cohesive service to be offered to clients. It was the reflection on client outcomes that moved the learning into the secondary level of transformation.

ORGANIZATIONAL LEARNING FOR TRANSFORMATION

Clients' stories fuelled the initial intervention of the Catalyst. Clients' stories fuelled the paradigm shift from reactive service to taking the initiative with the health service provision for clients. This proactive stance was supported by a survey of Centre users, which indicated as many as 75 per cent suffer health problems. The outreach work demanded effective collaboration with other agencies. This agenda was a high priority for Worker 'A', the Communications worker. This increased her ability to raise awareness of the whole range of services which should have been available to clients with health problems, services that Centre staff were only too aware was not accessible to all their clients. Once documentation was in place, she was able to secure funding which enabled the Centre to employ a mental health professional, formalizing this aspect of the Centre's work. This placed the Centre in a strong position to lobby health services for better provision of services for clients.

The increased profile of the Centre encouraged the workers to separate out Centre management and ongoing strategic planning. Previously the roles of the Management Committee and paid workers overlapped. There is still work to be done in role identification.

The role of the Management Committee

Originally the Management Committee members held a nominal role. They were generous with their support where appropriate and relied on the paid staff to manage the Centre. As the paid staff have expanded their influence, particularly in health and social services, they have perceived the need for an active committee to accept accountability for the services provided by the Centre. The Centre staff has worked hard to expand the size and increase the shared expertise of the Management Committee. The membership of the committee now includes an elected representative of the volunteers, and professional representation from bodies including law, accountancy, mental health, social services, faith and justice, and the diocese. This body is working on a new constitution and further policies. Strong leadership from this body, in consultation with paid workers, will greatly support the paid workers in their ongoing management role and facilitate liaison with associated services to better serve the clients.

The model of a learning organization was introduced to the Management Committee when the paid staff invited the committee to a joint away-day, which was carefully planned with myself as facilitator. The main aim of the day was to create understanding of each other's roles. The foundation for a good working relationship was laid by focusing on introductions of all present. The paid staff offered case studies of clients, which illustrated the essence of their work and kept the focus on client service.

The volunteer workforce

The management of the volunteer workforce of about sixty volunteers is under review. It is hoped that the learning process can now begin to be applied to developing volunteer policy.

It is intended to create a learning environment for volunteers to empower them to play a more active role in the organization of the Centre. Retreat days are currently organized for volunteers. It is envisaged that a more formal induction programme will be supplemented by more training and support.

Current scenario

Clients using the Centre now experience continuity in the services offered. Their health needs can be addressed more consistently alongside their physical and emotional needs. Health professionals, for example, doctor, dentist, podiatrist and reflexologist, offer services on Centre premises and can make appropriate referrals.

There are currently six paid Centre workers. Three of these workers were part of the whole process detailed above. Worker 'C' who drew the frightened rabbit has moved on and the team conducted an exit interview to help them in replacing her. Worker 'F' still is regarded as the overall manager. Worker 'K' supports her vigorously in the ongoing work of the Centre. Worker 'A' has left. Her exit interview was instrumental in having her job description redefined and the post upgraded. The post of communications officer is now a full-time position. A lot of changes have taken place over a relatively short period of time. I believe this is now a time for consolidation. I would like to reiterate my admiration for the staff, who have sacrificed their security to venture into uncertain territory and who trusted the Catalyst's vision that clients would benefit from this process. As the facilitator I very much appreciated the honesty of the managers at all times and their skill in offering positive feedback to each other.

UNRESOLVED ISSUE?

An unresolved issue I perceive seems to be 'Who is *the* manager?' As detailed above, the theory is one of consensus management, but in practice the founder member seems to be called upon to make the final decisions. Financial gifts from her order supplement funding of projects, for example, the funding of a kitchen worker. Financial aid is one power factor but not the most important. Her greatest power is the high esteem in which she is held. This manager does not accept this power so there is still no one named individual manager to whom correspondence can be addressed or who can make decisions for the team. This might need to be addressed. Team meetings continue and they need to be nurtured to preserve the learning community and to prevent task taking over from process as work pressures continue to increase. It is the intention of the workers to complement these informal team meetings with more formal away-days. One-to-one supervision has been requested by one worker and will hopefully be introduced for them all.

WHAT MOTIVATED ME TO STAY WITH THIS PROCESS?

The dedication of the team to their mission inspired me. Their honesty and genuineness was a pleasure to work with. Challenges were greeted as constructive interventions. The Catalyst inspired me by her belief that we could build a learning organization. Her management expertise complemented mine and we were able to process the work together. Above all the clients' stories motivated me to want to be a part of making a difference.

MY LEARNING

I was confirmed in my belief that experiential learning is successful in effecting change. As the facilitator it is important that I remain detached from the process. When necessary, I was reminded by individual responses, verbal and non-verbal, that the team agenda was the brief, not an agenda I might perceive to be important, although I did have a role in offering and highlighting agendas. I was both excited and slightly anxious when invited to facilitate the combined management team and paid staff away-day. Having worked so closely with the paid staff for a period of time, I was well aware of the tensions that might be around in establishing a new working group. The day was extremely successful in engaging the management team. The paid staff openly voiced many emotions as they attempted to identify their expectations of the new management team. I became more aware of my emotional attachment to the project, and valued supervision of my work to help me process this issue. My own learning developed during the supervision process where I experienced one of those 'light bulb' moments due to the skilful interventions of my supervisor. The value of supervision was reinforced for me.

WIDER OUTCOMES

The lobbying of local government, the raising of awareness in mental health and social services and the encouragement of participation from a wide range of professions are all very positive outcomes, which the Centre staff has achieved. The Cathedral Centre staff now offer its collaborative partners a real experience of non-traditional ways of working. They address the complex needs of clients and meet them in their own world. The team knowledge of their growing number of clients is impressive. Hopefully the enthusiasm and expertise of the team will be communicated to observers from other agencies who are currently studying their working methods, thus transforming other agencies who are in a position to make a valuable difference to their own clients' lives and those of the Centre.

17 Values Work in Health and Health Education

Bob Sang

Recently, I was invited by a relatively progressive university to help it look at its future in Management Education. In common with other institutions of further and higher education, my client was seeking to extend its relationships with local and regional employers by creating enhanced career opportunities for its graduates and post-graduates, whilst boosting income generation in the process. In parallel with this project I have been actively involved in facilitating major change in the health systems that constitute our National Health Service and its commercial suppliers.

In both cases the language of partnership and integration is now in common use. Similarly, in the commercial sector 'consolidation', principally through acquisitions and mergers, and the creation of consortia and alliances, is becoming increasingly commonplace. For managers and staff, for professionals and clients, and for investors and the wider public (tax payers), the effectiveness of *inter*organizational development is becoming as critical as the quality of *intra*organizational learning. My contribution to our understanding of reflective practice focuses on the former for two reasons. First, I believe we are at the beginning of getting to grips with the *inter*organizational development agenda. We have been seriously hampered by the easy rhetoric of partnership, which obscures the nature of the work that must be done to achieve the co-creation of the new organizational forms, common cultures, shared working practices, and so on. Second, the challenge for independent educators and facilitators and for internal change agents in developing appropriate practice is considerable.

This chapter is written for such people – the values workers who enable the participants in interorganizational change and development to address the fundamentals of partnership creation and organizational integration. My intention is to offer a set of frameworks and insights to aid the effective facilitation of such change. It is also aimed at all those academics who seek to work cooperatively with employers and development agencies. For the clear message from my recent project in Management Education is that educational institutions are not as highly valued partners as they might be. Their dominant values and practices (values-in-action) tend to get in the way of, rather than promote, the cooperation they seek.

My own experiences as an academic responsible for new business development, as a change agent within large and small organizations, and as a facilitator of major partnership initiatives, have surfaced the deeply challenging nature of this work. The personal challenge, 'What's in it for us?', raises both issues of responsibility and accountability for participants, forcing them to examine motivations and taken-for-granted assumptions afresh. By reflecting on the limited success of a management development partnership and on recent attempts to create merged organizations in the health sector, I shall endeavour to tease out a

basis for values work – the interventions we share with others in order to support their learning through the processes of complex *inter*organizational change.

Rationale and purpose: What's in it for me?

This chapter is grounded, of course, in my values, in my practice: values-in-action within a process of dissemination. I have chosen to write personally and to challenge and support the reader because I enjoy such a creative opportunity, and I want to stimulate a response. That is what's in it for *me*.

In common with every other writer-practitioner, I have struggled with my place in this process of exploration, reflection and synthesis; testing the ever-present tension between altruism, serving the greater good or some higher purpose, and self-actualization, giving meaningful expression to my own talent and sensitivities, and hoping to achieve a fruitful balance as the work emerges. Such is the real, often hidden, rationale for values work: 'I am simply conscious of the forces I am using, driven on by an idea that I really only grasp as it grows with the picture' (Matisse).

I have also been greatly encouraged by experience, empirical observation, and a reflective review of recent work in this field (Pattison 1998), which have led me to a number of presuppositions:

- Values work is primarily concerned with people's behaviour and its effects, intended or unintended, on other people. It cuts through the CRAP – crass rhetoric about partnership – to the facilitation of what is really going on.
- Most dissemination, but not all, results in a process of externalization, whereby people are encouraged to describe, analyse, espouse, or proselytize – without seeking to effect real, measurable, change in their own and others' behaviour: the process of mutual discovery and development and achievement. Not a comfortable test to impose on myself!
- The will to change, or not to change, relates dialectically with each individual's skills, knowledge, understanding, intuition, and so on. Will and personal capability are inseparable and dependent on the resources available for change – time, energy, circumstance. Values are contingent variables, just one dimension of sentient human complexity. This challenges the notion of values as formal moral imperatives. Our values wax and wane with our energy, competence, and even the time we have for reflection in action (see also, Figure 17.4, on page 163).
- There is a real risk associated with values work: that it becomes an end in itself. The most obvious symptom is attention to, and investment in, the institutionalization of values and their encryption in standards, principles and programmes. That is, the codification of values as dogma, usually presented as a hierarchy of values – a new trade in intellectual property.
- Finally, human history indicates that Maslow got it more and less right. We all value the basic means of existence, safe, social living, including sexual and cultural reproduction, and, when and wherever possible, the opportunity to express our creativity. If there is a natural hierarchy, it places survival above creativity ... just. Whatever the motivation, we all need purpose and meaning in our lives and it is healthy, literally, to surface and test these needs, especially during times of significant change: personal, organizational and societal.

In sum, if we try to analyse values too far, we reduce ourselves. Values work is much more about facilitating contexts where people can express their values – 'What's in it for me?' – and address the entirely contradictory nature of coexistence – 'What will be in it for us?' That is, values are the choices we actively make, consciously or unconsciously, about what is important ... at the time: 'Values have always arisen as the human response to persisting areas of relevant uncertainty' (Emery 1981, p. 431).

Values work can be understood and developed in four respects:

- personal learning and development
- working with groups and teams
- working in complex systems including organizations
- appreciating changing contexts.

Values are concerned with the 'Me', the 'We', and the purpose within the ever-changing environments over which we seek to gain some kind of control. Hence the need to create interorganizational structures and processes that, for example, give us some chance at improving health in impoverished communities, or improve the employment opportunities of disabled people, and so on.

The remainder of this chapter concentrates on the first of these aspects and then, in conclusion, endeavours to show how learning about values work was applied to a complementary set of field projects, all of which challenge the personal and professional values of diverse participants: in groups and in teams, in complex systems and in changing contexts.

Personal learning and development

Values work is, inevitably, change 'agentry'. Any intervention that initiates an exploration and clarification of values is inherently powerful. It immediately tests day-to-day assumptions such as 'the way we do things round here' or even 'the way things *are* round here'. Change agents are all those who are catalysts for change. They choose the role of facilitator within a proposed programme of change or within a defined change process. Paid or unpaid, formal or informal, they are prepared to enable the active engagement of all the other stakeholders. Change agentry is an intervention in the lives of others: a field of high-risk, often unrecognized, practice.

Such practitioners are immediately part of the situation and, if they choose a values-based approach, they rapidly are perceived to be part of the problem. The mere act of simple observation, noticing behaviour, conversations, symbols and artefacts, is significant. Values workers are the change agents who ensure that observation is a fundamental activity, integral to the processes of exploration and experiential learning. Values practitioners are highly observant, active listeners and memorizers ... and this can be very threatening, or even reassuring, for others. During some previous work (Sang and McLenaghan 1999), I was reminded by a medical records clerk that 'Little things mean a lot', while a nurse manager told me 'Change has become very, very personal'. Both were reflecting, confidentially, on the real values of their organization and the gap existing between their day-to-day experience and the espoused values of their employer, an NHS Trust. Here we were in an organization claiming to value the health of its employees, yet they were telling me, in confidence, that imposed restructuring was resulting in stress and a reduced and less safe quality of working life.

How was I to respond? My own values were immediately tested. My thoughts and feelings exposed in an instant ... and my conflict of interest. I was being paid to research workforce health; but did this include testing the values-in-action of the very organization that had granted me access? How would this situation unfold if I dug deeper? Recent King's Fund work, based on the stories of NHS people (Malby and Pattison 1998) helps us to see that individuals continuously try to make sense of their world as their experience is always at odds with the declared values of the organization, both formal and informal, with which they are associated. Further work from the Office for Public Management (Steele 1999) shows what happens when this dissonance becomes too great. It is, literally, personally destructive, leading to committed people leaving the public sector. My own work takes me into situations where there is bullying and abuse by people charged with the care of vulnerable others. I find partnerships that are riven with mistrust and petty competition. I am beginning to learn to facilitate such situations, confronting my own values as I go.

Addressing this personal tension lies at the heart of values work: facilitating the ever-present contradiction between personal values and expectations, and each individual's interpretation of others' behaviours and attitudes. I have found that personal thoughts and feelings are continuously tested as I tread the fragile path between my own learned values and the goals and aspirations that I have set for myself: 'What *is* in it for me?', I often ask.

We all engage in this internal dialogue. As we do so our own vulnerability becomes more apparent as we endeavour to assimilate and appreciate others' values – especially those with power (employers, managers, professionals, etc.). Health systems, for example, remain dominated by institutions and hierarchies designed to promote and protect powerful individuals and groups, posing particular challenges for those who choose to be change agents within the existing structures.

Values work makes this challenge explicit by facilitating an open disclosure of the relationship between personal and collective values. Collective may mean family, social group, community, association, corporation, and so on. Indeed, one way of defining a culture is to understand it as the outcome of the resolution of the necessary contradictions between personal and collective values. How this process of resolution takes place is an expression of the use of power, authority and influence within a culture. Values workers confront these forces and, in so doing, test themselves. Thus values workers demonstrate both their pluralistic commitment – 'Human difference is the ultimate renewable resource' (Ritchie 2001) – and their role in encouraging people to share their differences as well as celebrate their common humanity.

Nowhere is their challenge more evident than in the corporate world of organizations. John Ralston Saul (1997) has pointed out the dominance of corporatist ideology over other value systems, rendering whole populations unconscious of the values choices confronting them. He argues that, in our 'unconscious civilization' we have replaced the open and constructive challenge of values work with a managerial language and management consultancy practices whose function is to reinforce corporate culture rather than explore it and test it against individuals' and communities' experiences and values. Even muddled thinking and plain bad behaviour become legitimized when people are aligned within the corporate culture. Nowhere is this more evident than in hospitals that sustain abuse and neglect of patients, or in universities that suppress academic debate and fundamental research.

In the health field, those brave individuals willing to challenge dominant corporate values may be local citizens, patients and their carers, health workers and educators, managers and those with governance responsibilities. And, they may be required to engage with a

number of organizations within a health system, resulting in a relatively new language: 'joined up', 'seamless', 'partnerships', 'alliances', 'inclusion'. The domain of values work has gained a new order of complexity. Interorganizational facilitation, such as integrated supply chain, and whole systems approaches (Pratt et al. 1999) have opened up the demands on values workers to new levels of skill, understanding and personal appreciation – all of this at a time of globalization of socioeconomic forces and growing cultural and demographic diversity! (See Zadek 2000.)

Working with others to help make sense of this contradictory world places new responsibilities on all those whose work is change agentry – as opposed to the spectatorship and disengaged critique produced by values-free consultants, many academics and contract researchers. How can sufficient common ground be established and sustained in order to find a way forward towards, for example, better health? There is a real danger that, without proper and robust evaluation, the new structures emerging through the rhetoric of partnership and equality will, in effect, become the new health conglomerates. Power (that is, structure) will dominate purpose and meaning, resulting in the creation of unwieldy and over-complex corporations disconnected from staff and the communities they are supposed to serve. In the UK, the proposed Public Private Partnerships (PPPs), intended to run our local hospitals, make this risk very real – especially for those vulnerable patients who have no voice and no choice.

Whose different purposes will be served when such initiatives are taken forward? Are others' roles and responsibilities complementary or in conflict? When is dissent more significant than assent or affirmation? Can working practices be aligned and attuned, or will more be gained from conflict and dissonance? And, how will people learn to learn and work together ... or, will they be better suited by *ad hoc* personal development within the chaos? 'What *is* in it for me?' is the unspoken, ever-present question at meetings of the boards and teams of these new multi-agency, multi-professional bodies. It is small wonder that the announcement of a new partnership is greeted with a mixture of anxiety and scepticism by those most likely to be affected in the long run: local staff and local citizens.

One thing is clear, the glibness and superficiality of standardized training and consultancy programmes stands in stark contrast with the new challenges faced by values workers. Each personal tightrope – between personal goals and aspirations and our learned values – is strung along the edge of a crumbling cliff, at night, in a storm, with only our fragile sensitivities and sensibilities to help us. It feels dangerous and unstable. So, fundamentally, why bother? What *is* in it for *me*? ... And, how can I enable others to reflect on these questions whilst endeavouring to work in and between organizations, in communities, within diverse cultures, and so on?

Recent work on the Scottish Values Project forced a small team of colleagues to confront this sense of vulnerability, both in relation to our own roles and in respect of the contribution of courageous fieldworkers endeavouring to establish genuine cooperation between the agencies that work in some of Scotland's most impoverished communities (Whitney and Groves 1999). As a result, we began to tease out a framework that we tested in the field through a set of challenging projects. Significantly, I have found such frameworks are of equal value in my work with a relatively wealthy corporation that is growing its business through acquiring and integrating smaller competitors. In both cases, the internal and external change agents, my fellow values workers, negotiated the personal tightrope described above.

Values into practice

[NB: 'I' has been changed to 'We' as the remainder of this chapter reflects on and values the work of the teams who came together in both sectors.]

The framework set out in Figure 17.1 below emerged from observations and experience, and the more it is tested the more robust it appears to be. It is based on the premise that all human endeavour is in some way purposeful, that we all have roles to play, work to do, and that we are learning in the process. We bring our values, consciously and unconsciously, into all these aspects of our engagement with situations, tasks, projects, and so on. This construction creates some useful tensions.

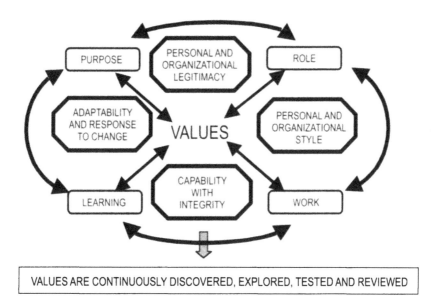

Figure 17.1 Values-in-change

For example, during a recent acquisition process, the senior management team of an 'ethical' Unites States company was required to comply with European Social Legislation. The purpose of the acquisition was clear and acceptable to the local owners and regulators, but the top team had to work hard to establish the legitimacy and style of working that ultimately resulted in a positive outcome. Behind the scenes the internal change agents (in this case the European human resources directors) worked intensively and reflectively with the external adviser/facilitator to enable acceptance of a fundamental shift in values in all aspects of the process. The above framework helped us to monitor and adapt our interventions as the whole complex story unfolded.

We have learned that, when working with groups and within complex organizational contexts, failure to attend to purpose, role, practice (the actual work), and learning, ensures that we are increasingly likely to find ourselves, and the others with whom we are working, blocked and unable to make progress. Hidden or assumed values that are not surfaced, shared and explored, may be expressed in the attitudes and behaviours that impact on the nature of

the relationships, emotional commitment to the endeavour, and the exercise of skills and capabilities by all participants. If we do not continuously aid this process of discovery, exploration and personal challenge, then:

- Legitimacy is not established – for both the endeavour itself and for those engaged in it.
- Appropriate and effective styles of working are not developed.
- Integrity is not sustained.
- People become less and less adaptable in their responses to change.
- Resistance to change, and worse, tokenism dominate the culture.

In effect, in all our fieldwork, we noted a failure of teams and boards to journey through the natural phases of group development: storming (establishing legitimacy), norming (accommodating styles), forming (achieving integrity as a group), and performing (responding well to change).

Elsewhere, during the creation of a partnership board to address children's health in a rural community, the espoused values concerning this sensitive and worthwhile project appeared to unite this newly formed group: 'We are all here for our local children ...'. But, as soon as a difference of view was aired, as soon as decisions had to be taken, that is, as soon as the possibility of conflict emerged, then values were revisited by the members: 'Why, really, am I here...?', 'What should I be doing...?', 'What is my (valid) contribution?', and, of course, *'What's in it for me ... now and for the future?'*

This is not an expression of self-seeking pragmatism. It is merely what we all rehearse when exposed and at risk. The impulse to fight or flight is rarely, if ever, discussed. As our colleague, Peter Ritchie of the Scottish Human Services Trust, has pointed out values work entails enabling others to 'discuss the undiscussable'. And, to discuss the undiscussable, people may have to think the unthinkable, surfacing powerful feelings of vulnerability in the process. Undiscussed discussables are a powerful blockage to engaging with values differences and to building a genuinely shared endeavour. Such situations are fraught with projection when powerful (and vulnerable) people displace their anxieties by blaming others for the failure of the process to deliver the task. The dynamics can rapidly break down if the facilitator is not aware and able to respond, appropriately and sensitively (see Figure 17.5, p. 163).

In health issues, shared endeavour inevitably concerns life and death, and matters of great sensitivity and contention. For example, the national–local deliberation on improving teenage sexual health in Scotland (Burtney and Sang 1999) and the similar deliberation on dietary inequalities (Whitney and Cogan 1999) were both designed to enable participants with strongly held values to work with a common evidence-base and to build a consensus that surpassed previous tensions and public conflict. The effective facilitation of these high-profile processes, in common with the facilitation of local health partnerships and cooperatives, depended on the creation of a safe enough environment for participants to share their emotional as well as their rational responses to the challenge. Two messages stand out. Never take on such work alone; and, always take time out to review the process and be prepared to adapt at least three times every day, openly and transparently.

Participation in any corporate or collective endeavour immediately grounds us all in our values – the fragile bridge between our thoughts and our feelings – that makes us tick as sentient beings. Values work engages with this deep complexity: actively, knowingly and reflectively. It is time we acknowledged the personal risks taken by the practitioners who

agree to facilitate partnership boards, mergers, or stakeholder events, and other processes which bring together and surface the multiple values held by each and every participant. Those who take on this challenge learn to develop a core set of skills that are fundamental to facilitating reflective learning in complex human situations.

Three competences are fundamental: listening, noticing and sensing. All require self-awareness and the ability to respond to inner tensions and signals. Let me explain. It is safe to assume that all facilitation is inherently dysfunctional, and even potentially dangerous. After all, if participants in a process or event can learn to learn to work and learn together, why should they need additional help? Then we all carry our stuff with us; our learned values and emotional histories. Like it or not, we approach every facilitation situation with a profound mix of subjectivity, experience and objectivity. We act as dynamic filters and channels for the energy and physical presence of everyone in the room. So, how can we deal with this built-in complexity and avoid becoming part of the problem, trapped in the values tensions and emerging dynamics of the larger group?

First of all, always work with a co-facilitator. Whilst values workers learn to listen to themselves – their tone of voice, choice of words, timing of interventions, use of language, and so on, they also need to be able to triangulate, test their inner senses both with the group and with a co-facilitator or fellow change agent. This principle applies to noticing what is going on in the room, especially in cross-cultural situations where it is often virtually impossible to spot and interpret all the titbits of behaviours, colour and tone that are ever-present in groups, large and small.

For example, recently, when working with the Board and Executive of a newly formed community health organization I began to notice the diverse ways in which members were engaging with each other and with the task – they were trying to get to grips with their new purpose, roles and functioning, and the need for recognition surfaced. For some, energy started slipping. My co-facilitator noted this apparent loss of momentum, so I stopped the process and asked *'What is going on here?'* The question created a space – an opportunity for a review, both of the engagement of new board members in the process, and of their relationship with more experienced professional staff. The timing of this intervention, prompted by my co-facilitator's observation, relied on my sensing the moment to call a halt and ask the question. Increasingly, I have come to rely on my own and others' gut feel. Above all, I no longer expect to facilitate well. My role is to leave the space and time for the real interests and concerns of all participants to emerge. Whether participants are angry, or despondent, or negative, or anxious, and so on – this is what is real.

Second, all feedback is good data in values work. What is behind the anger, anxiety, and so on? It is at the uncomfortable and even dangerous times in a process that the hidden values begin to surface. Facilitators can challenge their own inherent dysfunctionality by sensing and timing their own powerful interventions in order that the values tensions and contradictions in the larger group do not remain unnoticed, unheard and undiscussed. This realization raises a very uncomfortable question: how often does good facilitation get in the way? That is, how can we be sure that a process that appears to create common purpose amongst potential partners has actually produced sufficient resolution of conflicting or divergent values? All too often we may be happy to reach a comfortable conclusion, when we have not in practice enabled sufficient time and space for individuals and the group as a whole to address the inherent risks and conflicts associated with creating something that is new and potentially a fundamental threat to both the status quo and unspoken future aspirations.

Our values help us to define ourselves, for ourselves, for others, and for wider social purposes. New, or redefined, social purposes challenge us to determine new modes of working and, as such, they are in necessary tension with the established order (vested interests). In health, for example, two fundamental transformations are currently being proposed that will shake the foundations of vested interest:

- First, the search for whole systems or joined-up solutions challenges the basic structures of health and healthcare provision that are based on functional/expert and geographical/electoral structures.
- Second, the call for more democratic public participation and self-determination of people and communities is intended to break the culture of dependence ('doctor knows best') by creating health systems rooted in citizenships, community development and health education.

Such modern purposes have exposed the self-interested organizational complexity of local health services that are inevitably becoming chaotic while they endeavour to restructure and realign. Local government, health agencies and community organizations (and there may be dozens in any one locality), are struggling to understand the new agenda. For example, when proposals to change local hospital services are put forward, local action groups suddenly appear, the press have a field day, and straightforward consultation can turn into a local war of attrition. The facilitation and attainment of a reasonable consensus in such situations depends not only on the framework of competence described above, but also on creating safe spaces where the conflicting interests and values can be played out openly and constructively.

Three criteria matter:

- Independence – facilitators must be seen to be free of conflict of interest, and this includes a willingness to confront and question those who pay for their services (!).
- Openness to personal challenge – all feedback is useful data, including the anger and taunts of the more adversarial participants.
- Respect – a considered respectful approach with all comers must be modelled, especially paying attention to the participation needs of potentially disadvantaged individuals (for example, carers, elders with disabilities, people with poor mental health). The basic assumption is that we are all fellow citizens . . . including the facilitators.

Finally, in such situations, we re-emphasize, never work alone. In order to create a safe space two facilitation roles are needed: one to support the process from induction to closure; the other to look after the space itself and participants' needs, from temperature and light to refreshments and disability access.

Health practitioners, from direct services' provision, health promotion, and from health education, find themselves working in increasingly complex organizational structures. And local people face a two-edged challenge: understanding the changing systems and developing their own roles within them.

When we engage with such chaos and begin to clarify the emerging complexity, we inevitably face the fragile certainty and security of our own carefully constructed comfort zones. The structural chaos and associated role confusion surfaces a number of choices: avoidance; denial, retrenchment, resistance . . . or, engaging with and sharing the risks of

change. An appreciation of the new context really helps in building and sharing a vision that meets new purposes. However, when we do not feel in control of ourselves, when we feel threatened and deskilled by the prospects of change, then we are unlikely to engage with the risks – unless we are explicitly valued and supported in the process. One response is a vast literature on the management of change (Emery 1981). More recent work emphasizes the leadership implications (Quinn 1996; Mant 1998).

Values work is distinctive from the practice and theory of change management and organizational leadership, which emphasize the psychological and behavioural dimensions of transformation. Values workers recognize that, in order to address shared risks in our increasingly diverse cultures, we need to learn to depend on each other, enriched by our fundamental differences. These differences will change as we learn to work and to learn together, and to share the risks of the transformational changes, challenging the comfort of our established values in the process (Figure 172.) In plain terms, we learn to depend on our differences: 'Difference *is* the ultimate renewable resource' (Ritchie 2001).

Values work supports people as they surface and question their own purposes, roles, practices and learning ... together. Meaningful transformation will not occur unless and until participants regain a new sense of comfort with the diversity of values, the plurality and interdependence, inherent in our increasingly integrated systems. Such plurality and interdependence is necessary for us to take on the apparently intractable health inequalities that pervade society: locally and nationally.

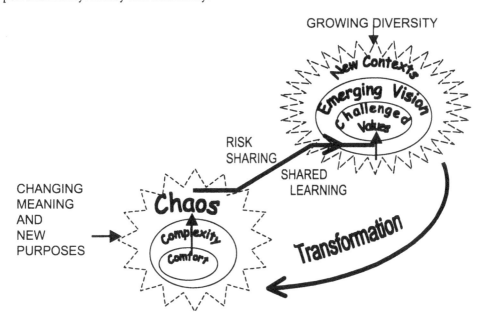

Figure 17.2 Breaking out of the comfort zone: challenging values

Unfortunately, values workers are usually involved once the chaos has begun! In complex organizations, boards and executives announce restructuring or closures or mergers and integration with little apparent understanding of the human consequences of their attempts to redesign the natural complexity of organizational life. One of the facilitator's first tasks is to assess and engage with the legacy of disturbance and the natural human responses to it:

rage, alienation, apathy, avoidance, collusion. Enabling leaders to share the inherent risks of change in order that everyone affected can participate is probably the most difficult task we face. It is also one of the reasons most partnerships fail and why reorganization rarely produces the potential benefits that are claimed at the outset. Facilitators need courage, assertiveness and determination to support processes intended to achieve real transformational change. They become, in effect, 'systems coaches'. So, where does this leave us as we seek, for example, to improve health and health services?

Values into action

WHO MAKES VALUES WORK WORK?

Development work, to an extent, consists of designing backwards: from the potential outcomes to the development process planning and the learners themselves. So, who are the potential learners and their chosen outcomes, and how might values work facilitate their development and contribution? Put another way: 'Who will be learning to create and sustain partnerships that foster improved health and increasing health equality within our diverse communities?'

Setting aside politicians, whose role is to proselytize and lead from a known ideological position, there are four key learners' groups:

- Enablers – the managers and professionals who, by reason of given authority and control of resources, can make or break the context of partnerships (chief executives, directors, and so on). Their contribution raises important questions about leadership in a world that still values power over diversity.

- Participants – the potential co-workers who will innovate and sustain the new working practices that will contribute to improved health and social inclusion. Such a group will include people such as service users, community activists, carers and community-based workers (GPs, nurses, therapists, and so on).

- Facilitators – the relatively small group of independent development workers who catalyse transformational, integrated innovation and learning.

- Influencers – all those, particularly educators and communicators including the media, who can prevent or create the contexts in which values work can be more or less explicitly explored.

However:

- *Enablers* traditionally direct and control resources from a defined organizational base. The partnership agenda demands that they learn new approaches to stewardship and leadership across complex, changing, systems, letting go of some of their power in the process.

- *Participants* usually work on the basis of dependency relationships, defined by the structural and functional assumptions of the dominant organizations and institutions. Can they learn interdependence, cooperation and mutual respect, especially when working with vulnerable or excluded people?

- *Facilitators* are usually kept in-the-box – as community development, health promotion, public involvement manager, for example. Their challenge is to effect fundamental shifts within both the above groups, whilst also developing themselves as change agents in the process.

- *Influencers* have grown and established themselves in past contexts. How will they take a risk and change their contribution – hidden though it may be – sharing useful knowledge about the wider environment, including learning about practice: the tools and interventions that are being used and evaluated elsewhere.

Whilst these are emergent whole systems roles, they cannot be viewed separately from either the considerable organizational development agenda facing national and local organizations, or from the work on capacity-building and citizenship that needs to be grounded in our communities. Facilitators tend to be absorbed in either or both of these agendas also, making them a particularly hard-pressed group of change agents. So, what can support the development of individuals in these four key roles – especially when many such colleagues will be unfamiliar with, or even resistant to, such a characterization?

EMERGING PRACTICE

Values work is risky and reflective because, like it or not, the first phases oblige all participants to revisit the basis of their self-esteem and given authority. For example, recent attempts to reform and integrate local health services has begun to surface the inherent contradictions between those who hold a medico-managerial model of the world of health and healthcare and those with strong social and community development values. These overt and potentially valuable differences tend to hide divergent personal and career expectations: 'What is in it for me?' becomes the core question for every participant; but who will help them share the question explicitly and usefully, and how?

We are at the beginning of understanding the challenge of values work, and we are producing some early helpful frameworks. First and foremost, we have begun to understand the relationship between risk and values. Risk is more and less evident and dynamic; values converge and diverge, continuously. Thus we can begin to map different phases.

The journey from engagement through acceptance to authenticity is a matter of developing competence and a willingness to participate with others who hold different values (see Figures 17.3 and 17.4). For example, active and attentive listening is a learned competence that is contingent on participants' willingness to appreciate, ever more deeply, the nuances and emphases of others' communications. Exercises that help multiple stakeholders rediscover and develop their listening capabilities help new partnerships get off to a much more grounded start.

We are learning that in order to move from the first level – and *not* to regress – a number of conditions must be articulated and sustained:

- Agreement about overarching purpose, sufficient shared understanding of the challenge, and commitment to the timing of the process. Time and pace are factors that are readily disregarded by policy makers and politicians.
- A 'contract' with the facilitators is needed that respects their independence and values their energy and sensitivity.
- A willingness to learn on all sides, without taking individual circumstances and constraints for granted.

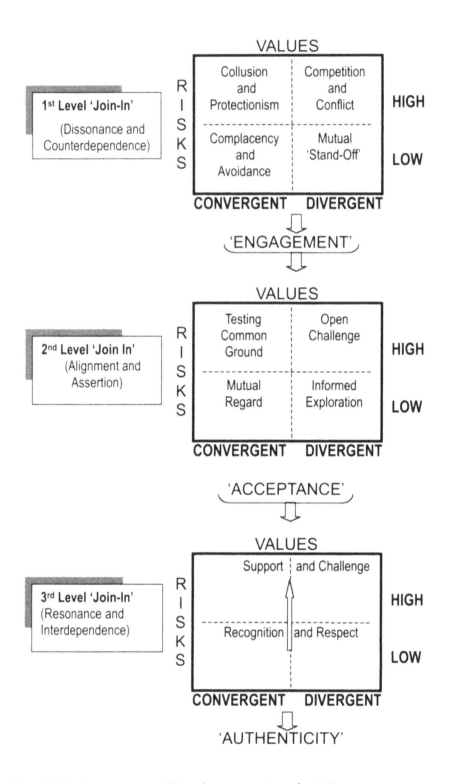

Figure 17.3 From engagement, through acceptance, to authenticity

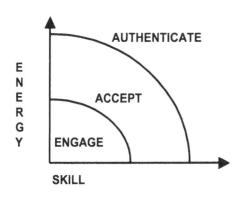

Figure 17.4 The 'skills-mix' matrix

- Recognition that everyone can move from being part of the problem to becoming part of the solution, developing and deploying their values in the process. Often this step requires one-to-one, confidential coaching work with those who feel they have most to lose. Senior people, for example, find it very hard to share their own vulnerability. Ironically, they find it easier to be blamed and to respond defensively.

- Learning to let go – of assumptions, prejudices, biases, and so on – is a deep personal challenge that ultimately strengthens personal integrity and the authenticity of the process also.

- Creating a safe, productive environment where participants can deliberate on evidence, drawing both on their own knowledge and experience and on the ordinary wisdom of local people of all ages and cultures.

- In order to break out of the comfort of Level 1 'Join-In' (with thanks to Martin Leith of the Innovation Agency for this helpful language), we have identified two relatively straight-forward keys to effective values work. The first is the uncomfortable exercise of undiscussability – and its hidden component unthinkability. Consider Figure 17.5 below.

Level 1

 Undiscussable undiscussability:

 'Problems, what problems? ... with me, with us, with our process'

 Discussing undiscussability:

Level 2

 'There are problems – I/we are struggling (to say what I am/we are thinking and feeling)'

 Everything is discussable:

Level 3

 'We clarify and resolve problems ... together.'

Growing Trust and Mutual Confidence

Figure 17.5 Achieving trust

Values workers sense and respond to the symptoms of the transitions between these levels. All feedback is helpful data: from anger and aggression, through encouragement and affirmation, to letting go and moving on. In such circumstances, participation is voluntary and participants learn to speak for themselves, not as representatives of particular groups, interests or organizations. Therefore the second requirement for effective values work rests with process participants themselves. If participants do not, cannot or will not, move themselves through the above framework illustrated in Figure 17.5, then partnership and inclusion will remain easy, dangerous rhetoric. A simple additional framework, illustrated in Figure 17.6, which people may choose to use, helps at and between every phase.

It takes time to appreciate and internalize this framework and then use it helpfully in different contexts. One simple, practical tip is to encourage people to learn to work without the barrier of tables and to move around as they get to grips with a shared challenge. By encouraging a large group of relative strangers, for example, a new partnership board, to pair up and walk together as they discover each other's histories and aspirations, it becomes possible to set up a much more free-flowing process of engagement and acceptance (see Figure 17.6). Chief Executives rapidly drop their labels and territories, service users learn to become thoughtful peers . . . everyone regains the status of fellow citizens.

Figure 17.6 Shifting values: 'The Words, the Music and the Dance'

Conclusion

Values workers are facilitators who have the scope to grasp the substance and complexity of transformational change and the tangle of personal negotiations and transitions it entails. They are instruments of change, the active catalysts who are learning all the time to question their own approach and sensitivity. They cannot do such work alone. They too need to ask 'What is in it for me?' in a supported context. Such work cannot be undertaken lightly: it requires careful preparation, planning, flexibility and a sense of humour. Such work is now crucial for the future of health and other complex human systems and it is in its infancy (see Figure 17.7).

Figure 17.7 The dialectic of complex human systems

What people need – in all the four roles noted in the previous section – is personal and shared development that ensures they can take responsibility for measurable improvement in the systems in which they coexist.

This chapter has endeavoured to highlight some key ingredients:

* Guidance, principles and supportive networking for those local facilitators who are endeavouring to catalyse sustainable, purposeful, partnerships
* An initial conceptual tool-kit for participants, which fosters the cooperative design of new working practices that sustain social inclusion and interorganizational cooperation
* Advice and personal development strategies for enablers and influencers seeking to manage the dynamic tension between formal accountability structures and diverse, complex, communities – as a joint venture with their peers from different organizational/institutional settings.

Above all, it is important to strengthen and promote recognition of the role of values workers

– those independent practitioners who will help to facilitate the multiple transformations envisaged in recent legislation and the growth of organizational mergers and integration. That is indeed 'what's in it for us'.

18 *A Life in Five Chapters*
Alison Lyon

1. I walked down the street. I fell into a deep dark hole. It was horrible. It wasn't my fault. It took me a long time to get out.

2. I walked down the street. I fell into a deep dark hole. I forgot it was there. It wasn't my fault. It was horrible. It still took me a long time to get out.

3. I walked down the street. I knew that hole was there. I fell into it anyway. It was my fault. It was horrible. I got out immediately.

4. I walked down the street. I remembered that the hole was there. I walked around it and didn't fall in.

5. I walked down a different street.

I learned this five-chapter analysis of learning in a personal-growth context but, as it fits just as well into the context of organizational reflective learning, it seems appropriate to quote it here. Most of my work experience has been in the voluntary sector and the experience of contributing this chapter is an interesting way of reflecting on reflecting, looking to see if there is anything distinctive about the ways that organizations in the voluntary sector learn, or fail to learn, to walk down different streets.

The ability to reflect and the inclination to make use of it are traits that can be found in a wide variety of individuals, filling a wide variety of roles in a wide variety of organizations. Being someone gifted with the inclination to reflect is, in my experience, a mixed blessing. One may be a natural-born reflector but until one's position carries the authority to introduce the lessons learned, the reflection may be of satisfaction to no one. And indeed a source of great dissatisfaction to the reflector!

My experience in the voluntary sector has lasted – so far – for 15 years, and I have worked in organizations of different sizes and with a variety of different purposes. They also have a variety of different approaches to the learning process. Some seem to spend all their time and efforts in the hole; some blame the hole for their falling in. None has consistently walked down a different street. I should add, though, that this failure to learn reflectively seems to be prevalent in all sectors. Most organizations, of course, are like us in life, doing some things well some of the time. For the last few years I have worked at NCH, the children's charity (founded in 1869, and formerly known as the National Children's Home), currently as communications manager. The examples in this chapter, about child migration and demands analysis, are drawn from my experiences there.

Child migration

In existence since 1869, NCH, like all the major child care organizations, was involved in the years around the Second World War in sending children from orphanages in the UK to Australia.

Child migration is a topic that has received, quite properly, a lot of media attention. Although NCH had previously been involved in child migration to Canada from 1873 to 1931, their involvement in child migration to Australia was small compared to that of the other agencies: a total of 129 children. Legally, NCH ceased to have responsibility for care and control of a child on their migration. At the time, NCH was fully satisfied that the legal requirements of the children were met and that their welfare seemed well addressed. NCH is no longer satisfied that the children's welfare was adequately addressed; at the time, though, it appears that the prevalent values – which said that it was reasonable, indeed good, to migrate children – were implicitly reflected in NCH policy. Although some members of staff, who had stayed in touch with the migrants, questioned the wisdom of the policy, NCH, and the child welfare assumptions of the time in pre- and post-war society, thought that this was a good strategy.

It was not until the 1950s that NCH policy changed; after then, no further children were sent to Australia. This sea change of attitudes went wider, and in 1998, the British government held an enquiry into the welfare of former British child migrants. This resulted in several recommendations, about identifying who they were, about offering access to records therapy and travel funds, and so on, so that those who had never returned to the UK could visit family, many of whom they had not previously even known about. NCH took these recommendations seriously and appointed an independent social worker, Joan Kerry, to make contact with as many of the people sent to Australia by NCH as possible to see if any services were needed. Joan's main tasks were to review the files, to make contact with as many former child migrants as possible, asking their views about what services were needed, and then to offer those support services, including reuniting them with lost relatives. She also, through these tasks, became the catalyst for much of the learning that followed.

This process uncovered some sad, and a few happy, stories. Contact was made with 82 of the 129; 14 were no longer alive. Many were helped to trace lost relatives, others were able to learn stories of their families. For some, what they learned was the location of graves of family members who had died. For example, a man who always believed his whole family had been killed in the war is now reunited with his 89-year-old mother. They have a family history for both themselves and the next generation. Talking about past experiences and searching for lost family is, of course, a highly emotional experience; emotions have swung from overwhelming joy to despair and anger at what has been lost and missed in the last fifty years. All those who have undertaken this emotional journey have said that they have found this of enormous benefit to both themselves and their children. The knowing is better than the not knowing. (And could this not be a key phrase for reflective learning?) Many have done well materially in Australia; many have steady jobs, good living conditions and loving families. But to only see this success ignores the hurt and loss inside and the struggles of a childhood without roots, which they have experienced. Some describe their childhood as one of loneliness and bewilderment about why they were sent 12 000 miles away from home.

This story is obviously not a wholly positive one. (Giving evidence at the 1998 Government enquiry, NCH said 'no one in their right mind today would seek to justify child migration.') But, of an event that 'finished' so long ago, was there anything that NCH could learn? Putting effort into redressing some of the balance for those affected by the child migration was one kind of learning, albeit one of basic courtesy. NCH, though no longer involved in child migration, is still working in areas that would benefit from learning from this part of NCH's history.

So this is not just an account of what happened over fifty years ago – a piece of social

history. Although children are no longer sent to orphanages across the world, they are, by other agencies (not by NCH) brought in from overseas countries for adoption through inter-country adoption schemes. They are moved from one part of the country to another into adoptive homes, foster care, residential schools and children's homes.

NCH has formulated a list of questions that are useful to both their own childcare projects and to other organizations with involvement in child migration (and indeed, more of this kind of interorganizational sharing later):

- Decision making – for example, who takes part in the decision to separate a child from its family? Have we recorded detail of the circumstances leading up to the child's separation?
- Preparation of children who have to move – for example, how do we help children understand what is happening in their lives?
- Collecting of information – for example, have we recorded and passed on details to new carers of who and what are important to the child?
- Culture and identity – for example, where does the child consider to be 'home'?
- Safeguarding the child's welfare – for example, do our reviewing systems provide adequate safety checks for children?

These questions are offered as a way of sharing best practice, and have been taken on board across many diverse areas of childcare. And, of course, asking questions stimulates more questions. Being seen to be open to learning encourages more learning.

Over the years many aspects of childcare policy have changed, and NCH is used to adapting its practices; indeed it is encouraging to work for an organization that often leads the way in establishing new, better ways of working with children and young people. Such changes, though, are more typically improvements rather than, as was the case with child migration, admissions of misguided practice. This may give a clue about how NCH was able to review its policies without blame or recrimination. The story is a relatively simple one and from today's viewpoint both the historic reasoning behind it and the later revision are easy to understand.

It has been refreshing to see how NCH has gone public with its activities in this learning process. When dealing with mistakes, even those that seemed like a good idea at the time, it is a temptation to learn in secret and not to publicize either the mistake or the learning process. NCH has exposed both its mistake – in sending the children in the first place – and its learning process. A video was made, in which former migrants tell their stories, and this has been shown to other agencies, which were also involved in child migration; copies were also sent to the British and Australian governments. Of more relevance here is that the video has also been shown to NCH staff, and proves to be popular. This is perhaps because it is an emotive topic – it includes wartime photographs of small children in belted mackintoshes, clutching teddy bears. But I also think that the staff who watch it are also intuitively appreciating that the organization they work so hard for, is owning up that they do not always get things right, and is showing that sometimes it can learn from its mistakes. That is a good lesson for staff to learn.

I think the video serves as a learning vehicle because of the simplicity of the story. Event = mistake → correction, *ergo* lesson learned. And aiding the success of the vehicle is the story's emotive nature: it makes a neat 'package' of the story and of both the implicit and explicit learning process.

Although walking down the different street cannot rub out the migration of those 129 children and their different stories, it can do something to optimize their situations now, and

can certainly lead to different streets for today's children in similar circumstances. The application of the questions above, and the lessons learned, will hopefully achieve this.

The benefits of learning lessons and introducing improvements can equally apply to organizational processes. While having less material significance than improved child welfare practices, more mundane new streets can be very rewarding, and such an application is explored below.

Demands analysis

One of my favourite ways of learning and making improvements is to perform a demands analysis, which does exactly what it says on the tin: analyses demands, and therefore allows one to see any patterns that emerge in those demands and then to make choices about them; in other words, to walk down a different street.

A service-based department in NCH had, over the space of several years, developed – through circumstance (primarily a lack of resources for the workload they were expected to deliver) – some moribund systems and rather pointless processes. The staff were fully committed to the work of the department, but the workload was so out of control that even if the inclination to reflect and learn had been there, it would have been hard to find the time to do it. We have always done it that way, was the reasoning, and any thought of looking at ways of improving, of becoming more effective and even a more pleasant working environment, were dismissed as extra effort and therefore merely adding to the already stretched workload. The demands analysis was not well received: it takes some effort and some consistency and is an added task. However, it is an added task that lasts only a week, and this is how it works.

Note that a demand is not necessarily someone being demanding. Demands can be politely expressed, reasonable, regular, expected. Typically, they will be for an action that fits – more or less – within someone's job description. Demands may come from above or below in the 'hierarchy', or from a peer. Required outcomes will vary, depending on the job in hand. Demands are defined as requests for action. For a period of time – a week is probably sufficient – all demands for an action must be logged. It is simplest to do this by preparing a blank form like the one in Figure 18.1. Then, everyone who is sharing the process logs every demand they get. At first, that is all they do. The analysis comes later.

It is worth saying, of course, that this exercise will not necessarily go down well, especially in a busy department. It is another piece of work. It is time consuming, and at this stage it is hard to see the benefit.

So it is worth putting effort into encouraging people to persevere, in whatever way works best for your particular team. Encouragement means different things to different people. It is important to enable learning, rather than precipitate a closing down! In my case, my strategy was to prime key people, whose desks were geographically well situated and whose temperaments were well suited both to the exercise itself and to encouraging others to maintain the process. Daily reminders also help.

If there are some natural reflectors in your team, or some process people, this will help. These are likely to be those with a sense of the big picture. If you have them, you will recognize them. If there are the opposite – people who see no value in reflection or who do not value process – it will be much harder. They are likely to offer resistance, and possibly to be vocal about it.

The value of the exercise depends upon the volume of data logged, and how closely it

Demands analysis form

(to build up a clearer picture of the demands on our time, please fill this in each time you receive an email, letter, phone call, visit, etc.)

Demands on ...'s time on ...

how it came	what it was about	want/don't want

Figure 18.1 Demands analysis form

reflects reality, so it is worth putting in the effort at this stage. Use whatever encouragements and rewards work best.

If you are a reflector, you will enjoy analysing the information that you find. It is a process of discovery to walk through the streets looking for the holes and helping your team to put in place some new routes.

In what will hopefully be seen as shared learning, a facilitator – probably you – sits down with each team member in turn and goes through their record of demands. For each demand, question them if it was a request for action that was wanted or not wanted. This does not mean whether or not they wanted to do it, or we might say no to everything. By 'wanted' is meant: was the action being demanded one that fits with an effective and clear way of doing the tasks that are relevant to that person's job description and workload?

At the first stage, that is all: just go through the list and decide – or help the person decide – whether each demand is wanted or not wanted. Different people will respond differently. For some it will largely be a fairly simple process, and they will see the patterns. Others – perhaps those who are more passive in how they handle themselves and their workload – will need help to see beyond the fact that they are 'required' to do things that are demanded of them. While it is possible to thrust learning upon people, it is worth encouraging them to think – even if it is not their own inclination – of the bigger picture.

It is difficult to explain the process in a way that will make sense to other people's situations. You need to try it for yourself. An example of a successful use of a demands analysis might help. The first time I did this exercise, some of those who joined in were designers and art workers in a publications design studio. One of the things the team was required to do was to send copies of the organization's logo and usage guidelines to external designers who were featuring the organization in their own materials. They could be sent on disc, on CD, or down an ISDN line. It is not a large or complex thing to do; it is a small task, but it is an interruption to the flow of other, more real, work. The demands analysis showed that requests were coming in all the time, and could be directed at any one in the team. Different people did different things with the requests: some attended to each request immediately, some saved the requests up and did a few at a time, some ignored them completely. Everyone grumbled about it. Of course, in a way we already knew this information. What the demands analysis allows is a way of articulating what the designers already knew: the process was inefficient and frustrating and had a lot of room for improvement. Going through the process legitimizes the knowledge, and allows one to learn from it. The knowledge is legitimized for everyone: a hole has been found in the street, and it is obviously a good idea to look for a different, safer, street. In this case what the designers decided to do was to ask one of them to spend half a day preparing a stock of the logo and guidelines on disc and CD, and to send an announcement to colleagues to state a minimum amount of notice required when requests were made for the logo to be sent. Then, when requests came in, they were collected until the appointed time, when the pre-prepared disc or CD was sent out. The system became clearer, was clearly communicated, and more effective, and the levels of frustration dropped.

Larger blocks of time were necessary initially: in discussing what the new process should be, in announcing it to colleagues, and in building up the stock of CDs and discs. They were time limited though. We did not do a precise measurement, because we knew instinctively that this was obviously the better way.

This may seem simplistic and I think some people might wonder 'what is the point?' As long as the CDs get sent out, what does it really matter whether the process is as neat and tidy as possible? Not everyone will agree about the best street, and some people like to have holes

to grumble about. We know that structure and pattern are important to some people and less so to others. Presumably not all reflectors are also structure people. But there must be a value in learning, and I believe that a lesson learned will often lead to the discernment of patterns, and the way they can be improved. At worst, this will merely bring satisfaction to those tidily minded structure people. At best, it will embed improved, more effective ways of working.

On the other hand, sometimes what one learns is to look at very different patterns, outside one's own box. This is why story-telling, poetry and art are such exciting means for learning about the way one is operating, running one's department, or organization: why not learn by reflecting on a metaphor, or a theme that emerges from a painting?

It is fascinating to observe how different people learn (or sometimes how they do not learn). One would think that being able to walk down the street without falling in a hole would be everyone's goal. But there are many other ways we can approach our journey. Some are determined to fail, and some are determined that others will fail. There is not, in any sector, a full complement of those who are eager for a positive outcome, or who agree what a positive outcome is. Taking time out to reflect, to learn, can seem like a waste, like taking the time to do a demands analysis.

Learning in public can seem dangerous. Although Brockbank, McGill and Beech point out in Part 1 that learning is a social experience, I think this can be quite scary. So learning is a risky thing to do. For one thing it requires one to say that there is room for improvement ... and this may not come easily to people.

Changing the culture of an organization is a major undertaking. But the change to embrace reflective learning surely brings exponential growth: the more one does it, the more it happens. There are some instances where this happens in the voluntary sector, where there are some networks that encourage good learning experiences. One of these is described below.

Resources, even in well-established charities, tend to be thinly stretched. And of course the resources are usually directed at the point of greatest need. I have never worked anywhere in the voluntary sector where there has been spare capacity. And so learning, and even more so, reflective learning, seems like a real luxury: if it is not built into the system or if the people in positions of influence are not by nature or aptitude reflective thinkers, then reflective learning will not happen. This is a shame. Perhaps because they have often been in straightened circumstances, I have known organizations fall – too easily – into a culture of blame, where individuals are afraid to take risks: they don't walk down any streets at all, for fear of falling down the hole; or they rush down a street without looking – because there are insufficient resources to enable careful walking – and thus fall in the hole.

We do not need to reinvent the wheel. If we need a thing that will help us propel something forward, we can look around and see if anyone else has invented a thing that looks like it might do the job. One of the ways in which the voluntary sector is very good at this is in the network of communicators who meet up a few times a year as part of a loose internal communications network to share ideas about best practice.

This valuable learning tool is organized by a small group, which sets up a few meetings each year and maps out a series of topics, inviting an organization known to know something about it to present on the topic. It is low key and low maintenance. In this way I have learned, for example about communicating brand identity within organizations, and about dos and don'ts when setting up an intranet. This information sharing is not done in an overtly reflective way, but it is I think something distinctive about learning in the voluntary sector. Certainly I have never known anything like it in the commercial sector. It does,

though, require an attitude of openness, both in the sharing of information – good and bad – and in the willingness to be seen to be learning.

For a brief example, our group once learned from a case study of how VSO (the charity that works through volunteers to promote sustainable development in the world's poorest countries) had defined their brand identity. In the space of an hour, and an informal question-and-answer session, the director of communications at VSO gave an overview of the key objectives, described the main successes, flagged a few mistakes he wishes they hadn't made, and outlined one or two things he would do differently. Commercially, some organizations would have regarded this as sensitive material. Instead, it was freely offered as best practice (and, presumably, as a well-deserved bit of PR). When NCH went through a similar exercise a year later, we were glad to be able to utilize several practical lessons learned via this informal network.

Undoubtedly there are some organizational secrets we keep to ourselves in this network, but I wonder how we have learned to learn in this simple, open way? Maybe it has something to do with us all being communicators? Maybe it is to do with shared understanding of our sector? Certainly we all benefit from this commitment to sharing our best practice.

19 *Creating a Learning Organization within Norwich Union*

Sue Dives

The financial services industry has been moving and developing very fast in all areas in the last twenty years. Organizations have been transformed through mergers and acquisitions, and through product, technology and service development. The Commercial and General Norwich Union was formed in 2000 through the merger of Norwich Union and the previously merged Commercial Union and General Accident. Norwich Union is the UK's largest insurance group and the world's sixth largest insurer. The company has assets of over £200 billion with approximately 15 million customers and employs 70 000 people worldwide.

Over the past two hundred years, Norwich Union has continuously been able to meet the challenges of a changing and competitive marketplace by developing a diverse and complex portfolio of products and services to meet their customers' needs. A key to Norwich Union's success has been its people and their ability to learn and develop in a fast-changing environment.

This case study illustrates double-loop learning in practice: first, in transforming how a team approached their customers, and team leaders developed their staff; and second, in facilitating a new e-commerce initiative. Learning achieved from the internally focused initiative was used to inform and guide the approach to achieve success in the new e-commerce marketplace.

Ammi Fuller of Norwich Union was responsible for leading both these projects and creating the learning environment which led to success.

The starting point – transforming the technology helpdesk

To enable the business to grow, Norwich Union identified the need to develop a new information technology (IT) platform to give broader-based and integrated information access across the key business areas. This would enable each department to be able to give a more comprehensive service to their customers. The new IT system had increased functionality, product access, complexity and capability, together with flexibility to support new initiatives. The roll-out of the new technology involved the replacement of computer hardware and software throughout the business and a comprehensive customer management training programme. It was estimated that the project would take approximately twelve months to complete.

First-line IT support for the Norwich Union head-office departments and the field was

provided by the in-house IT 'helpdesk' of approximately twenty consultants. The helpdesk provided a first-line support service providing diagnostics and advice via the telephone to find solutions to the majority of basic technology-based queries. In the event of the IT problem being more difficult to resolve, the helpdesk liaised with the user and engineering teams.

Unfortunately, the existing helpdesk did not enjoy a good reputation. Customer expectations were not met in terms of speed of answering, problem resolution and customer care, resulting in frequent complaints. The IT helpdesk team were trying to do the best they could with limited resources, servicing a complex system and helping an internal customer base of varying computer skills. Although the team was given some limited training regarding the specific systems, the team's IT literacy skills were largely self-taught. Some learning was shared across the team, however this was only on an *ad hoc* basis and not formalized. The team felt that their customers did not understand the pressures they were under and, consequently, the morale of the team was low.

It was identified that a critical factor in the successful launch and implementation of the new IT initiative would be the ability of the helpdesk to deliver a high-quality service from day one of the launch. In order to create the environment for success, Norwich Union recognized that the helpdesk had to be transformed. It would need to be able to service the new technology and simultaneously upgrade service to its customers. A new call centre manager, Ammi Fuller, was appointed from outside and given the challenge to create an IT helpdesk which would deliver a high-quality service and be respected from within. In addition, the helpdesk team would be required to help others learn and develop their skills so that the potential of the new technology could be fully realized in order to achieve business objectives.

Reading the map

The first steps were to understand the present position, looking at the issues from a variety of perspectives in order to develop the best way forward. The approach was to identify the specific groups who had a direct interest in the IT helpdesk service, stakeholder or customer groups, and understand their needs and expectations. The key stakeholder groups were identified as the:

- helpdesk team
- internal users
- engineers
- IT software suppliers
- project team.

Ammi Fuller developed a contact strategy for each of the stakeholder groups and identified gaps between the actual and proposed service delivery. This information was then used to develop a plan for the way forward.

THE HELPDESK TEAM

The call centre manager quickly set up formal and informal meetings with the helpdesk consultants. He spent time talking to each individual to begin to understand the situation from their point of view.

The team had been selected on the basis of their technical skills rather than their customer-service and problem-solving skills. The operational focus was one-dimensional, solely dealing with technical queries with little practical understanding of the customer's needs. This was reflected in the role of the team leader whose primary responsibility was the handling of more complex calls rather than managing and developing individuals within the team.

They knew that the new initiative would involve major change and they perceived that it would have a dramatic impact on them. They were nervous about the changes and felt ill-equipped to meet the expectations of the new manager. The team wanted their efforts to be recognized, respected, developed and valued; in addition, they wanted training to help them meet the new challenges.

Early in the project Ammi Fuller had identified that the team would need some behavioural skills training to complement their technical skills. He wanted to send a strong message that, although the team would be facing a new challenge, they would be given the support and help they needed to achieve success.

He commissioned the Oxford Group to design specific training for the helpdesk team and as part of the fact-finding exercise, consultants from the Oxford Group ran workshops and one-to-one interviews with the team and team leaders to assess the skills base and understand training needs.

OTHER STAKEHOLDER/CUSTOMER GROUPS

Ammi Fuller divided his time between the helpdesk team and the other key customer/stakeholder groups. He spent time with the engineers, third-party providers of computer services and end users to establish requirements, understand the problems with the existing service delivery and explore concerns about the new systems.

The stakeholders wanted improvements in both technical service delivery and the way in which the service was provided. Many of the users felt that the consultants did not effectively help them articulate the exact nature of the problems they were experiencing, understand their anxieties and difficulties or help them learn. Suppliers and engineers felt that there was a wide variance in the delivery of the service and had had little confidence in the information provided.

The project team knew that the users of the new system would need effective support for the first stages of the roll-out. They were aware that the success of the programme would be coloured by the experiences of the pilot groups. They were particularly keen that these new customers received high-quality help, felt confident in the new system and built expertise within the user group.

Planning the route

THE STRATEGY

The call centre manager recognized that the team needed to develop personal self-respect and belief in their ability to make the change, alongside learning a new set of technical and behavioural skills. The environment had to be created to support and reinforce a learning culture. In order to do this, a holistic strategy was created to transform the helpdesk operation and build the climate which encouraged self-esteem and confidence (see Figure 19.1).

Figure 19.1 Holistic strategy elements

Elements of that holistic strategy included reviewing the policies and procedures such as pay and reward, and a formal performance management system, as well as the environmental issues such as the management of customer expectation.

Pay and reward
The reward structure was realigned to reflect and recognize the ability and skills of the team in comparison to the rest of the business.

Working environment
The environment in which people were working was reviewed in order to create the most enabling conditions. The review examined the physical layout, displays and working areas, and improved tools to do the job, such as integrated technology solutions with intelligence-building facilities.

PR and marketing
An important task was to encourage the customer groups to use the new services being offered and help them understand what those new services were. A proactive strategy was developed to improve the PR and market the helpdesk in order to build confidence in the team and to change preconceptions.

Relationship management
In a time of change there is an important period of transition. During this time, learning is taking place; however, it takes time and can be compromised by the need to meet short-term goals. Ammi Fuller wanted to create 'breathing space' for the teams so that they could take the learning opportunities. He did this by visiting the stakeholder and customer groups, explaining the strategy and gaining their help and understanding during the transition period.

By working more closely with the stakeholders and developing greater mutual understanding, expectations were managed and the team was given the opportunity to learn. In addition, the improved relationship meant that the efforts of the team were better aligned to meet future customer needs.

Involvement and recognition

At the very beginning of the project, the message to the team was that they were key players in the change and that they were the customers. Every member of the team was involved in the plans through different activities, for example, visiting engineers, team meetings, discussions and sharing of learning through reflection and reflective dialogue.

Performance management

The team had grown offering support to customers, however there were no structured performance guidelines and processes in place. A structured performance management process was developed and implemented to support learning and continuous development.

The performance management process designed with the team recognized performance in terms of 'what' was done through results and 'how' it was done through competencies. The starting-point was for the team to have clarity and direction so that each individual knew where they were going and what was expected of them. Performance was then reviewed against those agreed expectations, an example of learning for improvement. This was done through an ongoing coaching process which helped individuals consider their own performance through reflection and reflective dialogue. This process was further reinforced with the team exploring and sharing their learning with each other as a continuous activity, building knowledge and confidence.

Training, learning and development

Comprehensive training and development was provided to help the team move forward in this important time of transition. Continuous development and learning was a fundamental requirement and, as a part of the performance management approach, every member of the team had an agreed and structured personal development plan.

Making the journey

At the start, the helpdesk was at crisis point in terms of the confidence of the rest of the organization and the confidence the helpdesk team had in themselves. Ammi Fuller wanted to create the environment where the team could begin to believe in themselves and to see that they could achieve success. He did this by bringing strong leadership in the form of a powerful, clear vision, a strategy for success and practical first steps to be taken. Through meetings and coaching, he helped the team members understand how the changes would affect them.

It is fair to say that the initial intervention from the call centre manager was not well received. The organization needed some quick service improvements from the helpdesk so that they could deliver business goals. In addition, Ammi Fuller wanted to help both the customers and the team believe that the helpdesk could be successful. The helpdesk team had to make certain immediate changes and to create some 'quick wins' which could be achieved and were very visible to the customer base. This was done through the focus of effort and commitment to the significant improvement of the quality of service in two key areas. Those

areas were improvements in the speed of answering the telephone calls in the first instance and the returning of customer calls as promised. Early success inspired the team and helped them begin to build confidence and belief in themselves. The way forward was to ensure that learning could be a constant feature of the operation in the present and the future. A competency framework was developed which provided the basis to assess performance in terms of the behaviours demonstrated and the achievement of business targets.

A modular management training programme lasting four months was developed and run by the Oxford Group, for the team leaders. The first stage of the programme was designed to help the team leaders learn how to learn and how they could help others learn. Using these skills they then developed their ability to coach and performance manage their teams using reflection and reflective dialogue. The modular design created the practical opportunity to reinforce and consolidate learning and to have time for reflection and reflective dialogue.

The performance management culture helped individuals to openly discuss their roles and responsibilities, gain clarity of what was expected of them and how this would be measured. In addition, it encouraged the learners to share and explore their feelings about 'how' they did their job as well as 'what' they did. Each individual had regular coaching from their team leader when performance was discussed. Learning was consolidated and continuously reinforced through the process of feedback and review. A high level of trust was built through the development of strong and supportive relationships within the team, which enabled team members to dare to think 'outside the box' and complete the double-loop learning process.

Learning was recognized as a key criterion for future success, which was measured by the increased capability of the team to support the changing customer and business needs. Systems were created to capture information about successes and effective problem solving between the helpdesk team and other stakeholders in order to build a new intelligence base. Regular workshops for staff and other stakeholders, were set up to create opportunities for open and honest reflection and reflective dialogue. The workshops were facilitated events where specific stakeholder groups were invited to identify and share feedback and learning with the helpdesk team. Continuous improvement and quality underpinned the ongoing effective development of the helpdesk. The new fully integrated IT initiative rolled out successfully throughout the organization with the full support of the IT helpdesk.

Completing the circuit – achieving success

The approach used meant that learning was embedded and became an automatic way of working. The helpdesk function achieved success and met the goals set. Success was measured against a range of criteria including the effectiveness of problem resolution and the way in which customer service was delivered. Importantly, the success was recognized and acknowledged by all of the key stakeholders, including the helpdesk team themselves. Continuous, sustainable improvement and learning was a constant theme throughout and individuals learned to develop their emotional intelligence as well as their technical intelligence. The new way of learning created the capability for them to take on further IT development challenges positively and broaden the scope of their expertise. Critically, they had learned how to learn through reflection and how to create the environment where others could learn. Working in such an environment offers the space and time for reflection and is typified by a coaching approach.

The contribution of the helpdesk was two-fold; it provided valuable first-line help and advice for its customers but also enhanced organizational capability through the education of the users. After two years, turnover is less than 5 per cent against an industry average of over 24 per cent, the team have real pride in what they do, and customers respect and value the help given.

The Contact Centre: building on double-loop learning

The opportunity to transfer the learning from this project came in the following year. As part of the strategic business development of the Norwich Union a new Web-based business was planned. Norwich Union.com was designed to offer an alternative product range and service to the general public through the Norwich Union's Internet network. Although the plan was that the customers would be largely self-supporting through the Web, it was recognized that there would need to be an on-line support service provided through a contact centre.

The creation of the contact centre presented a very new challenge. This being one of the first e-commerce initiatives to be taken, there were few precedents to inform the way forward. The sales and marketing plan forecasted the number of new customers attracted to the new portfolio of products and services. They knew the success of this important initiative would be very dependent on the ease for the customers of doing business through the Web. The plan was to roll out a broad range of new products and services in phases as the infrastructure was developed. The contact centre therefore would be in a constant process of change and learning. Predictions of traffic volumes indicated that a contact centre of approximately ninety advisers would be required in the first phase of the launch.

Ammi Fuller was invited to take up the role of creating a leading-edge, innovative contact centre building through the learning he had gained from the transformation of the IT helpdesk. The new contact centre required a fundamental change and a paradigm shift in thinking. In this context the typical ways of doing business were no longer valid. Customer contact would be remote and mainly though the Internet. This meant that all processes and procedures had to be re-thought and the implications considered very carefully. Customer needs would be fundamentally different from the typical telephone customer and the opportunity to build a relationship with the customer would be more limited. The e-commerce initiative was new ground for the business and although very exciting there were many uncertainties and risks to manage. The approach drew on the powerful learning from the previous experience and was an example of how new understanding could be achieved through transformative double-loop learning (see Figure 19.2).

THE CHALLENGE

The new contact centre would need to provide complex technical help to support external customers across a range of products and access options which were still being developed and tested. In addition, the challenge was to achieve success without yet knowing what customer expectations would be, emotionally and technically.

Using the experience and learning from the previous project, key preconditions for success were identified and used as the basis to develop the implementation strategy (see Figure 19.3).

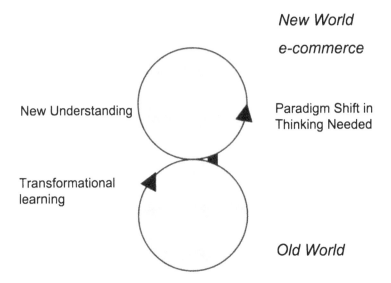

Figure 19.2　Double-loop learning

CLARITY AND DIRECTION

The first step was to define and understand the vision, mission and the role of the contact centre within the business. Although there was a level of clarity about the role, at this stage in the new project there were some major elements which were not yet clear or understood. This was accepted as the context for the initiative, which created excitement and, with previous experience, the management team had confidence in knowing that learning could be transferred to meet the unknown.

Figure 19.3　Preconditions for success

CULTURE

Ammi Fuller was clear about the type of culture he wanted to create for the contact centre. He wanted it to be an open environment built on trust and support, where learning and development could thrive and where teams and individuals felt valued. Above all, the culture would create the context for business success alongside personal growth, and enjoyable and fulfilling work and quality of life.

One of the important steps following recruitment and induction of the new team leaders and trainers was to design, develop and run a team-building day to reinforce the values and to have 'fun' – a key ingredient of effective learning.

Recruitment

The culture was reflected in the recruitment strategy. To support development of the contact centre, a team of trainers, team leaders and advisers needed to be recruited. The importance of recruiting the right staff who had the right behaviours and who were able to learn was key. Behavioural criteria within a competency framework were established and used in the selection process. Assessment centres were used for all roles, with applicants participating in a variety of activities designed to give them the opportunity to demonstrate their competencies and values. In addition, the call centre manager demonstrated his commitment to them by personally attending more than 80 per cent of the assessment centres to share the vision, answer questions and gain their feedback.

Reflecting the culture of involvement and learning, the recruitment process was phased to recruit the trainers and team leaders first so that they could be involved from the start in the design, development and delivery of training for the front-line teams. The driving philosophy was that they would be able to support and create the learning organization from scratch. It was critical that the team leaders themselves felt emotionally part of the new team and felt fully involved in developing and sharing their own learning to create the processes, procedures and behaviours that would form the culture of the new call centre.

Assessment centres are used for all ongoing recruitment, selection and promotion. Through coaching and an open environment, internal candidates are aware of development needs and have personal development plans to help them achieve the next steps.

TRAINING AND DEVELOPMENT

Team leaders and trainers were given initial people-skills training to help them develop and shape the agent-training and development suite. Key performance management skills were developed which involved coaching, feedback and managing learning. The team leaders themselves were part of the performance management system with regular one-to-one coaching and regular team meetings to support what they were doing and, more importantly, helping to create a learning environment.

During the set-up phase, there were times when product launches were delayed. Motivation and energy was maintained through training and development and involvement in generating knowledge, skills and operational intelligence. Teams developed flexibility and ability to explore and transfer learning.

The importance of the learning culture was reinforced by the decision to recruit only 50

per cent of the trainers and team leaders required initially so that there would be opportunities for personal development growth and recognition through promotion.

PERFORMANCE MANAGEMENT

As in the previous example, a robust performance management process was established to provide the framework for success. Through the preview coaching process, individuals were able to discuss and agree both technical and behavioural standards. Learning was reinforced through the review process of reflection and reflective dialogue. From the start the right behaviours were demonstrated, reinforced and recognized.

The culture, time, space and opportunities were created for people to talk to one another, learn from each other, share best practice and enhance their emotional intelligence.

The environment

The opening of a new centre provided the opportunity to design a physical environment which met emotional and operational needs. Team leaders and their teams formed physical units as well as intellectual units, increasing opportunities for reflective dialogue and shared learning.

Reward and recognition

Tailored reward-and-recognition systems were developed aligned to the culture and values of the organization. Building on the belief that if the right behaviours were demonstrated the desired results would be achieved, financial rewards were linked to behaviour. The performance management system introduced recognized the balance of performance between results and behaviour, which included learning and development.

Special awards were available of up to 15 per cent of salary on a quarterly basis, assessed purely on the demonstration of the right behaviours such as 'embracing change'.

Continuing the journey and sharing the learning

The contact centre is still developing. It has achieved success and has been able to flexibly deliver responsive customer service across all areas of the business. Learning continues and is shared openly across operational divisions who, in turn, are able to develop new understanding and create the potential to transform thinking.

Many organizations aspire to create a learning organization; however, often the reality in a pressurized working environment is that the aspiration is not fully realized. The management team at the contact centre continue to work hard to ensure that they are a learning organization in practice. Although there have been many challenges in the development of both the previously described initiatives, a critical review of the successes have highlighted some of the critical actions which have made that possible (see Box 19.1).

Above all, the key factor affecting success has been the total commitment by the senior team to ensure that long-term learning is not compromised by short-term responses to work pressures. In a rapidly changing and demanding business environment, the manager is continuously balancing needs and priorities and often must defend and actively reinforce the culture and philosophy. At first, this can be particularly difficult, however success generates belief and confidence in the reflective learning approach.

BOX 19.1

Key steps to a learning culture taken by Norwich Union

- Create a learning culture by actively planning, implementing and managing it as any other key element of business performance.
- Have a clear vision of what an effective learning organization is and how it would be measured.
- Develop an holistic strategy to achieve a learning culture.
- Create the framework for learning through performance management.
- Proactively manage the external and internal factors which will affect success.
- Create, recognize and take opportunities for learning.
- Use reflection and reflective dialogue to learn how to learn.
- Recognize that learning takes time. Long-term gains may be lost by short-term expediency.

- Proactively maintain the importance and profile of learning.
- Design modular training to provide opportunities for consolidation of skills in preview and review coaching.
- Develop 'heart and mind' with self-belief and knowledge. Use reflection and reflective dialogue to explore experiences and feelings.
- Support the achievements with strong leadership.
- Actively identify opportunities to transfer learning through reflective dialogue and double-loop learning. Use knowledge to transform and rethink ways to move forward.
- Build supportive relationships and learning champions.
- Celebrate success and have fun.

20 *Knowledge Management and CELT*

Nic Beech, George Cairns and Gerry Kincaid

In the postmodern era, there are pressures on the use of time and space which can have significant impacts on learning. In addition, the traditional ways of conceiving learning – a process of transferring knowledge – leads to a privileging of knowledge management systems which reduce, codify and transfer information as if it were usable knowledge.

In this chapter, we explore some of the problematic assumptions which lie behind such approaches to knowledge management and present an alternative, Computerized Evaluative Learning Tool (CELT), which is being used to facilitate the learning of GPs. It has been designed in a way which seeks to escape some of the problems of traditional knowledge management. We explore an alternative metaphor for learning – that of travel – and apply post-dichotomous thinking to the learning framework.

Potential problems with IT-centred learning

The postmodern world presents certain issues which have a strong impact on learning, especially a 'compression' of time and space (Lyotard 1984). Time is compressed in the sense that consumers of services and products hold expectations of speedy delivery, and production processes such as JIT (just-in-time) reinforce the idea that efficiency is achieved principally through having the right materials to hand at the moment they are needed and not either too early (which leads to increased costs through having to hold stock) nor too late (which leads to increased costs through unnecessary under-utilization of production capability). Maximizing control over time is, therefore, linked closely to conceptions of efficiency, which are paramount in many iterations of business culture. The concern with speed and timeliness is also reinforced through many symbols of societal culture including a perceived need for 'real-time' information, the illusion of news occurring before it is news – for example, through the key points of reports and speeches being 'leaked' to the press and made public before the report has been issued or the speech made, and frequent updates of IT software and hardware being regarded as *de rigueur*.

Similarly, traditional spatial barriers to communication and interaction have been reduced by various forms of technology. Virtual meetings can be held through video conferencing, and Web bulletin boards can 'bring people together' across the world without any physical movement being involved. In the workplace, the concern with space-usage is often linked to effectiveness. Many traditional workspaces have utilization rates which mean that

for much of the time space is unused. Various approaches such as teleworking and hot-desking have been adopted in order to increase effectiveness by decreasing the amount of space held and increasing its (flexible) utilization.

Whilst the compression of time and space may hold business advantages in creating efficiency and effectiveness gains (at least in the short term), they raise certain problems for learning. These problems can be accentuated depending on the way that learning is conceptualized. One way of understanding the conceptualization of learning is through the use of metaphors. Baets and Van der Linden (2000) highlight a number of pedagogical metaphors. The dominant traditional metaphor is that of 'transfer'. The learner is envisaged as a passive vessel, standing beside a dock and the teacher places the knowledge into the empty vessel until it is filled, at which point there may be a 'bill of loading' such as a certificate or a formal acknowledgement of competence. When things go wrong the teacher can blame the vessel, and the learner can blame the loader. Baets and Van der Linden identify the 'excellence literature' as an archetypal example of this metaphor. Conceptual routines and prescriptions are complemented by stories of the exploits of corporate heroes and 'excellent companies', and the role of the learner is to absorb (and subsequently apply) the learning in an unproblematized way.

The pressures of postmodernity and the transfer metaphor inform much practice in the field of knowledge management. In this field, IT systems are often used to abstract and codify knowledge (Hansen et al. 1999) in order to store and transmit 'packages of knowledge' which can be used by people throughout the organization (Bassi 1997) regardless of their position in time and space. Because the knowledge is centrally stored and accessible, organization members can retrieve it when and where they need it. The intention is to maximize the efficiency and effectiveness of knowledge transfer.

There are, however, potential problems with such approaches to IT-centred learning, and these can be identified in the following seven assumptions:

1. Learning occurs as a process of installing information in the learner (as opposed to assuming that learning is a heuristic process involving interpretation and activity on the part of the learner).

2. Learning is directly transferable from one context to another – so the learner can take knowledge from the teacher and apply it in their own circumstances unproblematically (as opposed to assuming that learning is context-specific, and that it will necessarily change and develop if it is to be operative in any new context of language, practice, skill and social structure).

3. Learning is personal and individual – in a sense knowledge is in the head of the beholder (as opposed to learning being a social activity that will usually entail social interaction).

4. Learning is deliberate and explicit – in other words, the content of knowledge that is transferred must be selected and packaged by the teacher (as opposed to knowledge being often tacit or implicit and not completely conscious on the part of the teacher or learner).

5. Useful learning is available at the moment it is needed, and there is a cultural propensity for newness in which being up-to-date may be more important that getting-it-right (as opposed to genuine learning being based on reflection, over time and often iteratively).

6. Learning will occur on the basis of rationally structuring and absorbing information, independent of emotion (as opposed to learning being regarded as embedded in emotion – either as a positive motivator or as a disenabling blockage to learning).

7. Human beings can make optimal (if not maximal) use of IT systems for learning (as opposed to IT systems being a barrier to really effective exploratory learning).

In summary, an approach to learning and knowledge management based on the transfer metaphor (Baets and Van der Linden 2000) and on codification and packaging processes (Bassi 1997) is likely to have weaknesses from assuming that learners are passive, that packages of knowledge can be captured and applied in new contexts through an individual and rational process. Our experience of seeking to manage, or enable, learning has indicated that such assumptions are questionable. The example outlined below aims to overcome some of these problems.

CELT

Computerized Evaluative Learning Tool (CELT) is an IT-based (but not simply IT-centred) learning support system which has been developed in the first instance for use by general medical practitioners (GPs). It seeks to make the most of technology in order to enable GP users to deal with the space and time pressures referred to above, whilst not becoming a slave to the technology. It is acknowledged that there are social, emotional and other factors in the learning process which can either stimulate or stifle the effective use of the system. The system design and operation are vitally important, but in and of themselves, they cannot guarantee useful learning. In order to increase efficacy, pedagogical issues as well as technical ones had to be addressed at the outset and throughout the project.

How CELT operates

The purpose of CELT is to help GPs respond to, and learn from, events in their everyday experience. It is not an expert system designed to assist in diagnostic decision making, rather the focus is on the GP as a learner. The system is database driven and has been designed to operate on the standard hardware that GPs have in their consulting rooms and offices. Although this may be regarded as a limiting factor, for CELT it was important to make the system accessible and easily affordable.

A typical learning process could occur as follows: a GP has an interaction with a patient which stimulates awareness of a learning need or possibility. It could be, for example, difficulty in diagnosing an uncommon illness, or an interaction which the GP felt could have gone better. Such a 'trigger event' can stimulate the GP to access the system in order to self-manage their learning. Figure 20.1 shows the main CELT splash screen. The initial screen identifies different routes into using the system. Main choices include:

- identification of an educational process to meet a specific need
- a practice-oriented reflection on a learning experience
- a reflection on emotional responses
- an analysis to inform future action.

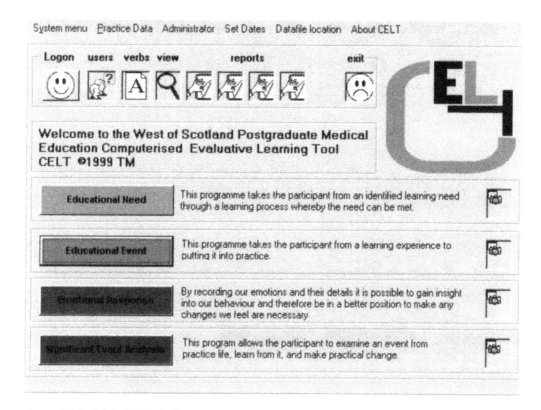

Figure 20.1 Main CELT splash sceen

The GP enters a record of the event and their learning needs and the system prompts them to manage their learning. The data entry encapsulates subjective narrative, but also prompts the GP to adopt an action–focus through the use of particular verbs. Initially the GP will explore the educational need. They are prompted to describe their learning need and the event that triggered their perception of the need (see Figure 20.2).

Once the learner has completed the initial screens, they can conduct further analysis. First, they are asked what current knowledge they have that might be applicable. Then they are asked to identify what area of practice the learning issue relates to, and to devise additional questions which will be used to direct the search for information and other sources of learning. The main purpose, individual learning, is served through recording, action planning and monitoring. Having recorded the initial event, the GP is prompted to decide on learning activities, which can include both technologically supported learning, for example operating a Web-based search for information, or identification and use of more traditional learning media, such as books and seminars available to the GPs. CELT structures the learning process in a mode that can be seen as the increasingly reflective dimensions of learning – moving from action through description to reflection on both reflection and action – described by Brockbank and McGill (1998). It relates to some of the principles of action learning (Revans 1980; McGill and Beaty 2001) in focusing on a specific event (or set of events) which is real and meaningful for the learner, prompting personal reflection through a combination of open expression and questioning, and subsequent action and 'report back' (see Figure 20.3).

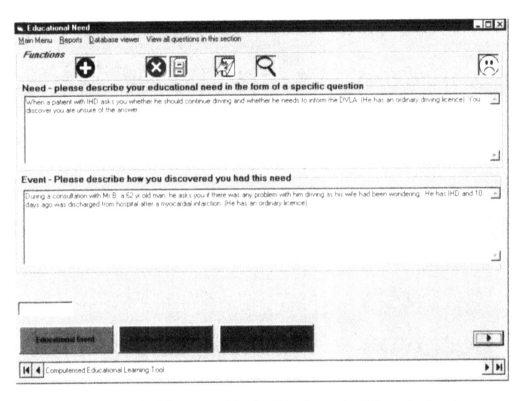

Figure 20.2 Education Need: first screen of five describing the event and the resultant need

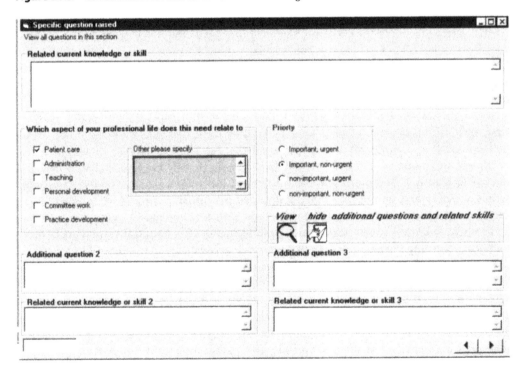

Figure 20.3 Second screen of five in the Educational Need system

The perspective adopted here is that it would be false to assume that learning is emotion-free. In the context of health care, there is a conjunction of evidence-based science and interpretative human issues. Stress rates amongst GPs are high, partly as a result of the human issues and it is important to acknowledge this in their learning. In addition, because the profession is regarded as scientific, in the popular mind there can be false expectations that correct answers to clear problems can be produced, whereas in reality diagnosis and cure are typically complicated by problems which are not reducible to formulae and facts. CELT focuses attention on the emotion surrounding the triggering event. The learner is guided to reflect on the type, intensity and impact of the emotion (see Figure 20.4).

Figure 20.4 Emotional Response form, outlining the event and the generated emotional response

The motivation for getting actively involved is two-fold: the intrinsic motivation of learning and the extrinsic motivation of recording learning events and processes which 'score continuous professional development (CPD) points'. GPs need to maintain a recognized amount of CPD activity each year in order to obtain the Postgraduate education allowance (PGEA), and CELT offers one way of achieving (and recording) part of this requirement (see Figure 20.5). GPs may plan to develop their knowledge by use of information put onto the system by other users, or they may devise learning actions which include getting information from other sources, such as the Internet, and formal training. A further development for CELT will be to enhance the searching facility and enable users to search a central database via the Web.

The system can also be used proactively by education or professional bodies. For example, where a problem arose repeatedly, targeted courses and information could be made available to the professional network.

In addition, the system provides an audit function. Currently it is self-driven, so that the GPs can track their own learning needs, actions and reflections over time. The profession is

Figure 20.5 Summary Credit dialogue box

aware of potential increases in litigation by dissatisfied patients, and of the need of GPs to be able to give evidence of their proactive development. The CELT system provides one way of tracing the data for these needs. It provides a reliable record of learning equivalent to a learning journal. It is a 'closed-loop' system in which, when a GP generates an event, they have to 'close it off' by taking some action which they decide on, and reporting it. The system prompts the GP on any outstanding action points so that they cannot be easily forgotten or ignored.

It is important to acknowledge the social environment of learning, particularly when the learning carries emotional connotations. The Web-site is being developed to facilitate on-line access to a central CELT database storing all anonymized CELT entries. Standard Web-site functionality such as discussion groups and newsgroups are also being considered. In addition, users will be able to correspond with relevant GPs based on individual entries or experiences. These developments will enhance the possibilities for communal learning. The learning already has a communal element in that the data is generated by a community of practitioners, but further enabled interaction would diminish the physical boundaries to interactive learning of a professional group which is necessarily dispersed.

No single system can enable best learning practice for all users; however, CELT does engage with a number of design issues which seek to cross some traditional boundaries in knowledge management, as well as those of physical space. It formalizes learning through questioning/analysis, action planning and monitored report-back. Public self-analysis is enabled, and there is acknowledgment that learning and knowledge are not just about facts and information. CELT seeks to acknowledge that learning and knowledge generation are not emotion-free activities.

In a sense, opening up to one's peers can be a form of confession which can be highly invasive when done face-to-face (Beech et al. 2000). The advantages of openness in a group setting are that there is often a realization that one is not alone in having a particular problem and the emotions associated with it, and it is possible to gain from questioning and advice which lead to action. The disadvantage is that once something is confessed (a fear, a failure, a worry, and so on) it cannot be unconfessed. That knowledge becomes public, and can potentially be used as a source of power against the individual. One of the key advantages of the CELT system is that a supportive peer group can be enacted whilst anonymity is maintained. Thus, openness and confidentiality can be achieved simultaneously.

Discussion

Baets and Van der Linden (2000) offer alternative metaphors to that of 'transfer', and one of these is the 'travel' metaphor. In this metaphor, learning is not simply a matter of packaging and transferring knowledge, rather it is an active process on the part of the learner. There is a sense in which there is no true path for the learner to follow – rather the path is only revealed when you turn around and look at your own footsteps in the sand leading up to where you

currently are. Teachers can facilitate the learning process, but they cannot prescribe which direction will be best for the individual learner, nor can they know all the possible paths that the learner might take. As a guide, a teacher may provide navigation tools and techniques – maps and compasses – and the process will be one of exploration in which knowledge may be transformed. In other words, through learning and applying knowledge in new situations, the learner may develop the current understanding of the terrain being travelled.

The CELT system fits more closely with the travelling metaphor than the transfer metaphor. It stimulates and enables the learner to take control of their own learning, offering a guide but not constraining choice. It acknowledges the possibility of using established knowledge and information (current maps), but also focuses on how the learner will develop ideas and awareness to improve their own practice (the use of navigation tools to move into uncharted territory).

However, the negative pressures on learning identified above were not derived only from the dominant metaphor, they also related to the compression of time and space, and CELT also addresses these issues. First, with regard to time, the system is available whenever the learner has the time to use it. Learning records can be stored and returned to later, and information and stored forms of knowledge are available at any time via the Web and search facilities. In addition, as learning events are increasingly stored on the system, a virtual community of users can be accessed through the narratives and other records they have created at any time. Second, with regard to space, the system can operate across geographical boundaries without any significant barriers. Learners operating in remote areas can be linked to each other, and groups can be established. Although this will not completely replace face-to-face learning, it can remove some of the obstacles to interaction where people with shared concerns or interests live and work at a distance from each other.

It was argued above that the transfer metaphor and compressions of time and space led to problems which could be identified in seven assumptions. The assumptions were presented dichotomously with an alternative, noted in parenthesis, which could be held in tension with the original assumption. Typically, dichotomies operate in such a way as to eliminate one or other end of the tension. We would argue that this approach is less productive than one which adopts post-dichotomous thinking (Beech and Cairns 2001). This does not seek to resolve the tension, but preserves it, recognizing that learning is often not about exclusion (either/or) thinking, but about inclusion (both/alongside) thinking which does not dissolve the two ends of the tension into a single solution. CELT operates in this manner with regard to the assumptions listed:

1. Learning is a process of the learner making sense of their experience, but this can run alongside absorbing information, for example, about the similar experiences others have previously had.

2. Learning needs to be context-specific in its development and application, it needs to work for the learner, and, in this case, their patients. But that is not to say that every situation is entirely unrelated to others, nor that elements of best practice can neither transfer to other contexts, or stimulate a new reaction in those contexts.

3. Learning is in the head of the beholder in that it is only when the learner recognizes the path they have travelled that there will be the possibility of new and improved behaviour in the future. Similar analyses and critiques by others (such as teachers) will only have impact to the extent that they are genuinely accepted by the learner. However, learning is

also social. Having a community of practice is vital to the development of many professionals, and there is a role for guides and supporters in professional learning.

4. Learning incorporates deliberate and unconscious elements. For example, the emotional force of an event that triggers learning may be outside the conscious control of the learner, but the way they plan their review of the event and its impact may be deliberate and rational. The CELT format seeks to help the learner bring out tacit elements of their knowledge and understanding whilst accepting that implicit and unconscious elements are likely to remain embedded in the learner's practice.

5. It is important to have information and a structure for learning available when the learner is willing and able to learn, but this in itself is not sufficient for useful learning to occur. The process must also encourage reflective learning over time. Hence, providing a learning framework which can be cumulative – developing insight from an event, taking further action and reflecting on that – is a significant part of CELT's purpose.

6. Emotional content and context of learning are acknowledged within CELT. However, this factor is not dominant to the level where gaining access to information, or reflective processes cannot occur unless or until there has been an emotional reflection. In some settings, emotion may be very important for the learner, in others it may be relatively unimportant and so as a focus it can be increased or decreased in use of the programme by the learner.

7. IT systems are probably never used to the optimum, but this does not negate the proposition that they can significantly add to learning. The crucial thing is not whether or not the system is fully utilized, but whether the system provides the opportunities for learning that are useful to the GP when and where they need them. CELT seeks to do this in a way that is cost- and time-efficient.

Conclusion

The purpose of networked knowledge systems, such as CELT, is to provide learning and decision support based on real events rather than hypothetical ones. In order to achieve this, we would argue that it is important to address certain dichotomies, and, where possible, to escape from traditional 'either/or' forms of thinking. Adopting a travel metaphor may be more productive than the traditional transfer metaphor, and this alters the thought processes of both designers and users towards providing an environment for the learner to direct their own learning, rather than providing expertise in the form of packaged knowledge. It lays the basis for learning in which the main principles/dimensions of experience, reflection and reflective dialogue, the three domains of thinking, doing and feeling and a relevance to renewed action are all present.

The psychological context of knowledge management must be supportive of the user's needs for expression of lack of knowledge and fear of failure – past and future – as well as of the positive aspects of knowledge acquisition. In support of the psychological context, the physical context must also be designed to suit the needs of the user. The IT system must be user friendly, accessible and responsive on the user's terms. It must also enable the user to access and interact with it and with others within a supportive physical environment of their own choosing.

There is a need for individual analysis, and action and collective learning, between peers.

There is also a need for contributors to be able to make deliberate choices about their learning, adopting forms of rational analysis, and to engage emotionally. The programme operates in a way that enables a process that is equivalent to reflective dialogue by learners who are subject to the pressures of compressed time and space.

21 *Transformation Management: Developing Communities of Practice*

Ronnie Lessem

Building communities of practice

NATURE OF TRANSFORMATION

The Transformation Management programme links the University of Buckingham with its public and private-sector partners; together they build communities of practice, in contrast to the conventional stand-alone degree course aimed at the development of the individual in isolation of their organization and society. Such communities, in our case, are functionally based or process oriented (for example Human Resource or Information Technology functions), but may also be interorganizational, and cross-cultural in their nature and scope.

Specifically the transformation management programme is focused on:

- creating healthy communities, at Ealing Social Services
- developing a nursery for human growth, at the Virgin One Account
- sustaining development locally and globally at the Anglian Water Group.

Four assumptions underlie our approach, duly aligned with that of the French-born American authority on communities of practice, Etienne Wenger (1997):

- Learning is inherent in our nature – it is an ongoing and integral part of our work and lives, individually and collectively, rather than a separable 'taught' activity; as such the transformation programme is aligned with the individual and the organization's development.

- Learning means dealing with boundaries: it creates bridges; it involves multi-membership in serving to evolve our individual and communal identities; to that extent business and academe, as well as one organization and another, are juxtaposed.

- Learning is becoming: it builds upon personal and institutional histories to facilitate the unfolding of ourselves and our communities, so that ultimately, to that extent the rhythm of our programme – from preparatory, to ordinary, to extraordinary development – is sacrosanct.

- Learning transforms our identities: it transforms our ability to participate in the world by changing all at once who we are, our practices and our communities; to date, this is where

our experience is mixed, in that the parallel evolution of individual and organization remains hit and miss.

Whereas conventionally based education and training aims to create targeted competence in a specific field, our approach opens up opportunities for the renegotiation of individual–organizational–societal identity. Such education is more than individually formative. It is, communally, transformative. To that extent, and for example, the separation between organizational and environmental development at Anglian Water, hitherto, has been bridged.

Scope of transformation

While the above four elements underlie the nature of our programme, four others define its scope:

* Learning becomes a matter of *engagement*: defining a common enterprise in the process of pursuing it with others, duly oriented towards adding economic value; to the extent that Virgin One Account becomes personally and communally more enriching, so it brings in more profitable business.

* Learning becomes a matter of *alignment*: investing energy in a directed way and creating focus, it is duly oriented towards enhancing organizational effectiveness; for example, enhancing the degree of integration between Ealing's social and health services.

* Learning is a matter of *imagination*: locating our engagement in the broader society, conceiving of such as a dynamic context for our communal practices; the very notion of creating healthy communities, through our transformation programme, is a reflection of such imagination.

* Learning involves an *interplay* between the local and the global: it takes place, altogether, locally set in the context of what surrounds it globally; the development of Anglian Water locally, into the Anglian Water Group, globally, is in at least small part facilitated by the interactions between the water treatment (English) and construction (Czech) oriented members of our learning set.

As we shall see, then, within the communities of practice that we are developing, inductions fostering 'participation', and workshops promoting 'reification' set the stage, while projects facilitating progressive transformation, and accreditation incorporating communal incorporation, make up the actual performance (see Box 21.1).

We start with the programme inductions, designed to promote meaningful participation.

The three inductions: communal engagement, alignment, imagination

Communities of practice are first characterized by meaningful participation, involving both membership of social communities, and also active engagement in public or private enter-

The transformation programme

Form	Phase	Description	Schedule
INDUCTIONS	1	Engagement: Self and enterprise	Two- to
Accumulative	2	Alignment: Organization and Environment	three-day
Participation	3	Imagination: Business and Society	workshops
WORKSHOPS	1	Marketing to Customer Empowerment; Finance to	
Modular		Intellectual Capital	
Reification	2	Human Resource to Organizational Learning;	Three-day
		Operations to Knowledge Management	module
	3	Corporate Strategy to Managing Complexity;	
		Environment to Organizational Ecology	
PROJECT 1	1/1	Germination – Practical Incorporation 1	2 months
Departmental	1/2	Assimilation – Conceptual Incorporation 1	2 months
Transformation	1/3	Momentum – Strategic Incorporation 1	2 months
CERTIFICATE	1/4	Completion – Communal Incorporation 1	2 months
PROJECT 2	2/1	Germination – Practical Incorporation 2	2 months
Organizational	2/2	Assimilation – Conceptual Incorporation 2	2 months
Transformational	2/3	Momentum – Strategic Incorporation 2	2 months
DIPLOMA	2/4	Completion – Communal Incorporation 2	2 months
PROJECT 3	3/1	Germination – Practical Incorporation 3	2 months
Social	3/2	Assimilation – Conceptual Incorporation 3	2 months
Innovation	3/3	Momentum – Strategic Incorporation 3	2 months
MASTERS	3/4	Completion – Communal Incorporation 3	2 months
ACCREDITATION	1	Accredit/Incorporate Departmental Transformation	Half-day
	2	Accredit/Incorporate Corporate Transformation	Presentation
	3	Accredit/Incorporate Communal Transformation	Ceremonies

prises. It is a complex process that combines doing, talking, thinking, feeling and belonging – involving the whole person, set in the context of mutual recognition. In this experience of mutuality, participation is a source of identity. By recognizing the mutuality of our participation we become part of each other, through engagement, alignment and imagination.

The programme inductions, run by the University of Buckingham then, set the stage for such participation in and across the sponsoring organizations and societies, involving:

- first, self and enterprise – engagement
- second, organizational and environmental – alignment
- third, social and cultural – imagination.

Placing the focus, in that combined context, on participation:

- for individuals so that learning becomes an issue of engaging in and contributing to the practices of communities, such as the evolution of human resources at Anglian Water towards sustainable development

- for communities so that learning is an issue of refining their practice and ensuring new generations of members, as is the case for Ealing Social Services, which is oriented towards re-directing its core function to attract new people

- for organizations so that learning is an issue of sustaining the interconnected communities of practice through which an organization knows what it knows and thus becomes effective and valuable; such an evolved state of being is still somewhat alien to our participating organizations.

FIRST INDUCTION: COMMUNAL ENGAGEMENT – TRANSFORMATIONAL LEADERSHIP

The work of engagement is first of all that of explicitly forming communities of practice, within which individual and enterprise identities are progressively transformed, through:

- developing individual trajectories that shape identities in relation to each other
- pursuing mutual engagement in shared economic and social activities
- accumulating a history of shared activities within the community of practice
- producing a local regime of economic and social competence
- developing interpersonal relationships within and without the enterprise
- managing boundaries between the enterprise and its customer-and-community
- ultimately defining a common enterprise in the process of pursuing it with others.

Alan Clark, Deputy Head of Social Services at Ealing, has developed the notion of creating healthy communities with us, and with the adjacent hospital trust; orienting individual participants to this forms the basis for the first induction to individual and communal self-actualization, through transformational leadership.

Traditionally speaking, at least within the Anglo-Saxon world, the concept of the individualistic and materially oriented 'self-made man' was equated with self-development. More recently in the West the idea of 'self-actualization' has evolved, with a broader psychological and social base to it. Through this first induction programme, focused on the engagement of self-in-enterprise, we recognize the development of individual and communal identities through transformative leadership, set in the context of building up a community of practice.

SECOND INDUCTION: COMMUNAL ALIGNMENT – ORGANIZATIONAL TRANSFORMATION

The work of alignment, the second induction, requires people to coordinate perspectives and actions in order to direct energies to a common purpose. The challenge is to connect local to global styles and perspectives in ways that allow communities of practice, and the individuals within them, to invest their energies effectively. This characteristically involves:

- investing energy in a directed way and enhancing quality and focus
- negotiating perspectives, finding common ground, articulating visions

- devising procedural, quantifiable and controllable structures/systems
- reconciling technical and social perspectives in managing knowledge.

Craig Williams, Director of Consultants' Vision into Reality, is engaged with our participating organizations in helping them to manage knowledge effectively, through the individual participants on our programme, and their adjacent internal communities.

From both a social and a technological perspective, the hierarchically based twentieth century is giving way to the network-based twenty-first century. Property-based relationships are being displaced by an age in which 'access', of both a social and technical nature, is becoming key to individual and organizational, if not also societal development. Managing such unrelenting organizational change, with a view to continually re-creating alignment, is one of the great challenges of our day.

THIRD INDUCTION: COMMUNAL IMAGINATION – SOCIAL INNOVATION

Imagination requires the ability to reinvent ourselves, our enterprises, our practices and our communities. It needs the willingness, freedom, energy and time to expose ourselves to the exotic, move around, try new identities, and explore new relations by:

- recognizing our experience in others, that is, being in someone else's shoes
- defining a trajectory that connects what we are doing to an extended identity
- locating our engagement in broader systems in time and space, conceiving of the multiple cultural constellations that become contexts for our practices
- documenting historical developments, events, and transitions; reinterpreting histories and trajectories in new terms
- generating scenarios, exploring other possible worlds, and identities.

We are helping Anglian Water create a new global unity out of its local variety, most especially though re-cognizing, and re-combining its Anglian 'western' and 'southern' and Czech 'northern' and 'eastern' identities on the one hand, and water treatment and asset management configurations on the other (Lessem and Palsule 1997).

Ultimately the notion of managing in four worlds – pragmatic, rational, holistic and humanistic – has been developed over the past 15 years in Britain and continental Europe, Asia and southern Africa. Most recently we have begun to apply it to the creation of healthy communities, through re-conceiving of capitalism and communism in terms of a newly emerging environmentalism and humanism. We now turn from participation to so-called 'reification'.

Reification workshops: enterprise, organization, society

So-called 'reification' gives form to our experience. Applying a financial formula, creating a computer programme, applying a management concept, or developing a marketing tool, are all cases in point. This form then becomes a focus for the negotiation of meaning. Such a meaningful process, then, occupies much of our collective energy: from making entries in a financial journal to completing personnel records, from developing customer databases to market segmentation, from preparing strategic plans to documenting best practices, from

developing computer programs to evolving more intricately networked systems, from applying single concepts to devising entire business theories. In all these cases, aspects of fluid human experience are congealed into fixed managerial forms (Wenger 1997).

A good leader can reify their followers' inarticulate longings in one phrase that galvanizes support. A good tool, like the balanced scorecard, for instance, can reify activity so as to amplify its effects while making the activity effortless. A good procedure can reify a concept so as to make its application automatic. But the power of reification is also its danger, for example, tools like Total Quality can ossify activity. Procedures can hide broader meanings. The evocative power of reification is thus double-edged. A value statement may be frozen into a text, a definition of our 'shared values' that does not capture the richness of lived and worked experience. The course modules then, run locally, serve to promote such 'reification', but not in isolation of prior participation. Moreover, and in each case, the 'reified' body of theory is conveyed in the process of its own progressive evolution, starting with the transformation of financial, into intellectual capital (see Figure 21.1).

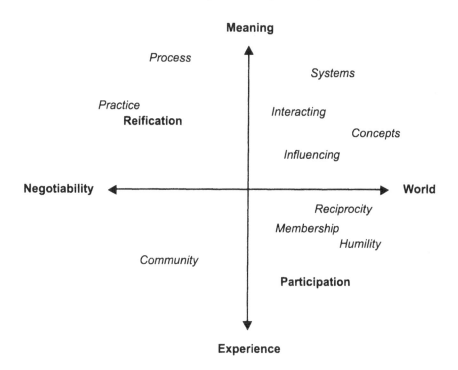

Figure 21.1 Participation and reification

Engagement: self and enterprise

COMMERCIAL ENGAGEMENT: FINANCE/INTELLECTUAL CAPITAL

The practice of finance and accounting can trace its origins back to a fifteenth-century Italian monk, Luca Pacioli. A Renaissance man and close friend of Leonardo da Vinci, he wrote a book on *Divine Proportion*. It involves a study of balance and proportion, potentially as relevant to the measurement of natural and human as to organizational and financial bal-

ance. Not surprisingly, therefore, there has recently been a resurgence of interest in the intelligent enterprise generally, and the balanced scorecard specifically. Communities of practice then, engaged internally with management control, and externally with investment analysis, need to evolve their identities accordingly. More specifically then, such a psychologically as well as economically oriented approach to self-and-enterprise involves a recognition of:

- the origin of finance and accounting
- the theory of the firm as a behavioural as well as an economic unit
- the development of financial as intellectual and social capital
- shareholder value, the 'triple scorecard' and the evolution of enterprise.

This is the terrain, most particularly, that Virgin One Account is entering into with us, thereby connecting up life balance with financial balance.

CUSTOMER ENGAGEMENT: PHYSICAL PRODUCT/SOCIAL SERVICE

The advent of the knowledge era is also affecting our customer orientation. In fact, as mass marketing evolves towards empowering the customer, so the needs of the frontline employee and individual customer, or patient or client, need to be taken more purposefully into account. The resulting interconnections and overlap between producer and consumer become accentuated by the shift in world economic activity from product and nationally based manufacturing to solution-focused and local/global-oriented services. As such, the self-actualization of the individual becomes a service imperative, from both an internal and external perspective, spanning:

- motivational thresholds, and the individual origins, of self-and-enterprise
- cycles of success and failure in marketing-and-service
- the enterprise as a nursery for human growth
- public and private enterprise and the development of the dream society.

Again the Virgin brand, in principle, is predisposed towards the realization of a dream, from both an external, customer-focused, and internal, employee-focused perspective; in principle engagement comes more naturally in the first respect than the second, so that our programme applies more of a corrective balance in the latter respect.

Alignment: enterprise and environment

ORGANIZATIONAL ALIGNMENT: HUMAN RESOURCES TO ORGANIZATIONAL LEARNING

Communities of practice engaged with people in organizations are going through turbulent times. On the one hand, within organizations as a whole, human resource management today is being pared down to its basic personnel management functions. On the other hand, the advent of a service economy, the new information technology, as well as the onset of individual and cultural diversity, is leading to increasing empowerment, networking and flexible work contracts, changing the nature of what is increasingly becoming knowledge-

based work. The need to be continually upgrading intellectual capital therefore could be placing a transformed human resource function in the forefront of management, specifically via organizational learning, duly recognizing:

- the way organizations are structurally evolving
- the role of IT in turning organizations into networks
- an ability to manage ever-increasing individual and cultural diversity
- the role of the learning organization in integrating all of these elements.

The emergence of asset management in the Anglian Water Group, and the participation of individuals engaged in it, for both Anglian and Morrison's, on our programme, serves potentially, if not yet actually, to foster such a transformation of old-style HR into a new style of composite physical and human asset management.

OPERATIONAL ENGAGEMENT – OPERATIONS MANAGEMENT/KNOWLEDGE MANAGEMENT

The material-intensive twentieth century is giving way to the knowledge-intensive twenty-first century, heralding the opportunity for applying a more sustainable waste-free technology. The evolution of the desktop computer, as a personal tool and gateway to larger systems, coupled with the growth of the Internet and telecommunications in general, has provided many new possibilities for public and private enterprises alike. The convergence of computing and telecommunications technologies, moreover, has had an enormous effect on the way organizations are structured, and on the nature of work. Specifically then, this module involves a recognition of:

- the nature and origins of quality
- operations management, information technology and knowledge management
- evolving towards knowledge creation, alongside
- total quality management and *kaizen* in the context of sustainable development.

The establishment of best-practice groups at Anglian Water Group, most specifically linking the English and Czech operations, represent an attempt to share knowledge and, to the extent that such sharing is aligned with our transformation programme, to create new knowledge; as such Petr Svab, on our programme from Ostrava, John Semjka in technology development and John Newell in organization development are combining forces with a view to ultimate knowledge creation.

Imagination: business in society

CORPORATE RENEWAL – STRATEGY/COMPLEXITY

The ultimate purpose of public and private enterprise is heavily preconditioned not only specifically by corporate and national culture, but also by the prevailing consciousness in society as a whole. The essence of managing complexity, compared and contrasted here with analytically based strategy, involves seeing whole patterns where others see only part activi-

ties and events. This gives rise to the need for complex learning which involves questioning and adjusting mental models. Such complex learning is destabilizing, but vitally necessary for transformation. Communities of practice, in that varied context, are exposed to a spectrum of change situations, from closed to contained to completely open-ended, including:

- new concepts of business and society
- the dynamics of self-organization
- the development of strategy towards complexity
- preparatory, ordinary, extraordinary and masterly management.

SOCIETAL RENEWAL – COMPETITIVE/CO-CREATIVE

This final module takes an ecological perspective on enterprise, both literally and metaphorically, rooting it in the natural as well as the digital and human environment. First and literally, it explores the impact that business is having upon the global environment today, both positive and negative, and what can be done to enhance the sustainability of social and economic enterprise. Second, and metaphorically, it develops the notion of an organization as a healthy or diseased community, creating or constraining knowledge and well-being. Third, it reveals how an ecosystemic perspective can pave the way for a parallel approach to individual, organizational and interorganizational development lacking today, through being engaged with:

- individuation – from youth to maturity
- organization development – from independence to interdependence
- interorganizational development, individual–organizational–societal
- creating healthy communities – public/private/civic.

The focus on sustainable development at Anglian Water, in which our environmentalist and organizational development (OD) practitioner Ken Smith are engaged, coupled with Alan Clark's aspiration to create healthy communities in Ealing are both germane here; however the gap between aspiration and realization is caused by the sponsoring organization's remaining hesitance to engage in a genuine act of co-creation with us.

Transformation

FROM KNOWING TO BECOMING

The programme inductions first establish the participative context for being and doing, that is communal engagement, alignment and imagination respectively. Second, the workshops or course modules provide the knowledge base (reification) for the cycles of transformation – alias projects – to follow, drawing then upon both participation and reification. At this third point we move from being (community) and doing (practice), through knowing (community of practice), to becoming (the transformative community).

What is being learnt in, and by, such a community is not a static subject matter but the very process of engaging with, and participating in developing, an ongoing practice.

Such individual and communal learning is not just the acquisition of knowledge, skills

and attitudes, but the formation of an identity, that is, becoming. Our experience and our membership inform each other, pull each other, transform each other. We create ways of participating in a community of practice in the very process of contributing to making that practice become what it is, by:

- evolving forms of mutual engagement – discovering how to engage, what helps and what hinders; developing mutual relationships; defining who is who, set in the context, for example, of a newly forged asset management

- understanding and tuning an enterprise – aligning your engagement with it; struggling to define the enterprise and reconcile different interpretations of, for example, creating healthy communities

- developing repertoire, style, perspective – renegotiating the meaning of various elements; producing or adopting tools, programmes, concepts; recording and recalling events; telling and retelling stories; creating and breaking routines, for instance in relation to a newly conceived call-centre paradise.

TRANSFORMING: THE LEARNING TRAJECTORY

Identity, for the individual and the community of practice, is not an object but a constant becoming. Our identity is something we constantly renegotiate during the course of our work and lives. Such a 'trajectory' suggests not a path that can be foreseen or charted but a continuous motion – one that has a momentum of its own combined with a field of influences. There can be various types of *trajectory*:

- inbound: the evolution of the practice – new events, demands, inventions – such as knowledge management
- boundary: identity formed by spanning boundaries, linking communities, sustaining identity across boundaries being the challenge of brokerage work, as, for instance between East Anglia and the Czech Republic
- outbound: leading out of a community, involving developing new relationships, seeing the world, such as that of community health, and oneself in new ways.

The cycle of transformation

PARTICIPATING PRACTICALLY: GERMINATION – TRANSFORMING THE AGENDA

Initially then, germination has a very special energy, the energy characteristic of any beginning. During the initial part of transition, excitement, keen interest and freshness abound.

Richard Lambert, at Virgin One Account for instance, gained fresh insight into the world of networks and felt impelled to take this forward, as part of his development role.

Such a creative cycle is therefore set in motion by the germination of an idea, with a view to its practical realization, born out of a combination of action and reflection. Moreover, and as such, it paradoxically needs a period of separation, as we have seen, from the world of action, whereby the reflection-upon-action leads to this new conception. Essentially, at this point, there is a need for the individual, and compositely for a community, to decide first

what transformation they aim for, personally and functionally, and thereafter to begin to activate such. In order for it to take hold, those on the transformation journey need to survey the practical and political lie of the land, and take due account of it, so that the transformation they aim to bring about is likely to stick. At the end of this germination phase then, to the extent that it is successful, the intended result to be created needs to be practically incorporated as a key point on the communal agenda, during the first two months.

PRACTICAL REIFICATION: ASSIMILATION – TRANSFORMING THE PRACTICE

What is lacking, up to this point, is sustained direction which serves, subsequently, to consolidate upon initial action. In other words, what is needed is an overall theoretical as well as practical framework for action, one that provides an underlying, and enduring, rationale. At this point, therefore, comes assimilation. If you are initially impelled to 'do something', for example, about organizational learning, it helps to have Peter Senge's *The Fifth Discipline* (1990) or McGill and Beaty's *Action Learning* (2001) as an overall framework in mind. Such a framework enables you to connect up, and consolidate upon, one learning activity with another. At Anglian Water, Etienne Wenger's (1997) communities of practice played that part.

An initial idea then, if it is to endure, needs to become aligned not only with the needs of the organization, practically, but also with the signs of the times, conceptually. For example, it is no accident that so many organizations, today, are aligning themselves with the 'Balanced Scorecard', with 'Intellectual Capital', with 'Outsourcing', or with 'E-Commerce'. These are altogether part of the knowledge era in which we are consciously or unconsciously becoming immersed. To the extent that we are able then, both individually and as a group, to assimilate the theory that serves to underline, or indeed connect up with, the signs of our times – most specifically in relation to the particular organization we are in – so we will be able to forge a better alignment between what we are seeking to create and our growing functional competence as an organization, particularly during months two to four.

COMMUNAL PARTICIPATION: MOMENTUM – TRANSFORMING THE COMMUNITY

Third, to build up a progressive momentum over a significant period of time is an accumulative process, whereby energy builds on itself. It does so, moreover, because connections are made with the intrinsic motivations of particular individuals, and communities. That is ultimately the aim at Ealing, creating healthy communities.

As such we tap into their ever-present origins. No part, that is action or connection, ultimately stands apart from the whole. No plot, or indeed sub-plot, remains disconnected from the passages of the overall story.

This is the trouble with programmes of individual development, whether or not they are accredited by an external agency, which are not specifically incorporated, within a sponsoring unit's strategy or story. Moreover, even in cases where such individual development programmes do become organizationally incorporated, over a period of time, a change in management regime, at the top, will more than likely put paid to them. The question then remains as to how such individually oriented, developmental activity can become communally and participatively ingrained. Realizing this is still a struggle in the individualistic culture in which we live and work, in Britain.

COMMUNAL REIFICATION: COMPLETION – TRANSFORMING THE COMMUNITY OF PRACTICE

Completion of a project, a would-be transformation, or a process of transition, is all too often disrupted because it is not embraced, culturally, by the organization as a community or practice. While disparate individuals may buy in to such a project, the community that it needs to embrace remains disaffected. All too often then, individualized development programmes fall foul of groups of people who never become more than peripherally engaged. Momentum is thereby curbed, connectedness is inhibited, and action is stymied. This remains par for the course in our sponsoring organizations, although somewhat less so than was the case several years ago. So where do we go from here?

The transformation, duly combining the germination and assimilation of ideas with the build-up of an initial momentum behind them, needs to be accepted by the community for what it is, involving rough exploration, abstruse conceptualization, vague bewilderment, and so on. We have not yet reached a point of final completion, nor should we have. After the initial point of target setting, the subsequent period of establishing new lines of connection, for the individual and the organization, followed by the build-up of a spiralling momentum, we now come back, full circle, to a new period of stability. While old habits and approaches are being discarded, and newly appropriate ones are being developed, a process of reformation is still being represented as work in progress.

Incorporation – becoming to being

SECURING AN ORGANIZATIONAL RETURN

Now we come to the nub of our transformational argument. Conventionally based accreditation, while generally serving to reward the individual for progress made, on a particular journey from action to reflection normally does little to benefit the community. In other words it is not sustainably incorporated into the institution's development. As a result, enormous investments made in developing people, leading to their individual accreditation or otherwise, conventionally has little impact on communal practice. It is for that very reason that we need to depart, further than we have currently done, from the conventional norms of modern academe, at least in so far as accreditation is concerned, and reconnected with communities of practice. This serves to establish a collective, as well as an individual, purpose to our transformation programme. In effect we have now instigated a process where the final viva, for each individual, is accompanied by a review of progress in the sponsoring organization, as a result of their participating individuals' projects, as a whole.

Conventionally speaking, then, in the course of an individual's transformation journey through an educational programme, there is, as it were, an individual departure without a built-in communal return. The returning heroes and heroines, and their transformations, are reintegrated into the corporate community. After eight months, in our terms then, the hitherto called project – now termed 'transformation' – needs to be organizationally, as well as individually, completed.

FROM PERFORMANCE REPORTING TO REPORTING TRANSFORMATION

As such, and in the interests of sustainable communal as well as individual development, the annual cycle of reporting on corporate performance, usually aimed at shareholders, needs to

be supplemented by a parallel transformational cycle. This would incorporate – subsequent to initiation, separation and transition – corporate transformation. In other words, while financially or statistically based reporting on how well the organization is doing, is the norm, communally based incorporating of progressively enhanced knowing (practice), becoming (emerging identity) and being (community) would serve to transform. Overall then, such incorporation would include a micro-cycle (two months) or project phase, a mini-cycle or complete project transformation (eight months) and a full programme maxi-cycle (two years). This is yet to be instigated.

During the mini and maxi 'graduation ceremonies', therefore, not only the individuals engaged in the Transformation Journey, but also the community of practice as a whole, would be reciprocally incorporated. In other words, the individual's, the community's, and the practice's re-storying, over the period of concern, would be newly engaged with, imagined and aligned. As such the role of each as protagonists would be incorporated into the unfolding history of the organization, to the extent that shared meaning could be recognised. The act of incorporation, then, would be signified by recognition of co-authorship between the individuals, the organization and the society. In fact, within Anglian Water, I instigated such a collective storytelling some two years ago, under the guise of Transition Management, with the management in attendance, to very good interim effect.

The cycle of creation, over the course of the Transformation Programme ultimately, is an iterative one, in that the four micro-cycles, from germination to completion, would need to be repeated three times – from preparatory to extraordinary – over the two years (see Figure 21.2). In that overall context, constituting the integrated journey towards mastery:

- The preparatory transformation of self-and-enterprise, over the first eight months, is focused most particularly on transforming the functioning of a department, as a community of practice, from both a customer and a financial perspective.
- The ordinary transformation of organization-in-environment, over the second eight months, is communally oriented outwards, towards the corporate entity as a whole, encompassing an organizational and operational perspective.
- The extraordinary transformation of the corporation in its society, over the course of the final eight months, is interorganizationally focused, via the management of complexity and through organizational ecology.
- Finally, the ongoing process of attaining mastery, combining engagement, alignment and imagination, on the one hand, and identification and negotiability on the other, involves three progressive communal transformations of practice.

Conclusion

In summary, all too often, programmes in management and leadership development, not to mention transformation management, fail because the development of the individual is cut off from that of the community. In order to try and ensure that this does not happen on our Transformation Management programme, we have lodged it firmly within the context of developing communities of practice.

Organizations in which conventionally commercial, technological and social functions are lodged, are institutional designs directed at practice. Indeed it is through the practices they bring together that organizations can do what they do, know what they know, and learn

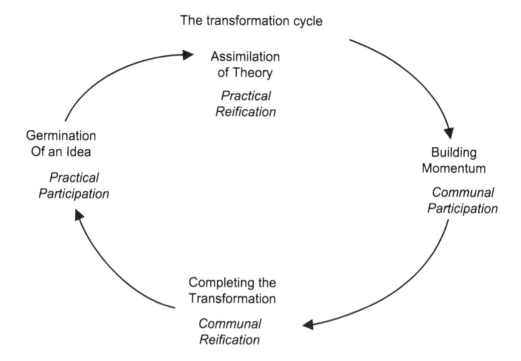

Figure 21.2 The transformation cycle

what they learn. Communities of practice, then, differ from such institutionally based entities along three dimensions:

- Communities of practice negotiate their own enterprise, such as a call-centre paradise.
- As such they arise, evolve into a healthy community and ultimately dissolve according to their own learning journey.
- These communities shape their own boundaries thereby becoming another entity, for example, the Anglian Water Group.

From this perspective there are two views of an organization:

- the designed organization which we term the 'institution', to distinguish it from the organization as lived in practice, incorporating the formal organization, be it Anglian Water Group, Ealing Social Services or Virgin One Account
- the practice, or constellation of practices, which gives life to the organization and is often a response to the designed organization, such as – in prospect if not yet in full reality – sustainable development as whole in AWG; creating healthy communities in Ealing; or developing whole life accounts at Virgin.

Both aspects contribute to making the organization what it is. An effective organization design connects communities of practices by enabling them to cross boundaries. It does not sit on top; it moves in between. It does not reign; it travels, to be shaped and appropriated in the context of specific practices.

Overall then, a focus on communities of practice does not entail paying less attention to individuals, such as the participants on our programme. On the contrary, it places a very specific focus on people, but not people in the abstract. It is commonplace to say that it is people who make the difference in an organization, but it is less commonplace to understand this truism in terms of focusing on what makes us human, on what enables us to make a difference – on the work of negotiating identities in knowledge-ability. What we learn with the greatest investment is what enables participation in the communities with which we identify, whether sustaining development, creating healthy communities or developing whole life accounts. That, overall, is what our transformation programme is about.

4 *In Conclusion*

22 *Conclusion*
Anne Brockbank, Ian McGill and Nic Beech

While the concept of the Learning Organization has been stimulating, in practice it still remains elusive. There are compelling reasons for seeking to be a learning organization, including the need to cope with the complexity and ambiguity of constant change, and the evidence of corporate success among companies that have invested in their people (Pedler et al, 1991). It is beneficial to move towards the end-point of being a learning organization whilst at the same time acknowledging that the target may be unachievable in full. One can never know all there is to know, and in management practice, 'perfection' is neither achievable nor desirable. It is not achievable because circumstances, goals, people and processes are constantly changing, and maximal prediction and control are not possible. It is not desirable because to try to achieve perfection would require so much resource and time that it would become dysfunctional. Given this argument, it is sensible to refocus on *activity*, rather than a 'state of being' or achievement, and to conceptualize learning as 'becoming' which emphasizes change.

Our first purpose was to seek to unlock the learning processes that can support improvements in organizational performance. This aim underlies the practice in many of the cases. For example, Sterling Bank, Pearl and Allied Distillers had pressing reasons to develop performance, and this was done partly through people development. Systems and structures were also changing and in these cases there was some evidence of cultural change, but the focus was on group and individual development. Similarly, in Thus, there were structural, cultural and skill changes and these impacted on key barriers to organizational performance – the problems of working across boundaries.

In the cases mentioned above many of the requirements established by Pettigrew and Whipp (1991) for successful change, and by Salaman (1995) for effective learning were in evidence. However, such change does not occur overnight. In these cases programmes were developed and implemented over time and with a degree of flexibility that enabled the learning processes themselves to adapt. In addition, developmental programmes were not regarded as sufficient in themselves. In all cases they were strongly linked to action in the workplace and to review of that action.

In other cases, there was less programme-based learning (for example, the Salford Cathedral Centre (Chapter 16) and the Coronary Heart Disease cases (Chapter 14) among others), but here there were strong links to the workplace and reflection on events in order to marshal evidence that would impact on performance.

In all these cases, there were group-based processes, but these processes were not regarded as ends-in-themselves. The aims were not principally concerned with team building (although this was a beneficial side-effect in many cases). Throughout they remained task-

focused and were conducting learning-with-purpose, aimed at performance analysis and improvement.

Our second purpose was to seek to get inside the 'black box' of learning. There is extensive theory and research in this area, and our aim was not to repeat that. Rather, we were interested in understanding patterns in what has and has not worked in the cases reported here. Our analysis led us to believe that there are no straight answers as to what constitutes best practice – that varies throughout the cases and there are no singular prescriptions for action. We would argue that it is necessary to keep an open mind, be aware of the socially constructed nature of the situation and the various actors involved, and seek to work proactively with constant change. There may be no straight answers, but there are some straight questions. The ones we found useful are as follows:

- Should time and space be 'carved out' and given exclusive priority?
- Is time conceived as progressive and linear in reflective learning?
- What media should be used for reflective learning?
- Who 'owns' the learning?
- What are the implications for management practice?
- What are the implications for organizational success?
- What issues do relationships raise for reflective learning and vice versa?
- How do emotions relate to reflective learning?
- What are the impacts of narratives and symbols on learning?
- How does reflective learning impact on people being different?

We would argue that those involved in learning – designers, planners, implementers, learners and clients – could benefit from overt consideration of these questions, not only at the outset but periodically as learning and development continue. Such consideration can help to deal with complexity, develop a positive challenge for learners, enable learning from critical incidents and stimulate collaboration – the themes that emerged as important in our cases. Finally, attention to the questions can help learners adopt a pragmatic stance and an action orientation which incorporates awareness of costs and benefits. For providers the questions may generate a willingness to be flexible and alter programmes and actions when feedback indicates that this is necessary. This requires effective and speedy feedback.

Our argument has been that Reflective Learning is one means towards achieving these targets. Reflective learning is likely to vary in different organizational and individual contexts, but it is likely to incorporate the following features:

- It focuses on activity.
- It is based on experience.
- It is developed within a social context, and potentially a community of practitioners/ learners.
- It is not a 'style', but a set of intentional processes.
- It aims to be holistic – concerned with crossing boundaries not creating them.
- It seeks to enrich knowledge – through questioning, information search, application and dialogue.
- It includes double-loop learning – reflexivity about processes, the nature of learning and projection of action into the future.
- It uses dialogue – which helps to increase active engagement, challenge, constructive criticism, support, improvement and transformation.

- It recognizes and values difference.
- It embraces the emotional domain.

We have argued that most organizations in postmodern conditions need not only grand structural and cultural change, but also must operate effectively at the local level on short time-scales. Efficiency is a driving requirement, as is the need for evidence of impact (usefulness) of learning in the current organizational discourses. The need for efficiency and impact on performance have, in the past, led some to denigrate learning as a longitudinal process that may have no effect and will be costly. The cases presented here challenge those assumptions. Reflective learning starts at the micro level with action and problems that are current in the work of the individual and proceeds to seek solutions and improvement. In a sense, this is an argument for increasing the 'granularity' of thinking about learning. Rather than concentrating on the *macro-policy* end of the scale, we would recommend developing policy on the basis of a developed and dynamic understanding of what works in *practice* in the particular organizational setting. However, to leave it there would be to achieve only part of the value of learning. Reflective dialogue has the potential to enable transformation: for individuals through empathic questioning of tfgs and assumptions embedded in their work practice; for organizations the dialogue process itself promotes the cascade of organizational learning. Further questions concern how single-loop answers and double-loop transformations may be expanded and applied in new situations in the future, and how others might both contribute to, and learn from the process. Pushing the learning to these further stages offers the potentiality of added-value learning.

Reflective learning, through the dialogue process seeks to achieve added-value learning in an effective and efficient manner. We would argue that such a micro-focused, efficient learning process offers a practical way forward, and further, for those in situations of individual and organizational change, we would see reflective learning as not merely a nice-to-have, but as a necessity.

Bibliography

Adlam, R. and Plumridge, M. (1990), 'Organisational Effectiveness and self-development: the essential tension', in Pedler, M., Burgoyne, J., Boydell, T. and Welshman, G. (eds), *Self Development in Organisations*, Maidenhead: McGraw-Hill.

Antonacopoulou, E. (1999), 'Developing learning managers within learning organisations: the Case of Three Major Retail Banks', in Easterby-Smith, M., Burgoyne, J. and Araujo, L. (eds), *Organisational Learning and the Learning Organisation*, London: Sage.

Argyris, C. (1991), 'Helping smart people to learn', *Harvard Business Review*, May–June.

Argyris, C. (1986), *Change and Defensive Routines*, Boston, MA: Pitman.

Argyris, C. and Schon, D. (1996), *Organisational Learning II: Theory, Method and Practice*, New York: Addison Wesley.

Argyris, C. and Schon, D. (1974), *Theory in Practice: increasing professional effectiveness*, London: Jossey-Bass.

Baets, W. and Van der Linden, G. (2000), *The Hybrid Business School: Developing knowledge management through management learning*, Amsterdam/Harlow: Prentice-Hall.

Balarajan, R. et al. (1984), 'Pattern of mortality among migrants to England and Wales from the Indian subcontinent', *British Medical Journal* 289: 1185–7.

Bassi, L.J. (1997), 'Harnessing the power of intellectual capital', *Training and Development*, **51** (12): 25–31.

Becker, B.E. and Huselid, M.A. (1999), 'Overview: Strategic Human Resource Management in Five Leading Firms', *Human Resource Management*, 38: 287–301.

Becker, B.E. and Huselid, M.A. (1998), 'High Performance Work Systems and Firm Performance: A synthesis of research and managerial implications', *Research in Personnel and Human Resource Management*, 16: 53–101.

Beech, N. (2000), 'Narrative Styles of Managers and Workers: A tale of star-crossed lovers?', *Journal of Applied Behavioural Science*, 36: 210–28.

Beech, N. and Cairns, G. (2001), 'Coping with Change: The contribution of postdichotomous ontologies', *Human Relations*, **54** (10): 1303–24.

Beech, N., Cairns, G. and Robertson, T. (2000), 'Transient transfusion; or the wearing-off of the governance of the soul', *Personnel Review*, 29 (4): 460–75.

Belenky, M.F., Clinchy, B. McV., Goldberger, N.R. and Tarule, J.M. (1986), *Women's ways of knowing*, New York: Basic Books.

Berger, P.L., and Luckmann, T. (1966), *The Social Construction of Reality*, Harmondsworth: Penguin.

Bohm, D. (1996), *On Dialogue*, L. Nichol (ed), London: Routledge.

Boisot, M. (1999), *Knowledge Assets*, Oxford: Oxford University Press

Bourner, T. and Weinstein, K. (1996), 'Just Another Talking Shop: Some Of The Pitfalls In Action Learning', *Employee Counselling Today: The Journal of Workplace Learning*, 8, (6): 54–65.

Bourner, T., Beaty, E. and Frost, P. (1997), 'Participating in Action Learning', in Pedler, M. (ed.), *Action Learning in Practice* (3rd edn), Aldershot: Gower.

Bourner, T., Cooper, A. and France, L. (2000), 'Action Learning Across the University Community', *Innovation in Education and Training International*, **37**, (1): 2–9.

Bourner, T., France, L. and O'Hara, S. (2000), 'Practitioner-Centred Research', in Bourner, T., Katz, T. and Watson, D. (eds), *New Directions in Professional Higher Education*, Buckingham: Society for Research into Higher Education and Open University Press.

Bray, J.N., Lee, J., Smith, L.L. and Yorks, L. (2000), *Collaborative Inquiry in Practice: Action, Reflection & Meaning Making*, London: Sage.

Brent and Harrow HA (1991), *Brent and Harrow ethnic groups, 1991 census*, London: Brent and Harrow Health Authority.

Brockbank, A. and McGill, I. (1998), *Facilitating Reflective Learning in Higher Education*, Buckingham: SRHE/Open University Press.

Brookfield, S.D. (1987), *Developing Critical Thinkers*, Buckingham: Open University Press.

Brown, A., Galloway, A. and Brennan, C. (1999), 'Videoconferencing: active reflection on new technologies when lecturing'. *Active Learning*, 11: 36–40.

Browning, G. (1998), 'Office Politics', *Guardian*, 24 October.

Brundage, D.H. and Mackeracher, D. (1980), *Adult Learning Principles and their application to Program Planning*, Toronto: Ministry of Education, Ontario.

Burr, V. (1995), *An Introduction to Social Constructionism*, New York: Routledge.

Burrell, G. (1988), 'Modernism: Post Modernism and Organisational Analysis 2: The Contribution of Michel Foucalt', *Organization Studies*, **9** (2): 221–35.

Burtney, E. and Sang, R. (1999), *A Healthier Sense of Self*, Report of the Deliberative Seminar, Edinburgh: Health Education Board for Scotland.

Chia, R. (1996), 'Metaphors and metaphorization in organizational analysis: Thinking beyond the thinkable', in Grant, D. and Oswick, C. (eds), *Metaphor and Organizations*, London: Sage.

Clutterbuck, D. (1994), *The Power of Empowerment*, London: Kogan Page.

Cooke, B.a.K., U, Ed. (2001), *Participation: the new tyranny*, London: Zed Press.

Cooper, R. and Sawaf, A. (1997), *Executive EQ*, London: Orion Publishing.

Coopey, J. (1995), 'The Learning Organisation: Power Politics and Ideology', *Management Learning* **26** (2): 193–213.

Cummings, T. (1995), 'From Programmed Change to Self-Design: Learning How to Change Organizations', *Organization Development Journal*, **13** (4): 20–31.

Daloz, L. (1986), *Effective Teaching and Mentoring: Realising the Transformational Power of Adult learning Experiences*, San Francisco: Jossey-Bass.

De Geus, A. (1992), 'Modelling to predict or to learn?', *European Journal of Operational Research*, 59: 1–5.

Delaney, J.T. and Huselid, M.A. (1996), 'The impact of human resource management practices on perceptions of organizational performance', *Academy of Management Journal* 39: 949–70.

Dulewicz, V. and Higgs, M. (1998), 'Soul Researching', *People Management*, 1 October.

Easterby-Smith, M. (1990), 'Creating a Learning Organisation', *Personnel Review*, **19** (5): 24–8.

Easterby-Smith, M., Burgoyne, J. and Araujo, L. (1999), *Organisational Learning and the Learning Organisation*, London: Sage.

Egan, G. (1990), *The Skilled Helper: A Systematic Approach To Effective Helping* (4th edn), Pacific Grove, CA: Brooks/Cole.

Emery, F.E. (1981), 'The Emergence of Ideal-Seeking Systems', in *Systems Thinking*, Vol. 2, London: Penguin Books.

Fineman, S. and Gabriel, Y. (1994), 'Paradigms of Organisations: An Exploration in Textbook Rhetorics', *Organisation*, **1** (2): 375–99.

Flood, R.A. and Romm, R.N.A. (1996), *Diversity management: triple loop learning*, Chichester: John Wiley.

Foucault, M. (1976), *The History of Sexuality*, Vol. 1, London: Penguin Books.

Frost, P.J., Mitchell, V.F. and Nord, W.R. (eds) (1992), *Organisational Reality: Reports from the Firing Line* (4th edn), New York: Harper Collins.

Gallwey, T. (1979), *The Inner Game of Tennis*, New York: Bantam.

Gardner, H. (1985), *Frames of Mind: The theory of multiple intelligences*, New York: Basic Books.

Garratt, B. (1987), *The Learning Organisation*, London: Fontana/Collins.

Gaunt, R. and Kendall, R. (1985), *Action Learning, A Short Manual for Set Members*, London: Greater London Education Authority.

Gergen, K. (1999), *An Invitation to Social Construction*, London: Sage.

Gergen, K.J. (1989), 'Warranting voice and the elaboration of self', in Shotter, J. and Gergen, K.J. (eds), *Texts of Identity*, London: Sage.

Glaser, B.G. (1992), *Basics of Grounded Theory Analysis*, Mill Valley, CA: Sociology Press.

Goffman, E. (1961), *Encounters: Two Studies in the Sociology of Interaction*, New York: Bobbs-Merril.

Goldberger, N., Tarule, J.M., Clinchy, B. and Belenky, M. (eds) (1996), *Knowledge, Difference and Power*, New York: Basic Books.

Goleman, D. (1995), *Emotional Intelligence*, London: Bloomsbury.

Grant, D., Keenoy, T. and Oswick, C. (1998), 'Organizational discourse: Of diversity, dichotomy and multi-disciplinarity', in Grant, D., Keenoy, T. and Oswick, C. (eds), *Discourse and Organization*, London: Sage.

Hansen, M.T., Nohria, N. and Tierney, T. (1999), 'What's your strategy for managing knowledge?', *Harvard Business Review*, March–April: 102–20.

Hawkins, P. (1994), 'The Changing View of Learning', in Pedler, M., Burgoyne, J. and Boydell, T., *Towards the Learning Company*, Maidenhead: McGraw-Hill.

Hendry, C. et al. (1997), 'Missed: A Motivator', *People Management*, 15 May.

Heron, J. (1996), *Co-operative inquiry. Research into the human condition*, London: Sage.

Heron, J. (1977), *Catharsis in Human Development*, University of Surrey, Guildford, UK: Human Potential Research Group.

Heron, J. and Reason, P. (1997), 'A participatory inquiry paradigm', *Qualitative Inquiry*, **3** (3): 274–94.

Hills, H. and Francis, P. (1999), 'Interaction Learning', *People Management*, 15 July.

Honey, P. and Mumford, A. (1992), *Capitalizing on your learning opportunities*, King of Prussia, PA: Organisation Design and Development.

Isaacs, W.N. (1993), 'Taking Flight: dialogue, collective thinking and organisational learning', *Organisational Dynamics* **22** (2): 24–39.

Johnson, G. and Scholes, K. (1993), *Exploring Corporate Strategy*, London: Prentice-Hall.

Keenoy, T. and Anthony, P. (1992), 'HRM: Metaphor, meaning and morality', in Blyton, P. and Turnbull, P. (eds), *Reassessing Human Resource Management*, London: Sage.

Kelly, G.A. (1955), *The Psychology of Personal Constructs*, Vols 1 & 2, New York: Norton.

Kets de Vries (1991), 'Whatever happened to the philosopher king? The leader's addiction to power', *Journal of Management Studies*, **28** (4): 339–51.

Kirby, A. (ed.) (1993), 'Icebreakers', (Exercise contributed by Kamp, D.), Aldershot: Gower.

Kleiner, A. and Roth, G. (1998), 'Learning histories: a new tool for turning organizational experience into action' <*http://ccs.mit.edu/lh/21cwp002.html*>.

Kolb, D. (1984), *Experiential Learning*, Englewood Cliffs, NJ: Prentice-Hall.

Lessem, R. and Palsule, S. (1997), *Managing in Four Worlds*, Oxford: Blackwell.

Lyotard, J.-F. (1984), *The Postmodern Condition: A report on knowledge*, Manchester: Manchester University Press.

McCaughan, N. and Palmer, B. (1994), *Systems Thinking for Harassed Managers*, London: Karnac Books.

McDonald, Stuart (1999), *Information for Innovation*, Oxford: Oxford University Press.

McGill, I. and Beaty, L. (1995), *Action Learning: A Guide for Professional, Management and Educational Development* (2nd edn), London: Kogan Page.

McGill, I., Segal-Horn, S., Bourner, T. and Frost, P., (1989), 'Action Learning: A Vehicle for Personal and Group Experiential Learning', in McGill, I. and Weill, S. (eds), *Diversity in Experiential Learning: Making Sense of Theory and Practice*, Milton Keynes: Open University Press with Society for Research into Higher Education.

McGill, I. and Beaty, L. (2001), 2nd edn (revised), *Action Learning: A Guide for Professional, Management & Educational Development*, London: Kogan Page.

McKeigue, P. and Marmot, M. (1988), 'Mortality from coronary heart disease in Asian communities in London', *British Medical Journal*, 287: 903.

Malby, B. and Pattison, S. (1998), *Living Values in the NHS*, London: King's Fund.

Mann, S. (1987), 'Knowing Ourselves as Learners and Researchers', in Richardson, J.T.E. et al. (eds), *Student Learning*, London: SRHE/Open University Press.

Mant, A. (1998), *Intelligent Leadership*, Sydney: Allen & Unwin.

Marshall, J. (1998), 'Living life as inquiry', *Systemic Practice and Action Research*, **12** (2): 155–71.

Martin, J. (1992) *Cultures in Organizations: Three Perspectives*, Oxford: Oxford University Press.

Marton, F. (1981), 'Phenomenography: Describing conceptions of the world around us', *Instructional Science*, 10: 177–200.

May, S. (1998), 'Some Reflections on Critical Multiculturalism', in Shacklock, D. and Smyth, J. (eds), *Being Reflexive in Critical Educational and Social Research*, London: Falmer Press.

Mayer, J. (1999), 'Emotional Intelligence', *People Management*, 28 October.

Mayo, A. (1998), 'Memory Bankers', *People Mangement*, 22 January.

Megginson, D. (1994), 'Planned and Emergent Learning: A Framework and a Method', *Executive Development*, **7** (6): 29–32.

Mezirow, J. (1994), 'Understanding Transformation Theory', *Adult Education Quarterly*, **44** (4): 222–44.

Mezirow, J. & Associates (1990), *Fostering Critical Reflection in Adulthood*, San Francisco: Jossey-Bass.

Midgley, G. (2000), *Systemic Intervention: philosophy, methodology and practice*, London: Kluwer Academic/Plenum Publishers.

Midgley, G. et al. (1998), 'The theory and practice of boundary critique: developing housing services for older people', *Journal of the Operational Research Society*, **49** (5): 467–78.

Millar, J. (1999),' A Most Peculiar Commodity', *Times Higher Educational Supplement*, 21 July.

Newman, J. (1996), *Shaping Organizational Cultures in Local Government*, London: Pitman.

Nonaka, I. (1988), 'Towards Middle up-down Management: Accelerating information creation', *Sloan Management Review*, Spring: 9–18.

Nowotny, H. et al. (2001), *Re-thinking Science: Knowledge and the Public in an Age of Uncertainty*, Cambridge and Oxford: Polity Press and Blackwell.

Patterson, M., West, M., Lawthorn, R. and Nickell, S. (1997), *The Impact of People Management Practice on Business Performance*, London: Institute of Personnel and Development.

Pattison, S. (1998), 'Questioning Values', *Health Care Analysis*, 6: 352–9.

Pedler, M. (1996), *Action Learning for Managers*, London: Lemos and Crane.

Pedler, M., Burgoyne, J. and Boydell, T. (1991), *The Learning Company*, Maidenhead: McGraw-Hill.

Pettigrew, A. and Whipp, R. (1991), *Managing Change for Competitive Success*, Oxford: Blackwell.

Pfeffer, J. and Veiga, J.F. (1999), 'Putting People First for Organizational Success', *Academy of Management Executive*, 13: 37–50.

Pines, A.L. and West, L.H.T. (1986), 'Conceptual Understanding and Science Learning: An interpretation of Research within a sources-of-knowledge framework', *Science Education*, 70: 583–604.

Potter, J. and Wetherell, M. (1987), *Discourse and Social Psychology: Beyond attitudes and behaviour*, London: Sage.

Pratt, J., Gordon, P., and Plamping, D. (1999), *Working Whole Systems*, London: King's Fund.

Prokesch, S. (1997), 'Unleashing the power of learning', *Harvard Business Review*, September–October.

Quinn, R.E. (1996), *Deep Change*, San Francisco: Jossey Bass.

Reason, P. and Bradbury, H. (eds) (2000), *Handbook of Action Research*, London: Sage.

Reason, P. and Goodwin, B. (1999), 'Toward a Science of Qualities in Organizations – Lessons from Complexity Theory and Postmodern Biology', *Concepts and Transformation*, **4** (3): 281–317.

Reason, P. and Hawkins, P. (1988), *Human inquiry in action: developments in new paradigm research*, London: Sage.

Reeves, T. (1994), *Managing Effectively*, London: Butterworth Heineman.

Revans, R. (1980), *Action Learning: New Techniques for Action Learning*, London: Blond and Briggs.

Reynolds, M. (1997), 'Learning Styles: A critique', *Management Learning*, **28** (2): 115–33.

Rigano, D. and Edwards, J. (1998), 'Incorporating Reflection into Work Practice', *Management Learning*, **29** (4): 431–46.

Ritchie, P. (2001), *Opening Address, The Future is Purple conference*, Edinburgh: Scottish Human Services Trust.

Rose, C. and Nicholl, M. (1997), *Accelerated Learning for the 21st Century*, London: Piatkus.

Rothenberg, A. (1979), *The Emerging Goddess: the creative process in art, science, and other fields*, Chicago: University of Chicago Press.

Salaman, G. (1995), *Managing*, Buckingham: Open University Press.

Saljo, R. (1988), 'Learning in Educational Settings: Methods of Inquiry', in Ramsden, P. (ed.), *Improving Learning: New Perspectives*, London: Kogan Page.

Salmon, P. (1980), *Coming to Know*, London: Routledge.

Salmon, P. (1992), *Achieving your PhD*, Stoke-on-Trent: Trentham Books.

Sang, B. and McLenaghan, J. (1999), *Up the Down Escalator*, London: HEA.

Saul, J.R. (1997), *The Unconscious Civilisation*, London: Penguin Books.

Schon, D. (1994), 'Organisational Learning: The Core Issues', transcription of address to Office for Public Management.

Schon, D. (1987), *Educating the Reflective Practitioner*, London: Jossey-Bass.

Schon, D.A. (1983), *The reflective practitioner*, London: Temple Smith.

Schon, D.A. (1971), *Beyond the stable state*, London: Temple Smith.

Seng, J.S. (1998), 'Praxis as a conceptual framework for participatory research in nursing', *Advanced Nursing Science*, **20** (4): 37–48.

Senge, P. (1990), *The Fifth Discipline*, London: Random House.

Stacey, R.D. (1995), 'The science of complexity: an alternative perspective for strategic change processes', *Strategic Management Journal*, 16: 477–95.

Steele, J. (1999), *Wasted Values*, London: Public Management Foundation.

Strauss, A. and Corbin, J. (1998), *Basics of Qualitative Research* (2nd edn), London: Sage.

Thatchenkery, T.J. (1996), Editorial to the special issues on 'Organisational Learning: Past, Present, Future', *Journal of Organisational Change Management*: 4–9.

Townley, B. (1994), *Reframing HRM*, London: Sage.

Walton, R.E. (1985), 'From Control to Commitment in the Workplace', *Harvard Business Review*, March/April: 77–84.

Weil, S. (2002, in progress), *Borderlands Inquiry: Making a difference through critical and creative knowledge co-generation in complex systems*.

Weil, S. (1999), 'Living and learning new cultures of inquiry: strangers on the shore?', *Professorial Inaugural Lecture*, <http.www.Northampton.ac.uk/solar>, Northampton: SOLAR-UCN.

Weil, S. (1998), 'Rhetorics and realities in public service organizations: systemic practice and organizational learning as critically reflexive action research (CRAR)', *Systemic Practice and Action Research*, **11** (1): 37–62.

Weil, S. (1997a), 'Postgraduate Education and Lifelong Learning as Collaborative Enquiry in Action: An Emergent Model', in Burgess, R. (ed.), *Beyond the First Degree*, Buckingham: SRHE/Open University Press.

Weil, S. (1997b), 'Reflexive Inquiry in Action', in Flood, R., Romm, N. and Weil, S., *Critical Reflexivity: A Multi-Dimensional Conversation*, paper presented at the Fourth Congress on Action Research, Cartagena, Colombia, June 1997.

Weil, S. (1994), 'Bringing about cultural change in colleges and universities: the power and potential of story', in *Introducing change 'from the top' in universities and colleges*, Buckingham: SRHE/Open University Press.

Weil, S.W. and McGill, I.J. (1990), *Making Sense of Experiential Learning*, Buckingham: Open University Press/SRHE.

Weil, S., Flood, B. and Romm, N.R. (1996), 'Critical Reflexivity: a multi-dimensional conversation', Conference Paper: The Fourth World Congress on Action Research, Action Learning and Process management and the Eighth World Congress on Participatory Action Research, Cartagena, Colombia, 1–5 June 1997.

Weil, S. and Samson-Barry, A. (2000), 'Learning on the Run: The End of the Beginning?' Video and accompanying material. Northampton: SOLAR Centre.

Weil, S., Wildemeersch, D. and Jansen, T. (2001), *Living dilemmas of social learning: exploring activation strategies with unemployed youth in Europe*, Book in progress based on report submitted to the EC, TSER Fourth Funding Project, Balancing Competencies.

Weinstein, K. (1995), *Action Learning: A Journey in Discovery and Development*, London: Harper-Collins.

Wenger, E. (1997), *Communities of Practice*, Cambridge: Cambridge University Press.

Whitehead, M. (1999), 'Collection Time', *People Management*, 28 October.

Whitney, E. and Cogan, H. (1999), '*People Eat Food Not Targets*', Report of the Deliberative Seminar, Edinburgh: HEBS.

Whitney, E. and Groves, J. (1999), *The Values Project*, report to the Gordon Cook Foundation, Edinburgh: HEBS.

Zadek, S. (2000), *The New Economy of Corporate Citizenship*, Copenhagen, Denmark: The Copenhagen Centre.

Zuboff, S. (1989), *In the Age of the Smart Machine*, London: Heinemann.

Zukar, G. (1980), *The Dancing Wu Li Masters*, London: Fontana.

Index